Dear Connie & Frank,

Your outstanding, generous services to the Churches, and humanity are greatly appreciated. May this book inspire you to this mission of love. Thanks for your love and friendship.

Rev. Dr Paul Nwobi
Bronx, New York
January, 2013

# POOR FORMATION
## AS A
# PRINCIPAL FACTOR
## TO THE
# CRISIS IN PRIESTHOOD
# TODAY

PAUL UCHE NWOBI

authorHOUSE®

AuthorHouse™
1663 Liberty Drive
Bloomington, IN 47403
www.authorhouse.com
Phone: 1-800-839-8640

ISBN: 978-1-4685-5317-8 (e)
ISBN: 978-1-4685-5315-4 (hc)
ISBN: 978-1-4685-5316-1 (sc)

First published by AuthorHouse 9/25/2012

Library of Congress Control Number: 2012903031

Printed in the United States of America

# ACKNOWLEDGEMENT

It takes many hands to make a loaf of bread. So, it is with this project. I, therefore, take this opportunity to express my heart-felt gratitude and appreciation of the generous hearts and helpful hands of the members of my family, colleagues, friends and associates, who in most wonderful ways help to make this project a reality.

To all of you, I am prayerfully thankful for the tremendous blessings, support and encouragement we lovingly celebrate and share with one another daily in our lives, works and relationships.

# TABLE OF CONTENTS

**Chapter One: The Biblical and the Historical Development of the Catholic Priesthood**     1

**1.1 The Biblical Development of the Catholic Priesthood**     1
   1.1.1   The Old Testament Period     1
   1.1.2   The New Testament Period     4

**1.2. The Historical Development of the Catholic Priesthood in the Catholic Church History**     7
   1.2.1   The Apostolic Phase (27 – 110)     8
   1.2.2   The Patristic Phase (2nd to 11th Centuries)     10
   1.2.3   The Medieval Phase (1050 -1414)     12
   1.2.4   The Reformation Phase (1415 – 1565)     15
   1.2.5   The Tridentine Phase (1565 – 1962)     18
   1.2.6   The Post-Tridentine Church     19
   1.2.7   The Post-Tridentine Theology     20
   1.2.8   The Post-Tridentine Spirituality     20
   1.2.9   The Period of Aggiornamento (1962 – 1965) and thereafter     23
   1.2.10  Vatican II and Ministries in the Church     23

**1.3. The Historical Development of the Catholic Priesthood in the African Church History**     24
   1.3.1   The First Phase of Christianity in Africa – North Africa     26
   1.3.2   The Apostolic Period (1st Century)     27
   1.3.3   The Expansion Period (2nd and 3rd Centuries)     27
   1.3.4   The Institutionalization of the African Church and the Barbarian Invasion (4th -7th Centuries)     29
   1.3.5   The Second Part: Seven Centuries of the Rise of Islamism and the Eradication of African Christianity     30
   1.3.6   The Last Six Centuries of Christianity in Sub-Saharan Africa     31
   1.3.7   The Colonization and Its Frustration of Evangelization (15th to 18th Centuries)     31

1.3.8    Missionary Revival (19th to Mid-20th Centuries)    32

1.3.9    The Independent and Christian Africa (1960 – to the present)    34

1.3.10   The Theological and Spiritual Implications for Priesthood in African Church    35

**Chapter Two: The Historical Development of Seminary Formation in the Catholic Church    43**

2.1.    Models of Seminary Formation in History    45

2.2    Tridentine Model of Priestly Formation    45

2.3    French School Model of Priestly Formation    46

2.4    Vatican II Model of Priestly Formation    51

2.5    The Seminary Model of Neo-Catechumenal Way    57

2.6    Implications for the Theology and Spirituality of Priesthood    58

2.7    New Foundation Model of Diocesan Seminary of Paris    60

2.8    Implications for the Theology and Spirituality of Priesthood    61

2.9    Priestly Formation in Nigeria    61

**Chapter Three: The Dimensions of Priestly/ Human Formation  67**

3.1    Priesthood and Human Development    67

3.2    Human Development in General    70

3.3    Erik Erikson and Human Development    72

3.4    Human Development and Priestly Life and Ministry    77

3.5    Ordination and the Task of Growing Up    78

3.6    Ordination and Professional Training (Learning in Skills)    80

3.7    Ordination and Community Leadership    81

3.8    Priest as a Human Person (the Human Self)    82

3.9    Priest as a Person-in-Relationships and a Person-in-Leadership    84

3.10   Human Development in African/ Nigerian Church and Culture    89

3.11   Priesthood and the Catholic Church in Igbo Land    92

**Chapter Four: The Dimensions of Spiritual Formation**      **99**

| | | |
|---|---|---|
| 4.1 | Spiritual Life and Relationship Questions | 99 |
| 4.2 | Meaning of Priestly Spirituality | 99 |
| 4.3 | Discerning One's Route to the Inner Center | 101 |
| 4.4 | Structures and Disciplines of Spirituality | 103 |
| 4.5 | Priestly Life and Spiritual Formation (A Moment of Truth) | 106 |
| 4.6 | Spirituality and the Lifestyles of Priests | 110 |
| 4.7 | True Self as a Key to Spiritual Formation | 114 |
| 4.8 | Moral Conversion (A Transformed Way of Living) | 115 |
| 4.9 | Affective Conversion (A Transformed Way of Loving) | 117 |
| 4.10 | Cognitive Conversion (A Transformed Way of Knowing) | 118 |
| 4.11 | Religious Conversion (A Transformed Way of Being) | 120 |
| 4.12 | Priesthood and the Crisis of Spiritual Abuse | 124 |
| 4.13 | Church Community and Spiritual Abuse | 125 |
| 4.14 | Neglecting Spiritual Growth | 125 |
| 4.15 | Neglecting Family Violence | 126 |
| 4.16 | Neglecting Stewardship | 127 |
| 4.17 | Neglecting Inclusive Spirituality | 127 |
| 4.18 | Neglecting Social Justice | 128 |
| 4.19 | Religion and Spiritual Abuse | 133 |
| 4.20 | Recommendations – Feedbacks from Questionnaire and Interviews | 140 |

**Chapter Five: The Dimensions of Priestly Identity**      **149**

| | | |
|---|---|---|
| 5.1 | Understanding the Priestly Identity | 149 |
| 5.2 | The Principles of Priestly Identity | 150 |
| 5.3 | The First Principle: Permanence of the Priesthood | 151 |
| 5.4 | The Second Principle: In Persona Christi | 154 |
| 5.5 | The Third Principle: In Persona Ecclesiae | 156 |
| 5.6 | The Fourth Principle: Priestly Presence | 159 |
| 5.7 | The Fifth Principle: Personal Identity | 161 |
| 5.8 | The Sixth Principle: Ongoing Formation | 163 |
| 5.9 | Unique Challenges to Priestly Identity Formation in African Church Today | 165 |

**Chapter Six: The Structuring of a Formative Community in the Catholic Church Today**    **177**

    6.1      Crisis, the Operative Principle    178
    6.2      Formation, the Task in Crisis    181
    6.3      Concluding Summary    184

**The Bibliography**    **188**

# PREFACE

This study explores the structures of crisis as a human and spiritual factor of formation and ongoing formation in the life and ministry of the Catholic priesthood. The term, crisis, is understood here as a "turning –point event." Any action or thing that creates a "turning-point" experience in the life of people will be qualified as a crisis. Formation here is understood as an "act" as well as a "process" in human and spiritual growth. Formation as an "act" refers to what we do or not do to foster human and spiritual growth. Formation as a "process" is a way we follow or not follow on our maturity journey through life.

Formation then, is a lifelong process. An ongoing formation process will guarantee a growing witness in the principles of priestly identity in priestly life and ministry. Whenever an on-going formation process is blocked or denied, a situation of crisis ensues. The crisis in priesthood then, is an "invitation-event" calling attention to a need for a proper formation and ongoing formation, not simply an "evil-event" that demands prosecution and punishment as it is being handled in the Catholic Church today.

Because the crisis in priesthood is structural, historical and cultural, this study adopts an exploratory method of investigation, not a comparative method of study. The exploratory method of investigation follows a two-way approach: historical and contemporary approaches. A historical approach looks into the history of the Church in general to investigate the structural roots of the crisis. A contemporary approach looks into a particular section of the Catholic priesthood, the Catholic priests in Igbo community in Nigeria, through interviews and questionnaires to investigate how the structures of crisis structure priestly life and ministry today.

This project discovers that a structure of crisis in priesthood is creating some attitudinal changes that are inimical to the principles of priestly life and ministry today at least in three forms: a) The priesthood is understood as a personal achievement; b) The priesthood is understood as a family investment; and c) The priesthood is understood as a social status. The attempted zero tolerance as a response to this crisis rather compounds the crisis. This study recommends that a proper response to the crisis in priesthood must include a focus on how to structure and maintain an appropriate, effective, formative community in seminary schools and an ongoing formation in priestly life and ministry. It also recommends a three-step *practical* approach to face the crisis and another three-step *process* approach to restructure the priestly life and ministry of today. The three-step *practical* approach is for priests and the lay faithful alike to develop and live out with commitment and faithfulness in life and ministry: a) a "courage to speak" honestly about their lives' needs and experiences; b) a "courage to listen" genuinely to individual and community needs and interests; and c) a "courage to affirm" and acknowledge in truth and compassion the dignity and respect of one another in all relationships, especially the most vulnerable, the children, the poor and women. Meanwhile, the Church is responding to the outrage of the people in reaction to the crisis. We are yet to face the deep crisis and deal with it.

The other three-step *process* approach to restructure the priestly life and ministry is: i) to restructure the seminary system from "a place" to study and prepare for ordination to be "a formative community" where seminarians discover and develop themselves, their gifts and their communities to serve God and the people of God. ii) To construct and restructure a human formation process or system that is more than a skill development training to include human formation and relationship /administrative skills formation. This is something to be added to the seminary system. In public life, school teachers, after completing their studies, go through a teacher's training process, priests who do more than a teaching ministry do so little or nothing in this regard. The grace of a priestly ordination may not supply the human training in relationship and administration skills. iii) To restructure a spiritual formation process that is more than the ancient monastic spiritual exercises to include an ongoing lifelong spiritual formation on conversion and renewal in the death and resurrection of Jesus Christ, in the divine Trinitarian community of God the Father, God the Son and God the Holy Spirit ( i.e. an ongoing spiritual formation and transformation lifestyle).

The case of the African/Nigerian Church and priesthood is a complex and complicated one due to an overshadowing confusion of a "White Church" syndrome and a cultural crisis of a "global pseudo-culture" (see chapter five). The African Church case may be seen from this wisdom statement from Pope John Paul II. The Pope stated in June, 1982 that "a faith which does not become culture is a faith which has not been fully received, not thoroughly thought through, not fully lived out." The cultural crisis of the global pseudo-culture is that African is a melting-pot of three powerful cultural forces: "the Western Capitalism with its unregulated, competitive, individualistic materialism; the Eastern Communism with its promotion of class struggle and its limited leadership of the few;" and the African Communion of all peoples and cultures with a blurred vision and corrupted leadership. In simple language, the West has the "wealth" with the "waste" and "wars," while the Africans have the "Way" without the "will." The challenge now is how to encourage the Africans to lead the "Way" with willingness in a communion of all peoples and cultures in true love, holiness, justice and peace; and the West to lead the "Way" on how to share the "wealth" without the "waste" and "wars." It is a challenge of an honest commitment and faithfulness to lead and follow the "Way" of a true communion of all peoples and cultures in a spirit of solidarity, collaboration, justice and peace, and not to follow the "way" of "waste" and "wars" of corruption, fanaticism, domination, destruction and indoctrination.

# INTRODUCTION

## *Defining the Problem*

We face different challenges in priesthood today. Many people call it "a crisis." Here, we understand the word "crisis" as a "turning-point event" that may cause emotional and spiritual upheaval.[1] Crisis is understood as an "invitation event," not just as an "evil event." An "event" is an encounter in life. It may be a physical encounter, moral encounter, emotional or psychological encounter, spiritual encounter, social encounter, political encounter, educational encounter, theological encounter, behavioral encounter, and so on. Crisis is not just an event. It is a turning-point event. Crisis affects our lives positively or negatively depending on the nature of the event itself or the nature of a response to the event.

The word, formation is understood here as an "act" and a "process" in human and spiritual growth. The concept of crisis and human formation as applied in this study is based on Erik Erikson's psychosocial theory of human development. Erikson's psychosocial theory teaches that "each individual proceeds through eight stages of development from the cradle to the grave. Each stage presents the individual with a crisis. If a particular crisis is handled well, a positive outcome ensues. If it is not handled well, the resulting outcome is negative."[2] The emphasis must be on how to handle crisis well, not just on how to contain the aftermath of a crisis.

What many authors call "crisis" in Catholic priesthood such as a sex scandal crisis, identity crisis and others are the "flower" events, not the "root" factors of the crisis. The real problem is a crisis of formation and ongoing formation in the Catholic priesthood. The crisis problem has a structural root in seminary education that is mainly intellectual. The main concern of this study is not on the interpretations and analyses of the flower-effects of crisis in priesthood. This study is an invitation to face the root crisis in Catholic priesthood which is to structure and maintain an appropriate, effective, formative community in our seminary schools and an ongoing formation in priestly life and ministry.

## Literature Review

Different authors give different interpretations and analyses of this issue of "crisis." A. W. Richard Sipe in his book, *Sex, Priests and Power: Anatomy of a Crisis* (1995) puts it in simple language: "The Roman Catholic priesthood is in crisis. It is obvious that the crisis is sexual." [3] Donald B. Cozzens in his book, *The Changing Face of the Priesthood: A Reflection on the Priest's Crisis of Soul* (2000) calls it "the priest's crisis of soul." For Cozzens, it has everything to do with "the changing face of the priesthood" in terms of "issues," "challenges," "concerns," and "realities" that have gone awry in priestly formation, life and ministries. [4]

Alan Abernethy in his own book, *Fulfillment and Frustration: Ministry in Today's Church* (2002) sees a crisis of balance between "fulfillment and frustration" in the life and ministry of priests which is often a challenge of "to be or not to be," "the unresolved questions," the realistic or unrealistic "expectations," and "the paradox." [5] Abernethy perceives an ongoing "crisis" in an unstructured lifestyle and ministry of priests as a daily struggle between fulfillment and frustration. In the same year, 2002, Michael S. Rose in his book, *Goodbye, Good Men: How Liberals Brought Corruption into the Catholic Church,* sees in it a crisis of a failed system and poor leadership in some levels of the Church life and education. [6] Rose believes that the people of power in the system have in many ways sabotaged the system and undermined the due processes to a level of an uncontained crisis of today in the priesthood.

Andrew M. Greeley in his own book, *Priests: A Calling in Crisis* (2004) looks deep into history to name it "a calling in crisis." Greeley describes "the year 2002, the year of pedophile and the fortieth anniversary of the convening of the Second Vatican Council." He claims that "the cracks and the fissures and fractures had been there a long time – inadequate leadership, low quality of service, dissatisfaction with the Vatican, and sex." [7] What Greeley describes as "the cracks and the fissures and the fractures that had been there a long time" in the Church in terms of "inadequate leadership, low quality of service, dissatisfaction with the Vatican and sex" are not without effects.

A survey released from Vatican two weeks before the death of Pope John Paul II on April 2, 2005 showed that the number of priests worldwide in 1975 was 405,000 and in 2005, it came to 397,000. At the same period, the number of Catholics "increased worldwide by 52%, to 1.1billion people." [8] In another survey release from Vatican City in

May 2006, it was indicated that there was an increase in the number of priests in Africa, from 16,926 in 1988 to 31,259 in 2006; and Asia, from 27,700 in 1988 to 48,222 in 2006. In Europe and America there was a decrease: 250,000 in 1988 to less than 200,000 in 2006 in Europe while the American stood around 120,000 in 2006.[9] What these two surveys showed was that the crisis affected the Church differently. While there was a decrease in the number of priests in Europe and America, there was an increase in the number of priests in African and some Eastern countries. However, when one considered the number of priests in relation to the number of the faithful, the picture was different. "While there were 893 Catholics for every priest worldwide in 1958, today there are 2,677. ... Meanwhile in Latin America today there are 8,000 for every priest. In Europe, the ratio is 1 to 1,400; in America it is 1 to 1,200; in Africa the ratio is 1 to 4000, according to the Vatican." [10]

The sexual abuse scandal had adversely affected the priests' crisis in the world. In United States of America alone, "the New York Times relying on court records, news reporters, church documents and interviews, found that 1,205 priests or 1.8 percent of all priests ordained from 1950 to 2001 had been accused of abuse." [11] It was not only priests who were affected, bishops were also involved. Since 1990, 10 Catholic bishops had resigned in connection with sexual abuse scandal in United States. Within the period (since 1990) 11 Catholic bishops had resigned worldwide in connection with sex scandal, in nine countries in the world: Argentina, one; Austria, one; Canada, two; Germany, one; Ireland, two; Poland, one; Scotland, one; Switzerland, one; and Wales, one.[12] In the recent sexual abuse crisis that engulfed the Catholic Church in Europe, five more bishops have resigned in connection with the sex scandal, bringing the total number of reigned bishops in Europe to seventeen: one more in Germany; one more in Belgium and three more in Ireland.

## The Focus of the Study

The focus of this study is on the crisis in priesthood as an "invitation event" to a neglected need for an ongoing formation in the life and ministry of priesthood in the Catholic Church over the years. There are problems in the Church today not because priests and bishops are now "criminals," but because there is a poor or lack of an ongoing formation in priestly life and ministry in general. The crisis in the Church today is not because there is no persecution and punishment of erring priests and bishops, even though it can be a contributing factor.

A major factor is a need for appropriate structures and maintenance of an ongoing formation in the lives and ministries of priests, bishops and priests-to-be in the Church at all times and seasons. This study makes a case that the Catholic priesthood is in crisis both as a *"content* issue" and as a *"context* issue." That is to say, we have not only "priesthood in crisis" but more so a "crisis in priesthood." Roderick Strange, a long time seminary rector in the Western Church, the European Church, in his book, *The Risk of Discipleship* (2004) perceives the situation as a "crisis of a missing piece." Roderick Strange, thus speaks of "recovering lost ground," "risking the cross," "a human calling," "loving and celibacy," "servant and leader," and "enduring commitment."[13] For Strange then a "missing piece" is an "enduring commitment" to the inner calling or a discipleship of the priesthood.

In the African Church, the Catholic Bishops of Nigeria in their 2004 Pastoral Letter, *I Chose You: The Nigerian Priest in the Third Millennium,* perceive the situation as a "great awakening" clouded with an identity crisis. The Nigerian prelates put it this way:

> There is a great awakening in Africa of a profound cultural, social, economic and political consciousness, which the Church does not ignore. This awakening includes a new quest for meaning, a search for fundamental values and a more radical expression of selfhood in one's native language and culture. Nigerian priests now seek their own identity, deriving from their particular socio-cultural, ecclesiastical and pastoral milieu.[14]

Indeed, the Church in Africa or elsewhere "does not ignore" the great awakening and the Church does not seem to have taken it seriously either. The feedback from the preparatory interviews and questionnaires on Nigerian priests and bishops which is discussed in chapter four of this project speaks for itself on this matter. There is a little awareness of the Church's problem in Africa but there is no grass-root focused approach to deal with it, as is indicative in the statements of the Nigerian Catholic Prelates:

> In the past, the problem for the Catholic Church in Nigeria was to attract, form, and ordain sufficient diocesan priests. Today the problem is the quality of the diocesan priesthood as it is lived. Each diocese has its own spirit or atmosphere. There is a growing danger of clerical arrogance, of materialism in an impoverished society, and of brazen disregard for the strategy that sustains a celibate life. Consequently, members of the laity are more and

more disedified by some Church leaders. When the laity are aware of the questionable conduct of a priest, that priest in turn is beholden to the laity, and loses his freedom, because of fear of revelation of his misdeeds. Media and video houses are beginning to search and reveal some of the greatest lapses in priestly life and ministry.[15]

According to the Nigerian Prelates, the problem today in the Church is no longer the *number* of priests – "to attract, form, and ordain sufficient diocesan priests" but "the *quality* of the diocesan priesthood as it is lived." The Prelates also foresee some dangers on the way to achieve the targeted quality issue. The first danger is a growing tendency to "clerical arrogance" and an addiction to "materialism in an impoverished society." The second danger, according to the Prelates, is the growing number of misled and disedified laity that is drawing the attention of the Media and video houses. And the third danger is that the controlling force in the misconducts of priests is "a fear of revelation of misdeeds" rather than a faith in their priestly vocation or the fidelity to their priestly identity and discipline. The irony of the whole situation is that the African Church is trying to repeat the mistakes the Western Church is trying to correct: sacrificing "quality" in an inordinate pursuit for "quantity." It is indeed a Church in great need to learn how to listen to God, to the genuine needs of one another, to the Gospel and the culture of the people of God.

Donald Cozzens, in a magazine's article in 2000, "Facing the crisis in the priesthood" suggested a three-step approach in addressing a situation where crisis is buried in fear and secrecy. The three steps approach according to Cozzens are: "Courage to speak" honestly about everything; "Courage to listen" genuinely and compassionately to individual and community's needs; and "Courage to affirm"[16] in truth and justice the dignity and respect of all in all relationships. David Toups, in his book: *Reclaiming Our Priestly Character* (2008) states that the key issue here is a distorted or lost of the priestly character in formation, life and mission of the priesthood. For David Toups, there are two root causes to this crisis: First, "a confusion regarding the exact nature of the priesthood among priests themselves;" and second, "a confusion among priests and laity alike about the difference between the priesthood of the faithful and the ministerial priesthood."[17] Toups sees a road to reclaim the priestly character in an "ongoing formation, not (just) education." He teaches that an "ongoing formation is essential for all Christian vocation"[18] – a stand this project supports and substantiates. An "ongoing formation," according to Toups, "is about deepening one's interiority and fostering a relationship with Jesus Christ. It is about an ongoing conversion that reminds the priest who he is as a minister of the Gospel and whose he is as a son of God." [19]

## Method of Study

This project makes a case that the crisis in priesthood today in the Catholic Church is a function of human and spiritual questions that have roots in the formation process. To substantiate this point, this study adopts a two-point methodical approach (exploratory in nature) to the issue of crisis in the Catholic priesthood today. The first is a historical method of investigation which looks into the history of the Catholic Church to explore the structures of crisis in the past. The second is a contemporary method of investigation which looks into a particular section of the Catholic priesthood, the priests and bishops of Igbo community in South-Eastern Nigeria, through interviews and questionnaires to explore how the structures of crisis structure the priestly life and ministry today.

## Analysis of the Study

For the purpose of our discussions in this study, priesthood is understood as a vocation and a way of life. The priesthood, so understood, has four roots: 1) Priesthood as an institution (the historical root, Chapter One); 2) Priesthood as a sacrament (the ritual root – ordination, Chapter Two); 3) Priesthood as a ministry (the human root, Chapter Three); and 4) Priesthood as a vocation (the spiritual root, Chapter Four). The chapter five discusses the dimensions of priestly identity; while the last chapter, chapter six concludes with a structuring of a formative community as a needed response to the issue of crisis in life. When a community lacks in its formative principles, the individual members lavish in crisis. The term, crisis, as was discussed earlier, is a turning-point event or situation which may cause emotional and spiritual upheaval. It may be applied in two forms: The first form is the normative or developmental crisis (positive crisis) which may tend towards greater growth and integration of the person in question. The other form of crisis is the neurotic crisis (negative crisis) which may create disruption and disintegration to some degree.

In the course of history, the Catholic Church underwent some structural changes that compromised some of the roots of the priesthood as we will see in chapter one. The priesthood in the Catholic Church underwent a structural process that tended to be somewhat reductionistic in nature. The structural process had been a part of the Catholic Church from the beginning. The effects are now becoming evident in three fundamental forms: The first structural form is the "episcopalization" and "sacerdotalization" of the Catholic Church and its priesthood whereby there is "over-concentration of leadership" in one person, a bishop (episcopalization) and the Church ministries on a person, a priest (sacerdotalization) with no "intrinsic reference to any given community." [20] This was between the first and fourth centuries. The Church shifted from a "house church" (a house to house celebration of a Eucharistic community) to a "basilica" (a court or a public meeting place); thus, a loss of the community roots. The Church becomes some "place" we go to, not who we are, a community of God's people. That is, there is overemphasis on the Church as a "place" (a building), not as a people of God.

The second structural form was the "monasticization" of the Catholic Church and its priesthood by the absorption of the ministries and spiritualities by the monasteries after the fourth century. With the institutionalization of this form, the Catholic Church lost its rich Trinitarian spirituality to monastic methods of prayer and religious exercises (a loss of the spiritual roots). The prayer life of the Church becomes some methodical formulae to be followed and the spiritual life is a series of religious exercises to be practiced in excluded areas (the monasteries). The Church became a separate entity from the world, thus, the dualism of the Church as "holy" and the world as "evil" was enthroned.

The third structural form was the "hierarchization" of the Catholic Church and its priesthood by the "over-structuring of its ministries and leadership into a cluster of offices" between the 8th and 14th centuries.[21] With this structural form, the Church ministry became a ritual power to do "something," a power to perform some ritual functions; and the Church leadership became a hierarchical office or position to be owned and protected. Consequently, the Church lost its human roots. As a result of the three structural changes in the Catholic Church, the Church came to be identified with "cultism."

These three fundamental losses in history: the loss of community roots, the loss of spiritual roots and the loss of human roots constituted the fundamental root causes of the crisis in priesthood today. It is quite interesting to observe some co-relatedness among these three fundamental root causes and what happened in the Catholic Church from the 15th century to the present day. The Protestant Reformation of the 16th and 17th centuries simply replaced cultism with secularization and western professionalization. While the Catholic Counter-Reformation, (the Councils of Trent and Vatican I – 16th to 19th centuries) only added legalism to cultism. Vatican II and everything after it are yet to get the attention, listening and learning they deserve to make a little difference in the whole system.

The more interesting part is the co-relatedness among the "ancient crisis" (the root crisis) and the "present crisis" (the three attitudinal tendencies among the priests of today: first, the priesthood is perceived as personal achievement; second, the priesthood is understood as a family investment; and third, the priesthood is appreciated as an accomplished social status) in the Catholic Church, as we shall see in chapter three. This co-relation between "the ancient root crisis" and "the present root crisis" makes a case to a claim that the crisis in the priesthood today is more than a socio-cultural problem of one particular area of the Church. It is not simply some "bad guys" scandalous behaviors or abuses that must be exposed, punished and corrected. The problem has deep roots that demand a radical approach and a radical solution – healing from the roots. It is both a human and spiritual formation and developmental problem that needs to be addressed from such fundamental perspectives.

The review of history and literature shows that the crisis in priesthood is a radical issue, demanding a radical approach. In chapter two, I address the issue of the "loss" of community roots through a review of seminary formation, its theories and models. This study makes a case that a seminary is not simply a "place of study" where seminarians are prepared for a priestly ordination. The seminary school is not a place to prepare for ordinations but a "formative community" which includes the seminarians, their families, the seminary staff, the bishops and the people of God. It is a formative community where candidates for priesthood discover, develop and dedicate themselves and their gifts in communion service of God and God's people. A seminary school is more than a place of intellectual education. It is a formative community in service of God and God's people at all times. What is true of seminary school education is very true of every school education in the outside world. The Church, the priesthood, and the people of God need to be continuously grounded in a formative community that is truly Godly (holy) and deeply human (compassionate, reconciliatory and respectful).

In chapter three, I addressed the issue of the "loss" of human roots with Erik Erikson's theory of psycho-social, lifelong human development. Erikson's theory holds a different ground against a cultural presumption that adulthood is attained once and for all in a lifetime or a religious belief that a liturgical ceremony in a form of public commitment like marriage or ordination guarantees automatic transition to a fully mature adulthood. Erikson teaches that whether as a child or as an adult, we move through and resolve a series of life dilemmas or crises at various stages in one's lifespan. We don't choose the life dilemmas, they choose us. Each person is pushed through this sequence of life dilemmas by three factors: 1) a biological maturation; 2) the social pressures; and 3) the demands of the roles one plays in a life journey. Crisis then, is not an "accident" or a mishap in human life. It is a part of the substance of human development.

Crisis is also an invitation to be fully grounded in a total acceptance and acknowledgment of our humanness as a God-given capacity to do good always. The capacity to choose the good is God's gift to us as free human beings; a commitment to live a good life is our gift to God. All human beings are therefore, invited to be grounded in humility, not humiliation of others; in forgiveness, not in fighting one another; in building bridges that connect, not walls that divide us; in reconciliation, not in revolting or renouncing one another. That is to say, no commitment is final. Every commitment is open to further opportunities and possibilities of new commitments. The invitation is to be constantly open to and accepting to new opportunities and possibilities to face the challenges of life. It calls for a radical spirit of patience, support and encouragement to one another.

In chapter four, I addressed the issue of the "loss" of spiritual roots. Chapter four proposes a point of departure from the monastic spirituality of methodical prayers and religious exercises (a spirituality of the head) that dominated the Catholic Church for many years. This chapter advocates for a new spirituality of interiority, a spirituality of living from the inside-out (a spirituality of the heart). That is to say, in the words of John Bradshaw, we are essentially spiritual beings on a human journey. To state that we are spiritual beings does not mean we don't need to grow spiritually. Spiritual growth is a journey of formation and transformation – an ongoing conversion process. Conversion is a key to spiritual growth. Conversion is not simply an act, it is also a process. Conversion, then, is "not just a matter of believing something new, of affirming a new faith, of adopting a new story" of life; a "change of content, a switching from one faith story to another" – an act or an event.[22] Conversion is not a program to be completed, an achievement to be accomplished. It is a human and spiritual challenge to live through in every point of life. No one, then, is converted for life, rather we are being converted every day, in fact, every minute. There is a need to be grounded in a spirit of ongoing formation.

## *The Message of the Study*

Human beings are essentially spiritual and in constant need of growth in all levels of life. As human beings in a common spiritual journey, we are either growing spiritually through an ongoing conversion or we are stuck in "spiritual bankruptcy." When people are growing physically but stuck spiritually, they become "adult children." According to John Bradshaw, "these adult children run our schools, our Churches and our government. They also create families ... the crisis in the families today is the crisis of adult children raising children who will become adult children."[23] The challenge then is to be grounded in an ongoing conversion in spiritual growth, morally, affectively, cognitively and religiously. The alternative is to be grounded in spiritual crisis and/or spiritual abuse of religion, whereby we remake our religious creeds or beliefs into idols; our rules of life into legalism; our rituals or celebrations of life into superstitions; and the people of God into ideologies. It is a death sentence to a sense of respect and responsibility to the "Beingness" of everything or every person including God; a death sentence to a sense of the Sacred, a sense of meaning, purpose and values in life.

This study is an invitation to a structural awareness of some out-of-touch issues in our lives and ministries as priests and the lay people of God and a need for a follow-through process of being grounded communally, humanly and spiritually. It is an invitation to a broad view of crisis, not simply as an evil to be punished and corrected, but more so as a call to a need of being fully grounded in life. This study is an exploratory approach in focusing on some structural issues of the crisis and their challenges in Catholic priesthood today. It is not an answer to all kinds of crisis in priesthood. It is not a comparative, sociological study of the crisis in priesthood but rather a theological/spiritual insight into the structural implications of crisis for Catholic priests in the world of today. I consider my task here an accomplished one if this study succeeds in opening a discussion on priestly crisis beyond accusations, litigations, and counterclaims in and outside the Church in today's world that is rapidly becoming a global village.

1  Webster's Universal College Dictionary (Random House, Inc., 1997), pp. 192-3

2  Kaplan, Paul S. (1993) The Human Odyssey: Life-Span Development, 2nd Edition, Minneapolis: West Publishing Company, p. 30

3  Sipe, A. W. Richard (1995) Sex, Priests and Power: Anatomy of a Crisis, New York: Brunner-Routledge, p. 6

4  Cozzens, D. B. (2000) The Changing Face of the Priesthood: A Reflection on the Priest's Crisis of Soul, Minnesota: The Liturgical Press

5  Abernethy, A. (2002) Fulfillment & Frustration: Ministry in Today's Church, Dublin: The Columba Press

6  Rose, M. S. (2002) Goodbye, Good Men: How liberals Brought Corruption into the Catholic Church, Washington DC: Regnery Publishing Inc.

7  Greeley, A. M. (2004) Priests: A Calling in Crisis, Chicago: The University Press, p. 1

8  Caldwell, Deborah "The New Pope's First Crisis, The Priest Shortage and Its Surprisingly Simple Solution: Allow Marriage as an Option for Priests," Dec. 6, 2009 [http://www.beliefnet.com/Faiths/Christianity/Catholic/2005/04/The-New-Popes-First-Crisis.aspx]

9  New Statistical Yearbook of the Church, "African and Asian Vocations Keep Growing," [Vatican City, May 22, 2006, Zenit.org]

10  Caldwell, Deborah "The New Pope's First Crisis, The Priest Shortage and Its Surprisingly Simple Solution: Allow Marriage as an Option for Priests," Dec. 6, 2009, [http://www.beliefnet.com/Faiths/Christianity/Catholic/2005/04/The-New-Popes-First-Crisis.aspx]

11  Current Issues in Catholicism "Crisis in the Priesthood: Priesthood Sexual Abuse Scandal" Dec. 8, 2009 [http://sfbayc.org/magazine/html/cbcrisis.html]

12  The Boston Globe, "Spotlight Investigation: Abuse in the Catholic Church," Dec. 8, 2009 [http://www.boston.com/globe/spotlight/abuse/extras/bishops_map.htm]

13  Strange, R. (2004) The Risk of Discipleship, London: Darton, Longman and Todd Ltd., pvii

14  Catholic Bishops Conference of Nigeria, (2004) I Chose You: The Nigerian Priest in the third Millennium, Lagos, Catholic Secretariat Press, p. 1

15  Ibid., p.29

16  Cozzens, D. in American Magazine, November 4, 2000 "Facing the Crisis in the Priesthood," December 8, 2009 [http://www.americanmagazine.org/content/article.cfm?article_id=2296]

17  Catholic Online, Featured Today "Priestly Identity: Crisis and Renewal (Part 1, 3/21/2008) Dec. 6, 2009 [http://www.catholic.org/featured/headline.php?ID=5458]

18  Ibid.

19  Ibid.

20  O'Meara, T. F. (1999)Theology of Ministry, New York: Paulist Press, pp. 88-89

21  O'Meara, T. F. (1999) Ibid., p. 89

22  Conn, W. E. (1998) The Desiring Self: Rooting Pastoral Counseling and Spiritual Direction in Self-Transcendence, New York: Paulist Press, pp.39-47

23  Bradshaw, J. (1996) The Family: A New Way of Creating Solid Self-Esteem, Revised Edition, Florida: Health Communications, Inc., p. 4

# CHAPTER ONE: THE BIBLICAL AND THE HISTORICAL DEVELOPMENT OF THE CATHOLIC PRIESTHOOD

## The Biblical Development of Priesthood
## - The Old Testament Period

A priest is "a person consecrated" or ordained "to the ministry of the Gospel" and the Holy Eucharist (the sacraments).[1] The priesthood, on the other hand, is "the office or character of a priest."[2] Priesthood, understood in this sense, it is a New Testament reality, the priesthood of Jesus Christ. However, one may speak of the biblical roots of this priesthood in the different calls of God to different persons in the Old Testament tradition. The "first" personal call of God is to the person of Abram. It is a call to "leave" everything and to "be a blessing:" "The Lord says to Abram, 'Leave your country, your relatives and your father's home, and go to a land that I am going to show you. I will give you many descendants, and they will become a great nation. I will bless you and make your name famous, so that you will be a blessing.'"[3] This primal root of the priesthood in the call of Abraham has in some ways highlighted a spirit of detachment as a condition of serving God among His people.

We see a similar case in the call of Moses in the "burning bush" in the desert mountain of Sinai. And the Lord says to Moses, "Do not come near; put off your shoes from your feet, for the place on which you are standing is holy ground." [27] The spirit of detachment implied here ("put off your shoes") is in a form of a respect for the sacredness of all that God created in doing the work of God.

When the work of service became too much for Moses to handle alone, through the advice of Jethro, his father-in-law and priest of Midian, he appointed twelve judges as "leaders of thousands, hundreds, fifties and tens."[4] God may call or choose us through other people. The required criterion for the choice of judges is: "They must be God-fearing men who can be trusted and who cannot be bribed."[5] This marks the "institution" of the royal priesthood. The judges are appointed to meet the needs of the people of God. The needs of the people of God define missions and ministries. Later on, God ordered Moses to "anoint Aaron and his sons, and ordain them as priests in my service."[6] This marks the "institution" of the domestic priesthood – the Levites.

When God called Samuel in sleep while he was "serving the Lord under the direction of Eli" the priest in Shiloh, Samuel answered Eli who directed him to answer the Lord: "Speak, Lord, your servant is listening."[7] God's call demanded a loving response and obedient listening. The Lord continued to call and to speak to His people. He never stopped calling and speaking to His people and their leaders. God led His people through the persons he chose to call. He ordered Samuel to listen to the needs of the people and anoint Saul, the son of Kish as the first king of the people Israel, saying: "The Lord anoints you as ruler of his people Israel. You will rule this people and protect them from all their enemies."[8]

When Saul failed God out of disobedience, Samuel anointed David to succeed him. [9] (This signals the genealogical lineage of Jesus Christ, the eternal High Priest). When God called Isaiah to be a prophet in the midst of his feeling of guilt and unworthiness, he answered: "I will go! Send me!"[10] Jeremiah, like Isaiah was overwhelmed with self inadequacies in spite of God's "elaborate calling" on his part ("I chose you before I gave you life, and before you were born I selected you to be a prophet to the nations." 1:4) Jeremiah's call was played out in a number of "visions."[11] Ezekiel was the same, as his call was played out in a number of visions. Thus he declared: "I fell face downwards on the ground, but God's Spirit entered me and raised me to my feet."[12] Ezekiel was a prophet of change and transition – the "old Jerusalem" and "the new Jerusalem." The frustration was on both sides. To the people, God says: "So my people crowd in to hear what you have to say, but they don't do what you tell them to do. Loving words are on their lips, but they continue their greedy ways. To them you are nothing more than an entertainer singing love songs or playing a harp. They listen to all your words but don't obey a single one of them."[13] God did not only call priests, he also called kings and prophets.

God said to the priests, prophets and kings together: "You are doomed, you shepherds of Israel! You take care of yourselves, but never tend the sheep. You drink the milk, wear clothes made from the wool, and kill and eat the finest sheep. But you never tend the sheep. You have not taken care of the weak ones, heal the ones that are sick, bandage the ones that are hurt, brought back the ones that wandered off, or look for the ones that were lost. Instead, you treat them cruelly."[14] The need for a change was inevitable. And God said: "I myself will be the shepherd of my sheep, and I will find them a place to rest. I, the Sovereign Lord have spoken. I will look for those that are lost, bring back those that wandered off, bandage those that are hurt, and heal those that are sick; but those that are fat and strong I will destroy, because I am a shepherd who does what is right."[15]

In the Book of Isaiah the prophet, "The Lord says, I am making a new earth and new heavens. The events of the past will be completely forgotten. Be glad and rejoice forever in what I create."[16] In the Book of Ezekiel, it was stated: "I, the Sovereign Lord have spoken. I will use you to show the nations that I am holy. I will take you from every nation and country and bring you back to your own land. I will sprinkle clean water on you and make you clean from all your idols and everything else that has defiled you. I will give you a new heart and a new mind. I will take away your stubborn heart of stone and give you an obedient heart. I will put my spirit in you and will see to it that you follow my laws and keep all the commands I have given you. Then you will live in the land I gave your ancestors. You will be my people, and I will be your God."[17]

In all, it was God who initiated every covenant relationship with His people through personal calls to some persons of the community. God had a plan and preparation for the "salvation of the whole human race" which He entrusted to persons and peoples He called at different places and periods. No one then was called for himself or for his own

agenda or purpose. God called us to Himself and to His mission. God's
call demanded a loving response and an obedient listening in a loving
service of all.


# The Biblical Development of Priesthood
# - The New Testament Period


John the Baptist was a "bridge-prophet-priest" between the Old and New
Testaments. In the Holy Scriptures we read: "A man named John was sent
from God. He came for testimony, to testify to the light, so that all might
believe through him. He was not the light, but came to testify to the light.
The true light, which enlightens everyone, was coming into the world."[18]
John bore that witness to the full. He declared: "I am not the Messiah ... I
am the voice of someone shouting in the desert: Make a straight path for the
Lord to travel!"[19] John did not only proclaim it in words, he demonstrated
it with his life (he even died to witness it, after handing over): "The next
day John was there again with two of his disciples, and as he watched Jesus
walk by, he said, 'Behold, the Lamb of God.' The two disciples heard what
he said and followed Jesus. Jesus turned and saw them following him and
said to them, 'What are you looking for?' They said to him, 'Rabbi, where
are you staying? He said to them, 'Come and you will see.'"[20]

Jesus presents Himself both as the continuity and the fulfillment of
the Old Testament promises: "Do not think that I have come to abolish
the law or the prophets. I have not come to abolish but to fulfill." [21] The
Letter to the Hebrews struggles with this message in emphasizing that
"it was on the basis of the levitical priesthood that the Law was given
to the people of Israel. Now, if the work of the levitical priests had been
perfected, there would have been no need for a difference of priest to
appear, one who is in the priestly order of Melchizedek, not of Aaron. For
when the priesthood is changed, there also has to be a change in the law.
And our Lord, of whom these things are said, belonged to a different tribe,
and no member of his tribe ever served as a priest. " [22] There is, then, some
uniqueness in the priesthood of Jesus Christ, the priesthood of the New
Testament. The priesthood of the New Testament is not simply a "copy"
of that of the Old Testament. Jesus Christ is both God and man.

The incarnation event leading to the paschal mystery constitutes a turning point in the history of humankind and the priesthood. Jesus Christ, while still in the womb of Virgin Mary did baptize (and ordained) John the Baptist in the womb of his mother, Elizabeth, during Mary's visitation. During His three years ministry on earth, Jesus chose the twelve apostles, ordained them during the Last Super and commissioned them before His ascension to His Father in heaven, saying: "All power in heaven and on earth has been given to me. Go, therefore and make disciples of all nations, baptizing them in the name of the Father, and of the Son, and of the Holy Spirit, teaching them to observe all that I have commanded you. And behold, I am with you always, until the end of the age."[23] The God of the New Testament is a Triune God. In similar manner, the priesthood of the New Testament is a triune priesthood. The first is the priesthood of Jesus Christ, who is the mediator between God and human beings, the Source and Sustainer of the priesthood of all the baptized.

The second is the priesthood of all the faithful, the common priesthood. In the words of Saint Peter, we are a priestly people and he urges all of us: "… and like living stones, let yourselves be built into a spiritual house to be a holy priesthood to offer spiritual sacrifices acceptable to God through Jesus Christ."[24] We become the universal priests of God through our baptism as to become the "moving altar" of God who sanctify and offer to God all we are and all we do in life, everywhere in the world.

The third form of priesthood is the ministerial priesthood of the ordained priests of God who are the spiritual leaders and sanctifiers of the common priesthood of God, though they are part of it. As a part of the common priesthood, through the power of Christian baptism, they are parts of the "moving altar" of God who sanctify and offer to God everywhere and in everything all they are and all they do in life in the whole world. Also, as the ordained ministerial priests of God, through the power of sacramental ordination, they are transformed into the "permanent altar" of God where Jesus Christ Himself is sacramentally sacrificed to sanctify the people and worship God. It is this third form of the priesthood, the ministerial priesthood that occupies our central interest in this project.

How would one define the theology and spirituality of the ministerial priesthood at that time of Jesus Christ? Jordan Aumann would like us to consider the spirituality of the priesthood of the time of Jesus Christ as the "Gospel spirituality" with a three-point caution to keep in mind.

The first word of caution is on how to read and interpret the New Testament. Aumann cautions that "we do not read the New Testament as we would read the biography of a great historical figure whom we wish to remember and perhaps imitate." He points out that "this could all too easily result in a religion of hero-worship, a liturgy of memorial services, and a spirituality of a nostalgia for the past."[25]

The second area of caution is on how we interpret the "code of morality" and the structures of the Church. Aumann claims that "Christ did not leave us a detailed code of morality, a fully explicated body of dogmas, a directory of liturgical rubrics and ceremonies, or even a completed pattern for the structure of his church."[26] There are no ready-made principles of disciplines or ready-made patterns or structures of the Church. He teaches that we may freely "allow for evolution in dogma, prudential decisions in morality, adaptation in liturgy, and the gradual development of the Church, not to mention the charismatic operations of the Holy Spirit." [27] The mentality or attitude of one size fits all is a death sentence to theology and spirituality.

The third area of caution is on the nature and quality of the spiritual life. It is not enough to have a historical or school spirituality. It must be a "Gospel" and/or Incarnational spirituality (that is, the spirituality of the Paschal mystery). Aumann reasons that "if Christian spirituality signifies a participation in the mystery of Christ, our first task is to contemplate that mystery with the help of the New Testament and then to discover how we share in it. Stated succinctly, the mystery of Christ is the mystery of the Incarnation, the Word made flesh and dwelling among us (John 1:14), the God made man."[28] To understand spirituality simply as sets of spiritual practices of some particular schools or institutional communities may tend to reductionism, a tendency to perceive spirituality as something to be owned and practiced at will. We will discover that this tendency to reductionism in the spirituality of the priesthood in history is the root cause of the crisis in priesthood today. Let us now look at the experiential development of the priesthood of Christ in the Catholic Church history.

## The Historical Development of Priesthood in the Catholic Church History

God still calls his people and gives them the gift of the priesthood now in the person of Jesus Christ, "in the priestly order of Melchizedek, not of Aaron" (Hebrew 5:6). It is still God's call to be his presence and gifts of sanctifying grace to his people. In the book of Exodus we read: "Now, if you will obey me and keep my covenant, you will be my own people. The whole earth is mine, but you will be my chosen people, a people dedicated to me alone, and you will serve me as priests." (In some other versions, "... and you shall be to me a kingdom of priests, a holy nation.")[29] Also in the first Letter of Peter we read: "But you are a chosen race, a royal priesthood, a holy nation, a people of his own, so that you may announce (proclaim) the praises of him who called you out of darkness into his marvelous light. Once you were 'no people' but now you are God's people; you had not received mercy but now you have received mercy."[30]

It follows then that "in the Old Covenant, even though Israel was a kingdom of priests (Exod. 19:6), the Lord called certain men to a special priestly ministry (Exod. 19:22). In the New Covenant, even though Christians are a kingdom of priests (1 Pet. 2:9), Jesus calls certain men to a special priestly ministry (Rom. 15:15-16."[31] Jesus confirms the men He calls to a special priestly ministry in the Catholic Church through a sacramental ordination, the Holy Orders. That is to say, "through the Sacrament of Holy Orders, priests are ordained and thus empowered to serve the Church (2 Tim. 1:6-7) as pastors, teachers, and spiritual fathers who heal, feed, and strengthen God's people – most importantly (but not exclusively) through preaching and the administration of the sacraments." [32]

The special priestly ministry began with Jesus Christ Himself. The priesthood in the Old Covenant was a prefiguration of the New Covenant priesthood of Jesus Christ. He, Jesus Christ chose the apostles and commissioned them with His own authority to teach and lead his Church. "Jesus gave Peter special authority among the apostles (John 21:15-17)" as signified in his giving Peter alone the "keys of the kingdom" (Matt. 16: 19)[33] Peter and the other apostles ordained other bishops, priests and deacons to serve and worship God and sanctify the people. This tradition was kept unbroken through history to our time and it continues, for Jesus promised to remain with His Church to the end of age. (Matt. 28: 20).

## The Apostolic Phase (27 – 110)

The people of Jesus' time (the apostolic age) knew who they were and lived in full commitment to what it entailed in their daily lives together as the people of God. They understood themselves as a priestly people, a priestly community, working together and sharing everything together as a community of God's people. In the Acts of the Apostles, we read: "They spent their time in learning from the apostles, taking part in the fellowship, and sharing in the fellowship meals and the prayers. … Day after day they meet as a group in the temple, and they had their meal together in the homes, eating with glad and humble hearts, praising God, and enjoying the good will of all the people"[34] The sense of the special callings (the apostles) and the general callings, (the other people of God) to community services in the priesthood of Jesus Christ were well appreciated, lived and witnessed in the apostolic community at that early period in the Catholic Church history. At this period, we have a "house Church." A "house Church" refers to a practice whereby an assembly of God's people is moved from house to house during the apostolic era.

Paul Bernier describes this period as "the foundations of ministry," stating that "this period takes in only the first generation of what is now known as Christianity. It runs from the ministry of Jesus around the year 27 A.D. through the destruction of the Temple in the year 70 A.D. During this time the foundations of the Church were laid."[35] As "the foundations of ministry" period, Thomas O'Meara describes the ministry of this period as the "primal ministry" which includes "kingdom, Spirit, freedom and charism." He explains it this way:

> The kingdom of God is the source, the milieu, the goal of ministry. The presence of God in our complex world enables ministry, gives ministry its life and its freedom. The Church, rather than being the sovereign dispenser of ministry, offers ministry within the

kingdom as something derivative, fragile, secondary, temporary. At
the end of the time, ministry and Church will be absorbed into our
life in God. A theology of ministry is basically a mediation on the
kingdom, a theology of the Holy Spirit, a contemplative analysis of
grace. [36]

O'Meara's basis for the above analysis is on his claim that "Jesus of
Nazareth preached neither a separate religion nor one institution; neither
did he teach esoteric information about God or himself. He preached
what he called the kingdom of God. Jesus invited followers to join his
ministry of evangelization, and the first Christians experienced his Spirit's
call to discipleship."[37] O'Meara is trying to emphasize that although Jesus
ministered in "a priestly society," he never addressed himself as a priest
and he was not of the priestly family of Aaron but of the royal family of
David. Reading from the historical background of Israelites, O'Meara
stresses Jesus is of "the prophetic line in Israel" not the priestly line, even in
his entire ministry on earth. O'Meara's emphasis here is on the historicity
of priesthood which is one way of looking at the issue of priesthood
of Christ. A word of caution here, I am using O'Meara's analysis of
the historicity of Christ's priesthood as "an illustration" (one way of
looking at Christ's priesthood, not as his (O'Meara) general teaching or
understanding of the priesthood of Jesus Christ.

Another way of looking at the priesthood of Christ is from the
spiritual point of view. Jordan Aumann emphasized this point well. For
him, the kingdom of God is not only historical, it is spiritual. It is not
only earthly, it is heavenly. It is not only of the Old Testament, it is of
the New Testament. It is not a divided kingdom, it is a united one. It is
not only external, it is within. Aumann explains:

> In the context of the spiritual life, the kingdom of God is interior,
> it is within us (Lk. 17:21), it is capable of growth and evolution,
> and from the individual it reaches out to all humanity, to the
> entire world. The kingdom is life in Christ, with whom the Father
> and the Holy Spirit are present (Jn. 14:23). It is a kingdom that is
> present but always evolving, and therefore we must always pray:
> "thy kingdom come." On several occasions Christ identified
> himself with the kingdom: "If it is through the finger of God
> that I cast out devils, then know that the kingdom of God has
> overtaken you" (Luke. 11:20); "I confer a kingdom on you, just
> as my Father conferred one on me: you will eat and drink at my
> table in my kingdom. [38]

Aumann likes to stress here that the kingdom is a life in God the Father, God the Son, and God the Holy Spirit. The priesthood is a call to life and ministry in the kingdom of God. The kingdom embraces all humanity, old, new and not yet. At the time of Jesus and the apostles, priesthood is more than "cultic functions." Even O'Meara himself is very emphatic of this point. O'Meara pointed out that toward the end of the apostolic age, we noticed a shift of emphasis in the understanding and practice of priesthood. He described it as "a move through communal diversity and universality to a small number of ministries with prominence given to the service of leadership (episcopalization) along with a further presentation of the ministry of the leadership (presbyter or bishop) as a priest (sacerdotalization)." [39] The first century of Christian spirituality witnessed both the laying of foundations of ministry and a methodical shift from the foundation.

## The Patristic Phase (2nd to 11th centuries)

The second phase of the history of Christian spirituality is the post-apostolic period. This period, according to Paul Bernier, begins with this short phase: 70 A.D. and 110 A.D. For him, it is a period of "re-foundation," a period in which "ministry" is understood or interpreted as "charism." Bernier points out that "the razing of the Temple in the year 70 was more than the ruin of a building, it was the final destruction of a way of life, a way of thinking for both Jews and Christians. A rethinking of enormous proportion was necessary." [40] The challenges of re-foundationing and rethinking are indeed widespread and deep. Bernier believes that it is evident in "the remaining books of the New Testament" which were written after the year 70 A.D. There is a challenge of continuity, the first generation of Christians is passing away and the second generation is setting in, what will "it" be? There is a challenge of "pluralism of practice" with the spread of the Gospel to different and diverse lands, cities and villages, whose practice will be followed or adopted? There is a challenge of legitimacy and consolidation, because "without a Temple, there was no longer a priesthood" and "the legitimacy of the Jewish religion and its law."[41]

These challenges raise some theological questions, such as "who had the right and responsibility of teaching authoritatively in the name of Jesus? How could one be sure that the teaching was authentic?"[42] The response to these questions took different forms. Raymond Brown points out that different biblical communities responded differently to this "challenge of survival." Brown "listed seven district communities: 1. Antioch, where Matthew was written, 2. The community of Ephesians and Colossians, 3. The community where Luke and Acts were written, 4. The community where John was written, 5. The community in which 1 and 2 John were written, 6. The community where 1 Peter was written, 7. The community of the pastoral epistles."[43] In other words, Brown is suggesting that the biblical books written after the destruction of the Temple in 70 A.D. were in response to the issue of continuity and authenticity in the Church's leadership.

Jordan Aumann, who adopted a broad perspective in his approach to the Christian spirituality in the Catholic tradition, understands the second period as beginning from the third century to the eleventh century, a period of "monasticization" of ministry (to use Thomas O'Meara's word). Aumann considers anything before the third century "the early Church" period. This period includes the Council of Jerusalem about the year 51 A.D. to the writing of the Didache (the Teaching of the Twelve Apostles) between 70 and 100 A.D.; then to the Apostolic Fathers who were the early Christian writers, the immediate transmitters of the teaching of the apostles, people like St. Clement, who wrote a *Letter to the Church of Corinth* in the year 95 or 96 during or immediately after the persecution by Domitian,"[44] St Irenaeus, Tertullian, Origen, Hermas, the author of *The Shepherd*, St. Ignatius of Antioch who wrote seven letters on his way to Rome where he eventually suffered martyrdom, St. Polycarp who wrote two extant documents: *Letter to the Philippians* and *Martyrium*, an account of his martyrdom, and Papias, Bishop of Hierapolis, a late addition to the list of the Apostolic Fathers. Aumann is of the view that these interventions in forms of Council meeting or documentaries are responses to some "occasional doctrinal disputes from within" the Church and some "periodic persecutions by Roman authority."[45] A drastic change occurred with the conversion of Constantine in 325 A.D. (a politicization of the Church) which aimed Christianity a legitimate religion and under the reign of Theodosius I (379-395), Christianity "became the official religion of the empire."[46]

Freedom comes with a price, a "loose living" at various levels of the Church's life and leadership (corruption in the "head and member").

The then pope, Damasus (366-384) responded with an aggressive "monastic movement" which "spread quickly to Egypt, Syria and Asia Minor." The writings of St. Athanasius, the *Life of Anthony the Hermit* helped to expand "monasticism in Italy and France." [47] The other key contributors were the Cappadocian Fathers, St. Basil (+ 379), St. Gregory of Nazianzem (+389), and St. Gregory of Nyssa, under them monasticism became "a school of learned spirituality" for all people; and also, other contributors were Evagrius Ponticus (+ 339), Pseudo-Dionysius and Maximus.

Then in the West, we have St. Jerome, St. Ambrose (+ 397), St. Paulinus of Nola (b. 353), St Martin of Tours, John Cassian (+ 435), St. Augustine (354-430) who influenced St. Benedict (480-547) to influence many with his monastic rules, St. Patrick and St Gregory the Great (+ 604) leading to Gregory VII. The price of this monastic influence in the whole Catholic tradition is diverse and deep. It is a two-way influence, as observed by Paul Bernier that it is "both a feudalization of the ministry and a sacerdotalization of monasticism itself." Bernier explains that "in many ways ministry was reduced to jobs within the monasteries themselves and to liturgical priesthood."[48]

## The Medieval Phase (1050 -1414)

The third phase in the history of Christian spirituality is the Middle Ages. Bernier describes this period as "the Age of Scholasticism (1055-1414),"a period in which "ministry" is understood as "hierarchy." He believes that this period falls "roughly between the Gregorian reforms and one of papacy's lower moments – the time when it was split between competing popes" and a period that "is overshadowed by the final schism that split Eastern and Western Christianity."[49] Bernier is of the view that this time of double split is "one of the saddest periods of Church history" as well as "a time of creativity whose influence is still felt in our own times (the worst time and the best time in the Church history)."[50] Some of the reasons for the negative categorization of this period are: a personality clash between Pope Leo IX and the Patriarch Michael Cerularius at that period; some theological and sacramental controversies like Iconoclasm, and the Filioque controversy, all leading to the eventual split of the Eastern and Western Christianity; (that is:) the conflicts between the papacy (Pope Gregory VII and the empire (Emperor Henry IV) in 1077; the schism of 1159-1177, the Avignon popes; and lay investiture.

On the positive, creative side, we have the outcomes of the Gregorian reforms: they introduced discipline, community life, the divine office and celibate life among the clergy; there were the four Lateran Councils, the first and second in 1123 and 1138 respectively which banned and invalidated clerical marriages; the lay investiture was stopped, a corruptive practice whereby the Church lands and titles were passed on to members of one's family; there was the collection and classification of the Canon laws by Gratian and the papal curia which extended the power of Rome over the entire Christendom as well as the liberation of the bishops from the feudal powers and the power of the nobles; there was the creation of "the college of cardinals" [51]which helped to streamline the flow of power, "from the pope through the bishops to the priests and laity (hierarchization);"[52] then, the ordination rituals were developed which emphasized "that priests were receiving the power to offer Mass and forgive sins."[53]

There were fall-outs from the developments of this period of hierarchization of ministry. The ordination rituals brought about the problems of "the multiplicity of rituals" of ordination and the scholastic controversy over the "exact moment when priesthood was conferred?" Bonaventure taught that it was the moment of "imposition of hands," while Aquinas and others said it "must be the handing over of the instruments, since these more clearly signified the transmission of priestly powers."[54] Aquinas' position held the way until Pius XII changed it to be at "the imposition of hands and the prayer of the bishop."[55] There was also a fall-out in the creation of the College of Cardinals. Bernier pointed out that "there was the disgraceful spectacle of papal power, politics and venality of the curia,"(whereby) Cardinalates could be bought if one had enough money, and many clergy seemed more interested in wealth and power than in spiritual realities."[56] This was the background that led to the Avignon schism because between 1309 and 1376, when all the cardinals and the popes were Frenchmen. Still another fall-out of this period of hierarchization of ministry was the Scholastic theory of "ex opere operato" that was understood in a "magical way" which encouraged poor education of priests and the "multiplication of Masses" because of the narrow belief that "priests (could) get people to heaven simply by the multiplication of Masses."[57]

On the other hand, Bernier also pointed out that everything was not totally negative. He observed that "despite the corruption of the age, there were popular movements of piety that kept the laity alive spiritually."[58] The "popular movements of piety" gave rise to new religious orders "especially the Dominicans and Franciscans" that "provided many preachers, theologians and bishops to the high Middle Ages."[59] The other new religious orders of this period were "the Carthusians, Premonstratensians, Carmelites, and the Hermits of St. Augustine."[60] There was also "the renaissance of the twelfth and thirteenth centuries" which "brought order to society," as well as some big "cities with the cathedral at the center (which) came into greater prominence."[61] The fall-out of this focus on big cities was the neglect of the "countryside" which left the rural clergy "often ill equipped." This gave rise to new religious orders "that specialized in this form of evangelization, such as the Redemptorists and the Vincentians."[62] In essence, it is a program-oriented process, new problems are treated with new programs.

The other important contribution of this period is the theories of priesthood. Paul Bernier pointed out three traditions of the theories of the priesthood within this period. One tradition followed from "Aristotelian categories of causality" which was put together by Albert the Great and insightfully systematized by Thomas Aquinas. For Aquinas, "mediation" is at "the heart of priesthood" and "he insisted that the action of mediating was essentially Christ's obedient acceptance of suffering and death."[63] In this sense, "an ordained minister (priest or bishop) acts as an instrument of Christ, who is the main agent of the sacraments."[64] It is interesting to note Bernier's assessment that "much of later theology on priesthood consists of repetition or comment on Thomas' explanations. Even Trent, though not tied to a particular school, is very open to Thomistic interpretation. "[65]

The other tradition in the theory of priesthood is by Bonaventure, followed by Duns Scotus (d. 1308) who interpreted the Catholic priesthood from the actions of Christ as a mediator and a redeemer. In other words, both Scotus and Aquinas share similar idea on the "cultic reality of the Catholic priesthood" but they differ on the philosophy of it. For Aquinas, an ordained minister presiding over the Mass acts "in persona Christi" (in the person of Christ) while for Duns Scotus, the president at the Eucharistic celebration acts "in persona ecclesiae" (in the person of the Church). The theology of the Christian priesthood, as noted above, has followed one school of thought, (the Thomistic interpretation). It will serve the Church better to look at the two schools of thought as complementary rather than contradictory.

The third school of thought within this period was that of Gabriel Biel (d. 1495), a staunch disciple of William of Ockham, the founder of Nominalism. Biel shifted his focus from Christ's priesthood to "the relation of substance and quantity in transubstantiation."[66] Paul Bernier believes that Biel's interpretation is "closer" to Scotistic interpretation but not the same thing. Both Scotus and Biel focused on the Eucharistic celebration from divine will, but Biel interpreted it from the point of view of transubstantiation. Biel taught that "God has so determined it (the Eucharistic action) that when a proper celebrant performs the proper external acts with proper intention, God's creative power will effect a change in the bread."[67]

Biel's notion of causality in the interpretation of the role of a priest in a Eucharistic celebration is "radically different" from Aquinas, (for Aquinas, a priest is an instrument of Christ's mediation event of His death and resurrection, while for Biel, a priest aligns himself to effect God's divine will in the transubstantiation), yet both agree that priest's dignity flows from his cultic function in the Eucharist. In other words, for Aquinas, a priest is called to do what Christ did – a priest sanctifies himself and others by doing what Christ did through the sacraments (especially the Holy Eucharist). For Biel, a priest is called to surrender to God's will, to be one with God's will in the transubstantiation (or in the sacraments). A priest sanctifies himself and others through a self-surrender to God's will in and through the sacraments. The undeveloped, if not forgotten, theology and spirituality of self-surrender in priesthood and in the Church is a terrible loss in Christian tradition. Because, with the theology and spirituality of the Catholic priesthood as "instruments of Christ" or "action of Christ" the Catholic priesthood loss the "Spirit" and the "Person" of Christ to become merely an instrument of Christ. Hence, the spirituality of self-surrender was overshadowed by the ideology of self-control. Life grows not by controlling but by surrendering and sharing.

## The Reformation Phase (1415-1565)

The fourth phase in the history of the Christian spirituality is the reformation of ministry (1415 – 1565). We saw in the third phase of the history of Christian spirituality that hierarchization of ministry and the somehow "sterile argumentation" of scholastic theology had left the Church in a bad scenario of neglect and abuses. While there was so much to complain against the Church's hierarchy, there was equally so much good to be affirmed on the grass-root level. Paul Bernier puts it this way: "However, this age of benefices, ecclesiastical patronage, increasing secularity and worldliness of the higher clergy, non-residence, and the theological ignorance, is also the age of the *devotio moderna* and many new religious orders."[68] It is indeed significant and critical to note that "most of the impetus for renewal welled up from the faithful, rather than from the authority structure of the Church itself. It came from below – a sign of the presence of the Holy Spirit in the entire assembly."[69] It means that the Holy Spirit is with the entire Church of God, not just with the hierarchy.

The Christian Church has gone through two great "ruptures:" the great split between the Eastern and Western Christendom in the medieval period. At this particular period in the history of the Church, the Western Christendom was at the verge of another schism of split – between the Catholics and the Protestants. Both sides had needs for reformation. Both sides misinterpreted and misapplied the needed strategies for the required renewal. In the end, both the Protestant's Reformation and the Catholic Counter-Reformation hopelessly missed their targets. The Reformation of ministry then, is not Reformation eventually. The Reformation agenda failed on both sides because "the question of ministry within the Church was not the primary focus of the Reformation."[70] The reasons are obvious.

On the Protestant's side, the "main theological issues" which Martin Luther presented in the 517 Theses he placed at "the door of the Wittenberg Cathedral in 1517" were: "1) the relationship of grace and good works, 2) the question of justification, 3) the place of the Scriptures, 4) and the role of the pope."[71] There is no doubt that these four theses are rooted in ministry. However, the Reformation process shifted from "a pastoral program to renew the life of the local Church" to be "a religious protest against the localization of God's activity in the human and the created."[72] The results are obvious.

Thomas O'Meara summarized them this way: "Paradoxically, the Churches of the Reformation were left with fewer ministries than the medieval Church, and unconsciously they seemed to have taken in the idea that there was only one ministry, not priest, but pastor."[73]

The Protestant Reformation achieved limited outcomes in many ways. The efforts to foster the "freedom and identity" of ministry turned out to be efforts to replace "the sacral-monastic (identity) with the secular (one)."[74] The marriage of the clergy did not liberate ministry from feudalism or the monasticism. The Reformation agenda to renew the "local Church along New Testament lines" was a great mixed up: ministry narrowed down to one ministry of the pastor and it became closely identified with Western profession that the sense of transcendence in services is lost; the furnishing of Churches slightly different from "law courts or theater." The "New Testament vision" of ministry targeted by the Protestant's Reformation never came through, rather what happened was a "secularization" of Church and ministry.[75]

On the Catholic side, the Council Fathers at Trent took a defensive approach to channel all efforts on "safeguarding priestly power by emphasizing even further the indelible character which was received at ordination" and "the essential difference between the clergy and the laity."[76] What happened was that the "cultic power" of the ordained was overemphasized and this power "resided in the individual rather than the Church."[77] The importance of the Sacred Scriptures and the pastoral ministry are ignored or neglected. At this period again, like the previous period, the needed renewal fails to happen from top-down.

In the medieval period, "New Orders" held a sign of hope for the Christian community. At this time, "New Movements" played the similar role like *"devotio moderna"* by John Busch. The frustration of the Christian community with the scholastic sterile speculation and high intellectualism at this time was unbearable. Jordan Aumann pointed out that "throughout the entire Church there was manifest need for reform: there was schism in the papacy, moral laxity among the clergy and religious, and false mysticism among the laity. There was a great need for a renewal of the Church and a complete overhaul of ecclesiastical structure. The externals of Christian life were deeply entrenched, but lifeless; basic theological principles were being contested; traditional ideals were taught but not practiced."[78]

In such a dark and desperate condition, a little light of effective spirituality made all the difference. It was this type of affective spirituality which *Devotio Moderna* provided for the Christian community of the period. The frustration of the Christian community with the speculative approach could be read in this passage from the *Imitation of Christ:*

> What does it avail you to discourse profoundly of the Trinity if you lack humility and, consequently, are displeasing to the Trinity? In truth, lofty words do not make a man holy and just, but a virtuous life makes him dear to God. I would rather experience compunction than know how to define it. ...
>
> Leave off that excessive desire to know, because it is the cause of much distraction and deceit. Men of learning are very glad to appear and be called wise. There are many things of which the knowledge is of little or no value to the soul. And he is most foolish who concerns himself with things that do not contribute to his salvation. ...[79]

When the spiritual initiatives came from below without strong support from the top (the hierarchy) their influence was quite limited. At the end of the day, the result was a Tridentine Church, a Church that "turns in on itself and irrelevant in the world;" a "defensive and apologetic" Church; a Church totally given to "orthodoxy and suspicion of innovations" in which "modernism" is a crime and "ecumenism," a dangerous word; a divided Church in a divided world.[80] The Reformation of ministry is simply adding legalism to cultism.

## The Tridentine Phase (1565 – 1962)

The fifth phase of the history of Christian spirituality is the Post-Tridentine period. Paul Bernier (*Ministry in the Church, 1992*) described this period as "the fortress Church" while Thomas O'Meara (*Theology of Ministry, 1999*) called it "the baroque Church." This period includes 1565 to 1962 and it is referred to, in terms of its spirituality as "ministry as cult." O'Meara claims that this period is "marked by five epochs: the Counter-Reformation; the Baroque, Late Baroque, and Rococo; the Romantic Renaissance of the early nineteenth century; the anti-modern atmosphere between 1860 and 1960; and the preparation for Vatican II after two world wars."[81] In O'Meara's analysis, it is difficult to see the epoch-making events of these five periods. The baroque spirit tends to pervade the whole period. I like to follow Paul Bernier's three parts approach: the characteristics of Post-Tridentine Church, its theology and spirituality.

## The Post-Tridentine Church

The Reformation period left the Church and the world divided. The Council of Trent with its "defensive and apologetic" agenda did little to save the situation. The Council Fathers had defined agenda: the organization of the Church under the pope; the structuring of a life of grace as the objective of every Christian and the mission of priests; and the structuring of the seminary training of priests. It is an inward-focused renewal of the Church, a "fortress Church" (Paul Bernier), a "baroque Church" (Thomas O'Meara). The Council Fathers stepped up efforts from the medieval theology that defined "the pope as vicar not only of Peter but also of Christ, and therefore head of the Church,"[82] to centralize Rome more by creating different curia offices for seminaries, religious orders, evangelization and so on. These efforts encouraged the establishment of new religious orders which followed the monastic model with emphasis on personal conversion and method of prayers in the enclosures. One exception at this time was the religious congregation of Francis de Sales which was meant to foster a life of holiness in the outside world. These religious orders powered the missionary activities in Africa, Asia and other parts of the world (an important feature of this period).

In terms of education, the Jesuits took the lead in education enterprises of this period, even the seminary education. The Jesuit's theology of obedience "which tended to identify the superior's will with the will of God" influenced the ecclesiastical structures. In such situations, those entrusted with ministries or the general Christian community were presumed to have "no rights, no question, no insight or appeal."[83] This is a further stage in the episcopalization of the Church, whereby the diocesan bishops were elevated from a coordinator of ministries to an authoritarian superior. The authority of the bishop did not stop in the diocese, it extended to Rome. The Vatican I Council formalized this process with "its definition of papal infallibility, the idea was firmly planted that the Church was a monarchy, and that this structure came from Christ himself."[84] It is important to point out that everything wasn't all that black and gray. There were some great events like the missionary activities on foreign lands, the establishment of the seminary schools for training of priests, the establishment of some women religious organizations like Jane de Chantal and St. Teresa of Avilla.

## The Post-Tridentine Theology

The Post-Tridentine theology was mainly defensive and apologetic, focusing more on the cultic function of priesthood. It was a tragedy of history even to this day that in "the post-Reformation period, Catholicism saw the Reformation, rather than modern rationalism, as the enemy."[85] This was because Trent relied heavily on St. Thomas and on the Council of Florence (1431-1445). One would understand why the Reformation never opened doors to "new depths of understanding." No wonder then the clerical culture continued to be emphasized by the French school and the principle of juridicalism continued to dominate the teachings of Robert Bellarmine and Francis Suarez. This conservative approach led the Church to lose sight of "the genuine understanding of sacramental symbolism" and "the evangelical, prophetic, or personal" dimensions of the priesthood of the twelfth century.[86]

## The Post-Tridentine Spirituality

The spirituality of the Post-Tridentine period was a sacramental spirituality, most importantly the sacramental characters of Baptism, Confirmation, Holy Orders and the Sacrament of Reconciliation. Paul Bernier pointed out that "the three poles on which Tridentine piety rested were: a revival of sacramental life, the spread and development of the Eucharistic devotions and techniques of mental prayer, and an urge to good works and outward activity as a factor in personal sanctification."[87] Put in other words, "the three poles" are: the means of grace, the methods of grace, and the works of grace. It is all about grace. Ministry is grace. Priesthood is an instrument of disseminating graces.

An important implicative point of the Post-Tridentine Church was that the Reformation efforts were turned into "religious wars," not a course of renewal. The more the Protestants attacked, the more defensive and apologetic the Catholics were committed to be. Theology and spirituality became "polemic" and intellectualistic. The Catholic efforts since then focused more on justifying the old practices and viewpoints rather than exploring new grounds of understanding and development to meet the new challenges in theology and spirituality of the priesthood. The inevitable outcome was a priesthood which became a dignified, clerical state of power to be defended against all attacks from the assumed religious enemy-combatant, the Protestants.

The Church then, became pocket-schools (like the French schools) of intellectual defense of "lofty dignity of clerical state" and ritualistic cultism.[88] This intellectualistic approach made the Church lose track of the twelfth and thirteenth centuries' "sacramental symbolism" to concentrate mainly on the Scholastic sacramental causality of the Eucharist. Two implicative outcomes of this scenario were: there was "a false opposition between evangelical and sacramental approaches to Eucharist and its ministry;" and there was the unresolved "basic question about the nature of Christ's own priestly ministry - and, therefore, the resultant questions about ordained ministry within the Church."[89]

The other area of great implication was the seminary formation which was formulated at this period. There were three outstanding theologians whose thoughts and teachings shaped the seminary educational structure up to the time of Vatican II Council. The first was an Englishman, Thomas Stapleton (d. 1598) who lived at the time of the council of Trent. His teaching maintained and extended the polemical approach of trying to justify the Catholic practices against those of the Protestants. For instance, Stapleton defended the "legitimacy" of the Catholic ordinations and their teachings against those of the Protestants on the ground of "apostolic succession" that came directly from Jesus Christ. In other words, Stapleton claimed a direct connection between *"potestas ordinis"* (the power of ordination) and *"potestas jurisdictionis"* (the power of jurisdiction) as the "two aspects of one office."[90] Stapleton's conclusion from a direct connection of linking the power of ordination and jurisdiction to one office of ministry is quite implicative. In a way, Stapleton was saying that "the reformers ' opposition to the Catholics (was) not a choice *for* the Scriptures, but one *against* the teaching authority of Rome." In effect, he was saying that "because they have rejected the authority of the true Church of Christ, neither their teaching nor their other ministerial acts can bear true witness to Christ."[91] This is a death-sentence to revamping the general studying of the Bible, the Word of God and meaningful attempts at ecumenism.

The second theologian who influenced the formulation of the seminary system was Robert Bellarmine (d. 1621). Bellarmine adopted a moderate polemic stance to the Protestants' opposition by making use of sound biblical and traditional approach. However, his teaching on the Church (*de ecclesia),* the priesthood and ministry modeled the

Catholic thought in these areas for three centuries after him. Like Stapleton, Bellarmine acknowledged the power of ordination which he identified with "order" and adopted many "Scriptural proofs" to demonstrate that it is "a sacrament."[92] In line with Thomistic tradition, he identified the power of ordination, not only as a sacrament but also a sacramental "character" which essentially differentiates the ordained from the laity. For Bellarmine, "the bishop is the *summus sacerdos,* or the *primus sacerdos,"* (an idea he borrowed from Hugh of St. Victor).[93] Bellarmine also believed that a bishop is different from a priest by virtue of wide extension "character" power which goes beyond his diocesan territory. He played down on the abstract sacramental concept of *"ex opera operato"* by emphasizing that every priest should minister "humanely."

The third great influence in the formulation of the seminary system at this time of Tridentine Church was Francis Suarez (d. 1617), a Jesuit and a Spanish theologian. His thought was more political. He teaches that "all structures of reality are ontologically monarchical" and that "all truth and life and grace come down to us in a chain of causes from the top."[94] For Suarez, a priest is a mediator of grace from Christ and the pope has the full "possession of the monarchial spiritual authority of Christ."[95]

Generally, Thomas O'Meara pointed out that "the theology of the ministry (of this period) is based upon two main operational principles: first, the organization of the Church in detail around the papacy; second, the designation of the interior life of grace as the object of Christian ministry."[96] This form of theology and its spirituality were promoted by three key principles: first, the principle of "Christification" (a form of sacerdotization), the theology and spirituality of the French school and the Neoplatonism of Pseudo-Dionysius helped to fashion a Christocentricity of life and ministry based on their emphasis on Christ's divine essence. The emphasis on the divine essence belittled (sometimes ignored) the humanness of Christ and all people of God. Second, "the centralization of vocations," the understanding of vocations of the Church as the religious or priestly vocations, and as the gift of the Holy Spirit and the Church office as the "gift of the papacy and of its representatives" greatly narrowed down the understanding of vocations in the Church.[97] There was then a tendency to regard some vocations as worldly and unholy. Third, "the monoform of delegation" of ministry, the seminary system of education and preparation for vocations in the Church which zeroed in on religious vocations, created one-way of delegation of ministry in the Church. The lines of grace, truth, authority, dignity and power of delegation and dialogue were reduced to a one-way process - top-down only. All these practical principles affected differently the theology and spirituality of priestly life and ministry in the Church.

## The period of Aggiornamento (1962-1965) and thereafter

Of all the twenty-one general councils of the Catholic Church, only the last Council, the Vatican II Council was convened without a motivating external threat. The reconvener, Pope John XXIII gave it its proper name: aggiornamento – a term defined by the Webster's College dictionary as "the act of bringing something up to date to meet current needs." In many ways, this is a turning-point period: The Western Church that has turned in on itself for more than a millennium is being invited into the modern world. The chaotic aftermath of war time of the World War II was drawing to a close. The Vatican II Council is indeed a strategic turning-point event both in the Church and in the world.

### The Vatican II Period and After

Pope John XXIII convened the Vatican II Council to "open the windows of the Church" which indeed opened a "window" of dialogue with the "world" that was once labeled an "enemy" and with other Christian Churches that were once perceived as the opposing-Christless-forces (the ecumenical movements). The "known" Church's (the Western Church) "doors" still remain closed to the so-called "mission" Churches (which Paul Bernier described as "carbon copies of the parent Church")[98] in some parts of the world such as Africa, Asia and Latin America. The challenge this scenario poses to mission and ministry in the Church of today is enormous. Further discussions on this issue will be developed later on.

Vatican II begins its documents with *Lumen Gentium,*(the Light of nations). Surprisingly, this "Light" is interpreted to mean the Light of Christ, not of the Church as well. Like the Tridentine Church that played down the humanity of Christ with its overemphasis on the ontological Christology, the Council Fathers defined Christ as "teacher, sanctifier, and leader" and also interpreted the Church in the same manner.[99] What is left out here is the "person" of Jesus Christ and the "person" of the Church. Fortunately, the Council Fathers included two important documents that discussed the Church not only as an agent of ministry but also as a mission in itself: 1. *Lumen Gentium* – the nature of the Church (*ad intra*) and 2. *Gaudium et Spes* - the mission of the Church (*ad extra*). This is a dramatic shift in a self-understanding of the Church in which the world is no longer seen as an "evil" to be avoided but as the context of the Church's life, mission and ministry. The Church of *Gaudium et Spes* "is open to and exists on behalf of the world. In fact, the world sets the agenda for the Church. She is not only in the world, she is the world, that community of people who have heard the Word of God."[100] The Church then is a mission and in mission to "save" the world and to "serve" the kingdom of God. The Church is the people of God. The people of God then is a mission and in mission to "save" the world and to "serve" the kingdom of God. It follows therefore that "a Christian is essentially a missionary. One is not saved by withdrawing from the world and concentrating on saving one's soul; it is by living in the world and committing oneself to saving others."[101] This is the challenge of today's Church and its ministry (the priests and the lay faithful alike) in the contemporary world.


# The Historical Development of the Catholic Priesthood in the African Church History


The understanding of the priesthood in the Catholic world did not change much over the years and at different epochs in history. It focused mostly on the ministry of the priesthood. The discussion here might sound more like a Church history 101 rather than a discussion on the development of the Catholic priesthood and priestly ministry in the African Church. This was because there was not only poor document of the Church history in African countries in those days. But also, the incessant religious or Jihad wars did a lot of damage to what was documented. Another contributing factor was the overwhelming emphasis on the ministry of the priesthood, the cultic nature of the

Church at that time, whereby so little or nothing was written on the "person" of the priesthood. Speaking on this cultic approach to the person of the priesthood within the period, Thomas O'Meara writes:

> The understanding of the priesthood moved within the celebration of the Eucharist (Trent) to the mission of the Church (Vatican II). The institution of the priesthood drew not only on the Last Supper (Trent) but on the institution of apostles and ministers in their totality. The specificity of the priesthood included not only the power of the Eucharist but action in the name of Christ, head of his body, the Church, and the priesthood as service was not only cultic (Trent) but apostolic (Vatican II). There was finally a movement from a theocentric ministry to the activity and presence of the priest in the world, from cult to a variety of ministries.[102]

O'Meara is of the view that over the years in the history of the Catholic priesthood, the Church had witnessed expansion-shifts on the conceptual understanding of the ministry of the priesthood of Christ. There had been some slight cultic shifts or changes in the nature and dignity of services in the priestly ministry. O'Meara would like us to believe that this scenario was not in any way peculiar to any particular period, from the time of the Council of Trent to the last ecumenical Council, the Vatican II Council of 1962 to 1965. History had known it that way:

> Every subsequent generation looks to that experience – not as a confining law but as a revelatory experience rich with more and more possibility for ministry. Modern theology interprets tradition not as written norms but as living consciousness of the Christian community reflecting upon itself (its world and its ministries) and its past. Similarly, change is neither an instant revolution nor a chain of successes. In old and huge organizations like the Catholic Church, change is a complex phenomenon. The past never fully disappears; old forms are not fully replaced; the new must be both incarnational and traditional. If these shifts in Church life are considerable and fraught with further implications, nonetheless, their day-to-day realization in the life of the local Church is ordinary. The Spirit never fails to offer the Church charisms adequate to the opportunities, and thus through pastoral responsibility rather than grandiose administrative centers, "We are shepherds of the future."[103]

O'Meara offers us here some insightful approaches to a healthy theological interpretation of tradition, not as "dead" (devilish or pagan) "norms" to be destroyed but "as a living consciousness" of the people that holds the grace of the past, the gifts of the present, and the promises of the future. The spirituality of change itself is equally noteworthy. The desired "new" that is sought for is neither a disappearance of the past, nor a total replacement of the "old forms," but a "new" that is radically "both incarnational and traditional" at the same time. With this background in mind, we turn to reflect on the development of priesthood in African Church which is indeed the development of the Catholic Church in Africa.

The Catholic Church in Africa historically falls into three major phases: 1. the first seven centuries of rise and fall of the Catholic Church in North Africa; 2. the second seven centuries of the rise of Islam and the eradication of Christianity in North Africa; and 3. the last six centuries of Christianization of sub-Saharan Africa. In order words, the Catholic Church flourished mainly in North Africa and its surroundings within the first seven hundred years, then came the unfavorable efforts of the Islamic Jihads which almost eradicated Christianity from the known African world, except for some pockets of underground Churches maintained by Coptic monks. The initial efforts of Christianization in sixteen to eighteen centuries failed under similar reasons. The actual Christianization of sub-Saharan Africa took place in just one century, the 19th century. Some historical documents, unfortunately have given undue emphasis or attention to the later part of the last phase as if it all began and ended with it.

## The First Phase of Christianity in Africa
## – North Africa (1st to 7th Century)

This period is made up of three stages. The inaugural period or the apostolic age of the first century; the expansion period of the second and third centuries – the period of persecution and martyrdom; and the institutionalization period of 4th to 7th centuries – a period of monasticism or monastic spirituality.

## The Apostolic Age (the First Century)

The African apostolic period began with the "escape trip" of the Holy Family, Mary and Joseph and the infant Jesus to Egypt;[104] then to Simon of Cyrene (Cyrene is close to Libya) who emerged from the crowd to help in carrying the Cross of Jesus Christ;[105] then to the Ethiopian eunuch who was baptized by Philip, one of the apostles.[106] We have also the pilgrims at the first Pentecost, the people "from Egypt and the regions of Libya near Cyrene," " … from Crete and Arabia."[107] Then there is the co-worker of Paul at Ephesus and Corinth, Apollos from Alexandria who was described as "an eloquent speaker and had a thorough knowledge of the Scriptures."[108] These biblical instances make an obvious case that African people and African cities are part and parcel of the Christian world of the apostolic age. Africa is part of the earliest tradition of "house church." We can see from this background how profound the reclaiming of the family as the model of the Church in Africa by the 1994 Synod of Africa. The African people are part of the inauguration of the Catholic Church on the first Pentecost as mentioned above. The African people are part of Jesus' disciples during the apostolic period.

## The Expansion Period (2nd and 3rd Centuries)

The Church of the Apostolic Age in Africa did not end with the period of the first century. It expanded through the forces of persecution and martyrdom in the second and third centuries. One of the great African theologians and a Christian apologist, Tertullian affirmed this historic fact in his prophetic statement: "The blood of martyrs is the seed of Christians."[109] So much went undocumented in regard to the magnitude of persecutions and martyrdom that the African Christian community suffered and continued to suffer during and after the so called "period of expansion." Vincent J. O'Malley, in the book, *Saints of Africa*, (2001) stated that "one of the earliest instances of Christian martyrdom ever recorded occurred in 180 AD. at Carthage, where Speratus and eleven companions from the town of Scillium (who) refused the proconsul's order to offer sacrifice to the emperor."[110] Because of this "defiance against paganism and defense of Christianity" so many African Christians and priests were murdered in cold blood. Some people were "thrown into the amphitheater" to be killed by wild animals like the two young mothers, Perpetua and Felicity with other three men.

The Roman civil wars were disaster for the conscripted African Christian soldiers who were forced to "worship Roman gods or be killed." Vincent J. O'Malley pointed out that about 287 A.D. Maurice and so many other African Christians were murdered under such pretenses. [111] The worst persecution took place between 297 and 311 during the reign of Emperor Diocletian. Many Christians were killed including Maximilian (from Numidia) who "refused to be a soldier for the emperor because he had dedicated his life to be a soldier for Christ."[112]

Before the terror period of Diocletian, there was a terrific persecution of Emperor Decian between 250 and 251 A.D. The Decian persecution forced many Christians as well as priests to seek refuge in remote desert places. For instance, Anthony, "from the city of Memphis," moved into the surrounding deserts and was joined by many other Christians who began the monastic movement in the Catholic Church.[113]

There were two forces at work at this period: "the defiance of paganism" (which was understood as the worship of emperors and/or his impositions) and "the defense of Christianity." This was what O'Malley described as "intense theological discussions" which were directed by "highly educated converts" from African Traditional Religion (ATR) to Christianity, persons like Tertullian (c. 160-220) and St. Cyprian (c.200-258).[114] While Tertullian focused on theological and doctrinal defense of the Catholic faith against some heretical teachings like Montanism and Manichaeanism, St. Cyprian of Carthage focused attention on moral and sacramental issues like lapses in Christian lives and "rebaptism of heretics." St. Cyprian and the reigning Pope, Sixtus II were both "beheaded by Roman authorities within a five-week span in 258," to tell us how bad it was then.[115] An important distinction however, needs to be noted here on the different understandings and application of the term, "paganism." At this period, paganism was applied mainly to the worship of emperor or obedience to his impositions; while later application tended to "label" the African traditional religions as "paganism" – an unfortunate misapplication or misinterpretation of history. The priesthood in the African Church at this period was mainly monastic.

## The institutionalization of the African Church and the Barbarian Invasion (4th to 7th Centuries)

The African Church moved from a "house church" of the apostolic period to a persecuted Church of the 1st and 2nd centuries, then to a monastic Church of the 3rd century. At this stage, the Church took another step to become a monarchical Church in the fourth and fifth centuries (the institutionalization of the Church in Africa). The institutionalization process began with the Edict of Milan in 312 which extended religious freedom to Christian religion, and thus ended the centuries of persecution of the Church. In 395 A.D., the Christian religion was recognized as the official religion of the Roman Empire which opened a "door" to a monarchical Church.

This period of the Church's freedom brought with it great growth in the number of Christians but not an active Christian faith. There were not only "nominal Christians" but also "lukewarm Churches."[116] This scenario pushed more Christians into the deserts in search of authentic spirituality and solid Christian communities. The existing monasteries were refurbished into community-based instruction centers while new ones were established. For instance, Saint Antony reorganized his monasteries around Saturdays and Sundays' community gathering, while Pachomius (c. 292-348) put together community life and activities like prayers and work. The new monasteries that were erected at this time were also significant. We had Ammon (d.c. 356) who founded one at the Nitrian mountains in 330; Also in 330, Macarius erected another monastery in the same Nitrian desert. There was development at various levels of the Church's life, the priestly life and ministries during this period of fifth and sixth centuries. O'Malley wrote that "ten Africans in toto are counted among the Church's eighty-seven Fathers, while three Africans, namely Athanasius, Augustine, and Cyril are included among the Church's thirty-three doctors."[117]

Everything was not "gold" and "silver" as there were some difficulties like "the threat of new heretics namely Arianism, Donatism, Montanism, and Monophysitism."[118] This form of internal threat influenced the Church towards apologetic and intellectualistic defense of itself at the expense of an evangelizing mission to other parts of Africa. Elizabeth Isichei observed that it was in the fourth century that "the Church conducted its first evangelization efforts into Ethiopia" through the evangelizing spirit of St. Frumentius (originally from Tyre) and the support of King Ella Amida and King Azana of Ethiopia.[119] The Ethiopian Church was the first to be evangelized but it failed to lead the "road" to an authentic African Church and the priesthood. Vincent J. O'Malley hinted this point in stating that even though the Ethiopian Church was given a bishop (Frumentius, ordained by Patriarch of Alexandria, Athanasius) yet "foreign clergy and a foreign mother Church continued to dominate the Ethiopian Church from its origin until the twentieth century."[120] This is not just a problem of the Ethiopian Church, it is probably a problem of many African Churches even in the twenty-first century. What has changed over the years in many African Churches is what Lawrence Lucas called "Black Priests" in "White Churches." That is to say, the African Churches are in many ways European and western, though administered and managed by indigenous African bishops and priests. Even some of the African bishops and priests battle with confused ideas in what is their true identity and mission in and to the African Church.

While the Western Church enjoyed relative freedom from persecution due to the Edict of Millan, the African Church and her priesthood continued to encounter serious persecution between 429 and 534. This was true especially in urban centers where "the six Germanic-speaking Vandal kings ruled in North Africa."[121] The destruction of the Church and human lives was so devastating that in "Carthage alone, under Genseric (428-477 – one of the Vandal kings) the number of Catholic bishops was reduced from one hundred and sixty-four to three" while his successor, "Huneric scourged and exiled five hundred clerics, five thousand laity, and, in an attempt to extirpate the monastic life, ordered all monks and monasteries to be handed over to the dreaded Mauri."[122] The worst was yet to happen with the introduction of the militaristic Islamic religion in the second part of the African Church history.

## The Second Part: the Seven Centuries of the Rise of Islamism and the Eradication of African Church

What remained from the menace of the Germanic-speaking Vandal Kings in the fifth and sixth centuries was taken out by "the Islamic Arab army" who started its military campaigns ten years after the death of Muhammad in 642. The Islamic Arab army combined political and economic exploitation or deprivation with "severe persecutions" in eliminating the Catholic faith and the Christians in Africa, through high taxations on Christians while the converts to Islam paid nothing. The climax was in 744 when an Arab governor in Egypt used high taxation exemption to force 24,000 Christians to convert to Islamism.[123] In such a terrible situation, the African Catholic priesthood and ministry suffered in so many ways. This condition of deprivation, exploitation, and persecutions continued unabated up to the fourteenth century while the Western Church paid little or no attention to the condition of the African Church.

## The Last Six Centuries of Christianity in Sub-Saharan Africa

The second part of the African Church history, the seven centuries of deprivation, exploitation and persecution was followed by the third part, the six centuries of restoration of Christianity in Africa. Vincent J. O'Malley divided this period of restoration into three sub-stages: 1. the "colonization and frustration at evangelization" (15th to 18th centuries); 2. "the missionary revival" (19th to mid-twentieth centuries); and 3. the "Independent and Christian Africa" (1960 to the present).[124]

## The Colonization and Frustration at Evangelization (15th to 18th Centuries)

The invention of the steam engine fueled the age of exploration into some unknown lands. There was a shift in focus from exploitation to exploration but the agenda was different for different groups. Vincent J. O'Malley pointed out that "the Portuguese led the procession of foreign powers, followed by the Dutch, French, and English people. Accompanying the sailors and governmental administrators were merchants and clergy."[125] Each of these groups followed the general motive of exploration within the context of its particular agenda. It followed then that "colonization and Christianization went hand in hand. The flag of a European country and the cross of Christianity were planted side by side on the African coast from Morocco, westward to the Azores and Cape Verde islands, southward to the Cape of Good Hope, and northward up to Madagascar and Ethiopia."[126] The obvious incompatibility of the two agendas (colonization and Christianization) created frustration rather than fulfillment at the evangelization of mission lands (in spite of some attempted efforts of a political solution

– the 1918 partitioning of African lands). However, we must commend and praise the courageous zeal and undaunted efforts of the early missionary priests and religious who spared nothing, even their lives to sow the seeds of the Christian faith in almost impossible situations and circumstances of the time.

It might be recalled that the 1400s and 1500s saw the introduction of some religious orders like "Augustinians, Carmelites, Discalced Carmelites, Dominicans, Franciscans and Jesuits in spreading the Word of God in Africa."[127] There was also the establishment of schools and seminaries for the training of priests for the Church. All these efforts not-with-standing, the period could not deliver as much good as was intended. Some of the reasons included internal factors like harsh weather, disease, tribal wars, etc. and some external factors like the influence of the Age of Enlightenment, the pagan/Muslim negative influences.

## Missionary Revival (19th to mid-20th Centuries)

The nineteenth and twentieth century was a period of missionary revival in African Church. The scramble for African lands at this period was streamlined by the 1918 partitioning of African states. The 1918 partitioning agreement fashioned unhealthy marriage between colonization and Christianization. This was how the pact was worked out among the foreign powers:

> The mother country supplied clergy for her colonies. The Belgium Congo was manned by Belgian missionaries while Italian served in Ethiopian and Somaliland. French West Africa, North Africa, Equatorial Africa, Senegal and Madagascar were reserved for the French clergy. South Africa, Rhodesia, Gambia, Nigeria, Gold Coast, Uganda, Sudan, Egypt, British East Africa, British Congo became the domain of Great Britain. The Portuguese ministered at Portuguese West Africa and Mozambique. Germany missioned their compatriot to German Southwest Africa, German East Africa, and Cameroom. Prior to European colonization, the political map of sub-Saharan Africa consisted of countless tribal lands, but between 1870 and the end of the World War I, the colonial powers carved out and parceled out the continent.[128]

The colonial powers "carved out and parceled out" the African continent with utter disregard of "the political map of sub-Saharan African tribal lands, religious and economic interests/boundaries was one of the worst casualties of history and the bane of religio-politico instability among the African States."[129] This scenario notwithstanding, the enthusiastic missionary spirit of the religious groups that were active in many places at this period encouraged and supported many vocations to priesthood and religious life in many African Churches. In connection to this fact, Vincent J. O'Malley observed: "While evangelization was not a primary intention of the European colonization, conversion to the religion of the mother country nonetheless occurred and supported the overall vision of the parent country."[130] A historian analyst, Joseph Bouchaud wanted us to know the numerical increase of the period:

> Thus it is clear that the Catholic Church has become present in everywhere in Africa, and that this presence is the result of only one century apostolate. The 50,000 Catholics in 1800 increased to 26 million by 1961. In 1800 ecclesiastical divisions were rare; in 1964 there were 312 dioceses, vicariates, or prefectures. ... The 50 missionaries of 1800 increased to 13,500 priests (2,500 Africans), 5,000 teaching brothers (1,200 Africans), 23, 000 religious women (7,000 Africans), and more than 100,000 African catechists or teachers. ... In a total population of 230 million in 1964, Christians numbered 50 million (26 million Catholics, 19 million Protestants, 5 million Orthodox); Muslims, 95 million; pagans, 85 million. Catholics represented about 12 per cent of the population.[131]

The above passage would imply that the twentieth century witnessed a growth in Catholic faith and the priestly vocation and ministry in African countries in different ways. However, it was a faith-growth in a borrowed system and in a culture in a Church that was yet to become an African Church. The issue here was that we needed not only a growth in numbers of the African Catholic priests and the lay faithful, there was also the greater need for the Christian faith and worship to become culture in the African Catholic Church. The context for a process to transform the Christian faith into the local cultures was set in motion with the event of the Second Vatican Council (1962-1965) on the universal level. The challenge then was how to translate the universal principles of inculturation outlined in the Second Vatican Council documents into the practical faith and witness of the local Churches, especially in the African Churches. The priesthood has to lead the way in the transformation process of the Christian faith and the African culture.

## The Independent and Christian Africa (1960 to the present)

A great obstacle to the founding of an independent, Christian African Church is the assumption that we are on the same page with the rest of the world or the Catholic world. Therefore the more we "photocopy" from the Western world the more authentic we are. The challenge is how to be an independent African Church without feeling separated or isolated from the mother Church. The point is that there is some fear of "the unknown" on both sides.

Milton Jay Belasco et al describes 1960 as "the year of African independence," a year in which eighteen nations gained independence from European colonial powers. Nine others regained their independence between 1961 and 1964, while the last to gain independence (Namibia) was in 1990.[132] During this period (1960 – 1964) the African nations and Churches were battling with political independence from colonial powers, while the rest of the world and the Western Catholic Church were fashioning spiritual independence in the event of the Second Vatican Council (1962 – 1965). Lawrence Cardinal Sheehan in his introduction to the Second Vatican Council's documents cautioned the Church of Christ everywhere on a need for a wise, open approach in reading and listening to the Second Vatican Council documents. He wrote: "'Beginning' is the key word, for much remains to be done. That is why it can be said, 'The Council has ended; the Council has just begun.'" [133] What has ended and what is beginning for the African Church? Following from the Council's spirit of aggiornamento, (an act of updating something to meet current needs) Pope Paul VI said: "From now on *aggiornamento* will signify for us a wisely undertaken quest for a deeper understanding of the spirit of the Council and the faithful application of the norms it has happily and prayerfully provided."[134] What is critical here for peoples, languages, cultures, religions, governments, etc is "a wise undertaken quest for a deeper understanding of the Spirit of" and "a faithful application of" whatever it is that happens to come on our ways of life in the community of God's people. How does God speak to us in all peoples, events, situations, and circumstances? And how do we listen to and apply them in our lives as a community of God's people? This indeed, is the crux of the matter. It makes all the difference.

For the Western Church, the key documents to begin to explore the Council's spirit of aggiornamento are the *Dogmatic Constitution on the*

*Church (Lumen Gentium)* and the *Pastoral Constitution on the Church in the Modern World (Gaudium Et Spes),* while for the African Church, the key documents to begin to explore the Council's spirit of aggiornamento are: the *Decree on the Church's Missionary Activity (Ad Gentes);* the *Declaration on the Relationship of the Church to Non-Christian Religions (Nostra Aetate);* and the *Declaration on Religious Freedom (Dignitatis Humanae).* A responsible awareness and appreciation of what is ending and what is beginning for the African Church is critical. The African priesthood must lead the way in this process and the road to go is "the Church as a family."

The 1994 African synod did well to reclaim the family as the model for the African Church. But the Synod Fathers shied away from discussing the fundamental issue that gives meaning and structure to the Church as a family, marriage. A living meaning and a culturally-grounded structure of marriage in African culture and people stand on the road to an authentic African Church and community.

## Theological and Spiritual Implications for the Priesthood in African Church

African theology as well as African spirituality is an incubated child, yet to resume its normal life. Colonialism "incubated" African culture and labeled it "barbaric." We, the African priests and the lay faithful have a challenge at hand, to continue the colonial agenda or the African Church/people agenda. John Baur hinted to this point very clearly:

> The birth of an authentic African Christianity has been intimately connected with the rebirth of African culture. Colonialism had denied Africans their own proper civilization and decried their cultural traditions as barbaric. How could a genuine African Christianity develop in a cultural vacuum? The Christian faith could but vegetate as an imported, "second-hand" Western Christianity. The result has been the so often deplored dichotomy of the African Christian personality: Christianity was grafted on to the person as an alien faith and exercised on the surface, while deeper convictions and reactions remained rooted in traditional religion. In order that Christianity might establish roots in the traditional culture with its specific religiosity, it was necessary to re-evaluate this culture.[135]

The problem is not whether the Africa Church has wise and

knowledgeable theologians. It has. John Baur has named some of them: "Vincent Mulago from Bantu, Tharcisse Tshibangu from Zaire, Engelbert Mveng ,( a Jesuit from Cameroon), Anselme T. Sannon from Burkina Faso, Jea-Marc Ela, (a priest from Cameroon), Harry Sawyerr from Sierra Leone, Emmanuel Bolaji Idowu from Nigeria, Kwesi Dictkson from Ghana, Mercy Amba Oduyoye, (an African leading woman theologian from Ghana), Byang Kato from Nigeria, John Mbiti from Kenya, Charles Nyamiti from Tanzania, Manas Buthelezi from South Africa" and many more modern theologians, too many to be mentioned here.[136]

The problem is not with the persons of the theologians but with their language, agenda and approach. An "authentic African Christianity" requires a "rebirth of African culture." An authentic African theology requires a "rebirth of African culture" and spirituality.[137] It is painful that African theologians distracted themselves with irrelevant agendas and wasteful fighting over some methods or some intellectual concepts. Whether we are talking of adaptation, inculturation, contextualization, liberation or black theology, the fundamental question raised by John Baur continued to hunt us: "How could a genuine African Christianity develop in a cultural vacuum?"[138]

The issues here are deeper and all-embracing that the surface issues of methods and intellectual wars on concepts are not just enough, they are not real to life however important they may appear. We must all address with all honesty and total commitment the deep-rooted issue of the African Christian spirituality and culture. Do we continue with what John Baur called "grafting programs" or do we engage on a "deep-rooting process"? Do we, the Africans want to continue with the colonial agenda or with an authentic African agenda? What kinds of theology and spirituality do we want - a theology and spirituality of dichotomy (of wars and jihads) or a theology and spirituality of a listening presence, whereby we see and recognize differences as an invitation to listen to what God is saying to us through others as different ways to hear and witness the Good news of Jesus Christ. It is a commitment to a sincere spirit of compassion and of sharing the Gospel truth in love. Without a wholehearted commitment to a spirit of compassion and a sharing of truth in love in a respectful community life, a theology of listening presence will soon degenerate into a theology of dichotomy and wars.

The issue of a "cultural vacuum" is not simply an African case. The issue of a cultural vacuum" is a concern of all peoples and of all nations in the world. In essence, a "cultural vacuum" depicts some deep-felt emptiness and a lack of a mutuality of care and respect of persons, peoples and environment in every community of God's people. We can do better and we must do better.

**Conclusion**

In this chapter, we looked at the theological and spiritual understanding as it related to the priesthood in the history of the Western and African Catholic Churches. Here, the priesthood was understood as a call of God to His chosen ones to be God's presence and to a life of self-sacrifice in sharing God's gift of service to God and to God's people. A priest is to be a blessing of God, a compassionate, forgiving presence of God, and a loving service of God and the people of God.

We are "the people of God," all of us, without exceptions. One of the greatest accomplishment in the history of the Church is the recovery and reclaiming of the peoples of all countries, all races, all cultures, all religions, all sexes, all colors as "the people of God" by the Council Fathers of the Second Vatican Council. It is a "grace of God" which is yet to be received and shared. Over the years, God continually and consistently declared Himself as the God of the people. In the Bible, more than two hundred and eleven times, God addressed us as "My people." For instance, in the Old Testament (the book of Exodus) we read: "… and you shall be to me a kingdom of priests and a holy nation."[139] Again, in the New Testament (in the first epistle of Peter) it is stated: "But you are a chosen race, a royal priesthood, a holy nation, God's own people, that you may declare the wonderful deeds of him who called you out of darkness into his marvelous light. Once you were no people but now you are God's people; once you have not received mercy but now you have received mercy."[140] We are the kingdom of God and the people of God. The on-going challenge for the priests and the lay faithful is to respect and serve every person and every nation as the "kingdom of God" and the "people of God." We are not "ideas" or "concepts." We are the people of the kingdom of God, a community of the people of God. In the next chapter, we consider how to transform our seminary school and our education system into a "formative community" that forms people into a community life and leadership.

1    The Webster's New Encyclopedic International Dictionary of the English language, The Publishers Guild, Inc. New York: 1975, p. 756
2    Ibid,.
3    Genesis 12: 1-2 (Today's English Version – TEV)
4    Exodus 3: 4 (Good News Bible – GNB)
5    Exodus 18: 25 (GNB)
6    Exodus 18: 21 (GNB)
7    Exodus 30:30 (GNB)
8    1 Samuel 3: 9 (GNB)
9    1Samuel 10: 1 (GNB)
10   I Samuel 16: 1-13 (GNB)
11   Isaiah 6: 8 (GNB)
12   Jeremiah 1: 1-19 (GNB)
13   Ezekiel 3:24 (GNB)
14   Ezekiel 33: 31-32 (Today's English Version - TEV)
15   Ezekiel 34: 2-4 (TEV)
16   Ezekiel 34: 15-16 (TEV)
17   Isaiah 65: 17-18 (TEV)
18   Ezekiel 36: 23-28 (TEV)
19   John 1: 6-9 (TNAB)
20   John 1: 19-28 (TEV)
21   John 2: 36-39 (TNAB)
22   John 5: 17 (TNAB)
23   Hebrew 7: 11-17 (TEV)
24   Matthew 28: 18-20 (The New American Bible – TNA)
25   1 Peter 2:5 (TNA)
26   Aumann, J. (1985). Ibid., pp. 9-10
27   Ibid.
28   Ibid.
29   Aumann, J. (1985) Ibid., p. 10
30   Exodus 19: 5-6 (TEV)
31   I Peter 2: 9-10 (The New American Bible – TNA)
32   Catholic Answers Inc. (1997) Pillar of Fire, Pillar of Truth: The Catholic Church and God's Plan for You, San Diego, California, p. 19
33   Ibid.
34   Catholic Answers (1997) Ibid, p. 8
35   Acts of the Apostles 2: 42, 46-47
36   Bernier, P. (1992). Ministry in the Church: A Historical and Pastoral Approach, Connecticut: Twenty-Third Publications, p. 11

37 O'Meara, Thomas F. (1999) Theology of Ministry, Revised Edition, New York: Paulist Press, p. 38

38 O'Meara, Thomas F. (1999) Ibid., p. 35

39 Aumann, Jordan (1985) Ibid., p. 13

40 O'Meara, Thomas F. (1999). Theology of Ministry, Revised Edition, New York: Paulist press, p. 88

41 Bernier, P. (1992) Ibid., p. 31

42 Ibid.

43 Ibid., p. 33

44 Brown, R. (1984) The Churches the Apostles Left Behind, New Jersey: Paulist Press, quoted in Bernier, P. (1992) Ibid, p. 33

45 Aumann, J. (1992) Ibid., p. 20

46 Ibid., p. 33

47 Ibid.

48 Ibid., p. 34

49 Bernier, P. (1992) Ibid., p. 108

50 Bernier, P. (1992) Ibid., p. 125

51 Ibid.

52 Bernier, P. (1992) Ibid., p.129

53 Ibid.

54 Ibid.

55 Ibid.

56 Ibid.

57 Bernier, P. (1992) Ibid., p. 130

58 Ibid.

59 Ibid., p. 131

60 Ibid.

61 Ibid.

62 Ibid.

63 Ibid.

64 Ibid., p. 138

65 Ibid.

66 Ibid.

67 Ibid., p. 140

68 Ibid.

69 Bernier, P. (1992) Ibid., p. 150

70 Ibid.

71 Ibid., p. 151

72 Ibid.

73 Ibid.

74 O'Meara, Thomas F. (1999) Theology of Ministry, New York: Paulist, p. 112

75 Ibid.

76 Ibid.

77 Strange, R. (2004) The Risk of Discipleship: The Catholic Priest Today, London: Darton, Longman, & Todd Ltd, p. 42

78 Ibid.

79 Ibid., p. 163

80 Imitation of Christ, I, chaps. 1-3.

81 Bernier, P.(1992) Ibid., pp. 176-7

82 O'Meara, Thomas F. (1999) Ibid., p. 114

83 Bernier, P. (1992) Ibid., p. 178

84 Bernier, P. (1992) Ibid., pp. 179-0)

85 Bernier, P. (1992) Ibid., p. 180

86 Bernier, P. (1992) Ibid., p.180

87 Bernier, P. (1992) Ibid., pp. 181-2

88 Bernier, P. (1992) Ibid., p. 185

89 Bernier, P. (1992) Ibid., p. 181

90 Bernier, P. (1992) Ibid., p. 182

91 Ibid.

92 Ibid.

93 Bernier, P. (1992) Ibid., p. 83

94 Ibid.

95 Ibid.

96 Ibid.

97 O'Meara, Thomas F. (1999) Ibid., pp. 116-7

98 O'Meara, Thomas F. (1999) Ibid., p. 119

99 Bernier, P. (1992) Ibid., p. 203

100 Bernier, P. (1992) Ibid., p. 203

101 Bernier, P. (1992) Ibid., p. 204

102 Ibid.

103 O'Meara, Thomas F. (1999) Ibid., p. 134

104 O'Meara, Thomas F. (1999) Ibid., p. 138

105 See Matthew 2: 13-14

106 See Matthew 27:32

107 See Acts 13: 1

108 See Act 2:5-12

109 Acts 18:24

110 O'Malley, Vincent J. (2001) Saints of Africa, Indiana: Our Sunday Visitor Inc. p. 177

111 O'Malley, Vincent J. (2001) Ibid., p. 175

112 O'Malley, Vincent J. (2001) Ibid., p. 176

113 Ibid.

114 Ibid.

115 O'Malley Vincent J. (2001) Ibid., p. 178

116 Ibid.

117 O'Malley, Vincent J. (2001) Ibid., p. 178

118 O'Malley, Vincent J. (2001) Ibid., 179

119 Ibid.

120 Isichei, Elizabeth (1995) A History of Christianity in Africa: From Antiquity to the Present, Grand Rapids, Michigan: William B. Eerdmans Publishing Co. pp. 32-33 in O'Malley, Vincent J. (2001) Ibid., p. 180

121 O'Malley, Vincent J. (2001) Ibid, p. 180

122 Ibid.

123 O'Malley Vincent J. (2001) Ibid., p. 181

124 O'Malley, Vincent J. (2001) Ibid., p. 183

125 O'Malley, Vincent J. (2001) Ibid., pp. 187-195

126 O'Malley, Vincent J. (2001)Ibid., p. 187

127 Ibid.

128 O'Malley, Vincent J. (2001) Ibid., p. 188

129 Ibid., p. 190

130 Ibid.

131 Ibid.

132 Bouchaud, Joseph. "Africa" in New Catholic Encyclopedia, vol. I, p. 176 in O'Malley, Vincent J. (2001) Ibid., p. 191

133 Belasco, Milton Jay and Hammond, Harold E. (1970) The New Africa: History, Culture, People, ed. by Edward Graff, Bronxville, New York: Cambridge Book Co., Inc., pp.150-151 quoted in O'Malley, Vincent J. (2001) Ibid., p.191

134 Lawrence Cardinal Sheehan, "Introduction" in The documents of Vatican II, ed. by Walter Abbot, tr. by Joseph Gallapher (New York: Guild Press, 1966), p. xviii

135 Ibid.

136 Baur, John (1998) 2000 Years of Christianity in Africa: An African Church History, 2nd Revised Edition, Nairobi, Kenya: Paulines Publications Africa, p. 430

137 Baur, John (1998) Ibid., pp. 439-444

138 Baur, John (1998) Ibid., p. 430

139 Ibid.

140 Exodus 19: 6 (RSV, Catholic Edition)

141 I Peter 2: 9-10 (RSV, Catholic Edition)

# CHAPTER TWO: THE HISTORICAL DEVELOPMENT OF SEMINARY FORMATION IN THE CATHOLIC CHURCH

## Priesthood and Seminary Formation before and after Vatican II

The seminary education system is a child of the 16th century, the Council of Trent. Before the 16th century, there was no standardized or structured education of priests, except some forms of individual tutoring. From the Apostolic Age to the introduction of seminary school for training of priests at the Council of Trent, everything was mission-oriented and mission-defined. That is to say, a candidate for priesthood was selected and tutored based on the need of a particular mission. Today, it is different. We have mass "production" of priests who are ordained and then wait to be called to mission (a kind of professionalization of priesthood). The structure of priestly ordination was only put together in the first and second Lateran Councils in 1123 and 1138 respectively during the Medieval period. Even at this, the Scholastic theory of *ex opere operato*[1] which led to multiplication of Masses further encouraged the poor education of priests. The need for the Council Fathers to step in to save the situation was inevitable.

The Council of Trent was called together on December 13, 1545 by Pope Paul III (1534-1549) who presided over two of its sessions, 1545-47 and 1550-55. He was known to have introduced "genuine reformation" in the Church. For instance, Pope Paul III supported new religious orders like the Jesuits with the Bull, *Regimini militantis ecclesiae* in 1540. He restored the Inquisition in 1542 and "commissioned Michelangelo to complete the 'Last Judgment' in the Sistine Chapel (in order) to continue the construction of St. Peter's Basilica."[2] His idea was to reform the clergy and the clergy would reform the Church. However, his successor, Pope Paul IV (1555-1559) did not believe that the reform of the clergy and the Church could be achieved through decrees. It was the successor of Pope Paul IV, Gianangelo Medici, Pope Pius IV (1559-1565) who reconvened and completed the Council of Trent on January 18, 1562, ten years after it was suspended in 1552. It was during the last session (the twenty-third session) which was conducted by Giovanni Cardinal Morone that the decrees on the reform of clergy were enacted. And it was "Reginald Cardinal Pole of England, who ... drew on his experience in the training of priests (helped to) give shape to the institution of the seminary."[3] The actual decree of the Council of Trent, the twenty-third session had these specifications about the training of candidates for priesthood:

> The age of adolescence, unless it is properly guided, is given to the pursuit of worldly pleasures. Unless from their most impressionable years youth are shaped toward religious piety before the habits of vice invade, never perfectly and without the greatest and singular help of our omnipotent God would they persevere in the discipline of the Church. This synod therefore decrees that a certain number of the youth of its city be nourished and religiously educated in the discipline of the Church.[4]

Even though there were these specifications for the Tridentine seminary, yet "it was only in the late nineteenth and early twentieth centuries that attendance in the seminary would be required, and even then there were exceptions like Pope Pius XII, who as a member of the Roman nobility was tutored at home."[5] Nonetheless, the great contributions of the Tridentine seminary system in the education and training of candidates for priesthood in the Catholic Church are immeasurable. Even at this, I strongly believe that the true spirit of the Tridentine decree on seminary education is yet to be reclaimed. A lot has been said and done about the legalistic interpretation and implementation of the said decree. The spirit of the decree lies dead in history waiting to be recognized, reclaimed, interpreted and implemented.

## Models of Seminary Formation in History

Over the years, there was a development of different models of seminary education in the Catholic world. Msgr. Charles M. Murphy, in his book, *Models of Priestly Formation (2006)* highlighted five models of priestly education with their distinctive spirituality, system of education, theology and missionary spirit. They are: the Tridentine model, the French School model, the Second Vatican Council model, the Neocatechumenal Way model, and the New Foundation model of a diocesan seminary in Paris. Let us now discuss each of these models in some details and their lessons for priestly formation.

## Tridentine Model of Priestly Formation

The first model of seminary education according to Msgr. Charles Murphy was the Tridentine model. The chief protagonist of this model was St. Charles Borromeo (1538-1584) the bishop of Milan, who opened a seminary school six months after the conclusion of the Council of Trent. Boromeo modeled his seminary school in line with the Ignatian spirituality. This spirituality emphasized "the practice of mental prayer, regular examination of conscience, personal mortification, and spiritual direction."[6] With its form of spiritual asceticism, a priest was identified with his two major "roles at the altar (the power to celebrate the Eucharist) and in the confessional" (the power to forgive sins).[7] Another outstanding feature of the Tridentine model was its militaristic system of education which understood the Church on earth as "the Church militant" and priests as "soldiers of Christ" leading the people of God in a battle against the enemies of God.

What are the implications of the Tridentine model in the understanding of priesthood today? From the point of view of a predominantly Ignatian spirituality, the Tridentine seminary model is "more suited to produce monks than parish priests."[8] The relational problems of priests that tend to be more individualistic and isolationalistic may find some roots in this model. From the Tridentine model of education that is more of "military training institutions" or camps, "a recent study by David Lipsky" pointed out four unhealthy implications for the priesthood of Christ: First, like military training school, Tridentine seminary "emphasizes separation from the world and its values."[9] Second, like military training schools which "produce" (professional) soldiers with "ready-made identity," the Tridentine seminary schools "produce" (professional) priests with "ready-made identity." [10] It is a heavily structured, regimented lifestyle. The bell is the voice of God that tells everyone when or where or how or what of every detail of daily lives. The priests-to-be put their lives on-hold to follow a ready-made life or identity. They are to obey without questions, follow rules and regulations without personal touch or to do what others do. Third, like military training schools, the Tridentine seminary schools encouraged priests to develop stereotypical character of flat obedience to the rules with a shallow sense of responsibility and accountability in life issues.[11] And Four, it is a life oriented to doing duties with a superiority complex or the elite complexity of knowing all the answers to all problems. Most of these debilitating factors are living realities in many seminary schools today.

## French School Model of Priestly Formation

The second seminary model was the French school model which was dominated by the teachings of Cardinal Pierre de Berulle (1575-1629). The French school came together as a reaction against the intellectualistic theology of Scholasticism of the Middle Ages. Different groups came under the French school: we had the society of Saint-Sulpice founded by Jean-Jacques Olier (1608-1657), the Congregation of the Mission founded by St. Vincent de Paul (1580-1660), the Eudist Fathers founded by John Eudes (1606-1680) and the religious society of diocesan priests (the Oratory Fathers) founded by St. Philip Neri (1515-1595) in Rome which was brought to France by Cardinal Berulle.

One thing about these religious societies of the French school was their unique contributions to spirituality of the priesthood which were related to and yet different from the spirituality of Cardinal Berulle. First of all, they were all focused on the renewal of the lives of diocesan priests, (with different emphasis) which in turn, would ensure the renewal of the lives of the people of God in the community. For instance, Jean Jacques Olier, like Cardinal Berulle, taught a religious spirituality grounded on the mystery of the incarnation of Jesus Christ but he interpreted the mystery of incarnation differently. For Olier, Christ's incarnation was not a unity of the human and the divine, rather the divine "annihilated" the human. To grow in holiness for Olier was to "disown the 'flesh' and to live entirely on the plane of the Spirit."[12] Olier came very close to Jansenism and Calvinistic Puritanism by insisting that our humanity and its proper care (foods and drinks) might create "obstacles" to spiritual life. For Olier, food and drink might be "tolerated" to sustain life, not to be enjoyed. On the other hand, Cardinal Berulle taught that the goal of spiritual life was a harmonious living of both the Spirit and the "flesh." And this harmonious living was to be achieved on three levels of life - "the authority, holiness, and doctrine" which were similar to St. Philip Neri's "the faith, Fire and Iron."[13] Different schools had different virtues they taught and modeled in spirituality. For instance, "the Franciscans modeled poverty, the Cathusians, solitude, the Jesuits, obedience," and the priests of the Oratory, love of Christ and prayer for the people.[14]

What are the implications of the French school model of seminary education to the understanding of the priesthood of today? There are so many good contributions from the French school model of seminary education. I would like to focus more on the challenges we faced today as results of this model which constituted a strong influence on the Catholic Church up to the time of Vatican II Council. According to Monsignor Charles Murphy, the author of the book, *Models of Priestly Formation, 2006*, there were at least three tensions to be noted here: "the human versus the divine, the diocese versus the seminary, and the pastoral versus the clerical."[15]

The first tension was "the human versus the divine" which was the stand of Jean-Jacques Olier who taught that growth in spiritual life was by disowning one's "flesh" while growing in the Spirit. For him, human nature was an obstacle to be overcome, food and drinks to be kept to their barest minimum for sustaining life only. The influence of this tension had left the Catholic Church with great suspicion with regard to human sciences like psychology, sociology, anthropology, etc. in seminary education except lately, in the second part of the twentieth century. Even today, these human sciences are treated as merely classroom subjects to be read and passed in exams. The critical human formation aspect of these human sciences is at best ignored. Faith and feelings are not enemies. They are great friends, great energy-sources to be harmonized in honest and mature life. The growing crisis in priesthood today pushes the argument in the other direction that intellectual intelligence is not enough. Howard Gardner's *Theory of Multiple Intelligences* teaches eloquently that we don't have "one" intelligence but seven or more. Definitely, social and emotional intelligences cannot be ignored in mature human relationships with others.

The second tension was the diocese versus the seminary. The idea of Cardinal Berulle was to create in the seminary school a strong "formative community" of priests-seminarian mentorship in an understanding that the relationships established in the seminary would form a foundation of priest-priest relationships years after the seminary education. In pushing for a strong formative community in the seminary, Cardinal Berulle taught that "the seminary faculty alone, not the bishop was better equipped to determine the worthiness of candidates for ordination."[16] The Council Fathers of Vatican II pushed this point to the other extreme to emphasize the position of the bishop. This ongoing authority tussle between the bishops and the seminary authority kills formation in many seminary schools today. What may be needed is a collaborative leadership between the bishops and the seminary community. We need a seminary system which is truly and fully a "formative community" which includes bishops, the seminary community, and the diocesan community (priests and people) as a collaborative, formative family of God. There is a great need for a seminary community that is both "a family" and "a formative community."

The third tension was the pastoral versus the clerical. The Scholastic cultic understanding of a priest was adopted and strengthened by the Council of Trent. The Saint-Sulphice society's emphasis on the divinity of Christ against his humanity extended the cultic understanding of priesthood in the French school, thereby furthering the gap between the priest and the people. The challenge of this situation was brought to light with the "priest-worker" in France after the World War II. The growing gap between the priest and the people is a real concern today. Some modern theologians like Yves Congar have insisted on a new understanding of a priest as one "who is 'in front of the people" as a servant leader. [17] In recent times, one may notice some gradual language shift: from a so-called "secular priest" to a "diocesan priest;" from a "parish priest" to a pastor (though the term, pastor is more a language of the Protestant Churches than Catholic. Today, the term, pastor is a household term for both Catholics and Protestants).

In my country, Nigeria, we have the Fulani people who pasture sheep and cattle all over the country. They go in groups of twos, threes or fours depending on the number of sheep or cows in a group. The first person walks in front of the sheep and the others walk behind or at the sides. In rain or in sunshine, these shepherds are always and everywhere with their sheep. They never abandon them or leave them alone unattended. The sheep literally follow the shepherd's steps to find pasture and safety. At times, the shepherds may carry the weak ones when circumstances demand it. This may serve as a model for priests in the parish. A priest is not simply at the front or at the back or at the sides all the time. The important thing is that the people are always at the center, at the heart of every priest in all decisions, policies and programs in the Parish. The people of God are not "means" to be used but "ends" to be served. Priests are servant-leaders, not task-masters. Collaborative spirit, holiness and humility define a leader, not simply a position of authority or the years of ordination.

I would like to suggest that appointments to offices and ministries in the Catholic Church be done through an **Appointment Evaluation Board (AEB)** and that this board (AEB) oversees the on-going evaluation process of the priests and the lay people in offices and ministries in the Catholic Church and then make recommendations to the local ordinary or to the National Bishops' Conference or the Pope as the case may be. The **Priest Appointment Evaluation Board (PAEB)** operates on a diocesan level and makes recommendations to local ordinaries on diocesan appointments and their on-going evaluations. The **Bishop Appointment Evaluation Board (BAEB)** operates on national level in co-ordination/collaboration with the diocesan PAEB, makes recommendations to the National Bishops Conference and to the Pope on the appointment of bishops and their on-going evaluations. There are two separate issues here: we have an **Evaluation Process** for appointments to Church's offices and ministries on the one hand. There is also an **On-going Evaluation Process** at intervals of two or three years for all serving in Church offices and ministries. The idea is to inject some form of accountability in the entire system of the Church's life, mission and ministries. The existing Board of Consultors , the Pastoral Councils and the Presbyteral Councils have overwhelmingly responsibilities to handle that the creating of this special board for accountability and appointments in the Catholic Church does not render these boards redundant. It does not also constitute a duplication of office or duty.

The **Evaluation Process** will take this form: the intended candidate will submit and defend before the evaluation board a self evaluation, fully illustrated with challenging personal experienced stories on the following areas of life:[18]

1. **Description of Self:** Here, the candidate gives a comprehensive analysis of family background, family roots, religious background, personal education and employment, cultural and social challenges, difficulties and experiences in life.

2. **Intrapersonal Awareness and Growth:** The candidate illustrates with examples an understanding and knowledge of areas of growth and improvement on the self, strengths, weaknesses and gifts as well as areas for further growth.

3. **Interpersonal Awareness and Growth:** The candidate gives evidences of gained insights and skills on some personality inventories like pastoral identity, relational skills, awareness of his/her attitudes, values and assumptions in relationships, relationship qualities with superiors, colleagues, friends and the general people at various levels of life. The candidate's level of tolerance and capacity in handling hot emotions of anger, guilt and shame, challenges, ability to resolve conflicts and make peace and areas for further growth and development.

4. **Theological Competence:** The candidate's theological education and awareness; Concrete evidences of accomplishments like certifications, degrees, awards and knowledge of current theological issues and their connections to current life and ministry. The social justice issues, advocacies for the common good and human right issues as well as areas for further studies and ongoing formation.

5. **Spiritual/Religious Competence:** The candidate gives witness to his/her spiritual identity, the sense of personal holiness and sacredness of life, the prayer life, skills in scriptural reflection and meditation and areas of future growth. The spiritual skills in naming, respecting and affirming other faith groups and individuals, their beliefs, and their religious and ethnic backgrounds and needs. The capability to offer spiritual directions, spiritual companioning and to identify areas of further spiritual growth.

6. **Professional Competence:** The candidate's ability to gain insight and integrate lessons and learning in the practice of ministry; The ability to initiate, deepen, and terminate pastoral relationships; The capacity to understand and recognize personal dynamics and relational dynamics within the context of a group and pastoral functioning; The relational skills to involve and promote interdisciplinary teams and integral involvement in working with interreligious and inter-faith groups. The institutional experience and competence with people of diverse religious background and disciplines. The knowledge and understanding of institutional structures and their operational working in the system. And the knowledge of and capacity to give and receive referrals in a timely and proper manner.

This evaluation process serves at least on two occasions: when one opts for an office of service and during annual evaluation. The purpose of the on-going evaluation process is not to blame or to find faults but to encourage and foster responsible pastoral functioning, effective leadership and on-going formation in ministry.

**Vatican II Model of Priestly Formation**

The Vatican II model of priestly education was the third model in order of our discussion. Gabriel Marie Cardinal Garrone, who was once the Prefect of the Congregation for Catholic Education and who took active part in Vatican II Council had instructed that the priestly education model of Vatican II would be best understood if read from the Council's two great constitutions: the *Dogmatic Constitution on the Church (Lumen Gentium, November 21, 1964)* and the *Pastoral Constitution on the Church in the Modern World (Gaudium Et Spes, December 7, 1965)* and its two other decrees relating to priesthood: the *Decree on Priestly Formation (Optatam Totius)* and the *Decree on the Ministry and Life of Priests (Presbyterorum Ordinis)*. However, our discussion here will focus on the Council's Decree on Priestly Formation (Optatam Totius) and how its teachings are explained and elaborated in the subsequent 1970 Synod of Bishops on priestly identity and the 1990 Synod of Bishops on further formation of priests as well as its aftermath, the 1992 Apostolic Exhortation of Pope John Paul II, *Pastores Dabo*

*Vobis.* What does the Optatam Totius teach us on priestly education and how are these teachings reflected in subsequent Vatican documents?

The Decree on Priestly education is divided into seven parts: The first part is an instruction to all nations to "develop its program of priestly education based upon the principles outlined in this decree."[19] Among other things, this will mean to develop an inclusive "formative community" in the seminaries that includes the diocesan bishop as a principal formator in each seminary. The second part is on "fostering of vocations" which the Council Fathers considered as the mission of all the entire Church, the whole Christian community. The importance of minor seminaries was highlighted and the value of using psychological evaluation as criteria for the measuring of the maturity of candidates. The third part of Optatam Totius is on programs in major seminaries. The programs are oriented to ministry of the Gospel and grounded in pastoral goals.

The fourth part is "deepening the spiritual formation" which must be connected with "doctrinal and pastoral training."[20] Two new practices are recommended at this time: the first is for "bishops to establish an appropriate period of time for more intensive spiritual apprenticeship, so that spiritual training can rest upon a firmer base and students can embrace their vocation with a decision maturely weighed."[21] This recommendation has given rise to what we have seen operating in some dioceses (especially in Nigeria) as the "spiritual year" program. The challenge is how to keep the spiritual year deeply spiritual without turning it into an "academic year" mingled with some spiritual exercises. The second newly recommended practice is "for bishops to consider the opportuneness of deciding on a certain interruption of studies or arranging for a suitable pastoral apprenticeship so that a more rounded test can be made of priestly candidates."[22] In some countries like Nigeria, this practice is what is known today as one year apostolic work after philosophical studies in the major seminary schools. From my experience in my studies, the one year apostolic work (as well as other periods of apostolic work during the formation period) is perceived by most candidates for priesthood as a tolerated added-delay year to the expected time of priestly ordination. To the priests and people of the local community, it is an added-grace time of catechism preparation for children's reception of sacraments. The challenge now is to restructure the one-year period into an action-reflection learning process of a well-supervised suitable pastoral apprenticeship experience for the candidates. The period must be perceived and appreciated as an extension of the seminary formation process and not as a distraction from it.

The fifth part of Optatam Totius is "the revision of ecclesiastical studies" with greater emphasis on integration of all philosophical and theological studies into a unified whole. The seminary training, the Council Fathers insisted, should not "aim at a mere communication of ideas, but at a genuine and deep formation of students. Teaching methods should be revised as they apply to lectures, discussions, and seminars and with respect to the promotion of study among students, whether individually or in small groups."[23] It is not simply an issue of integration of all studies, there must be standardized quality to it. By "standardized quality" I mean a shift of emphasis from mere paper-qualifications or certifications to a more personalized formation and transformation that can be evidenced and evaluated from time to time in the formation process.

The sixth section is on "the promotion of strictly pastoral training." The focus is on "careful instruction in the art of guiding souls" and to develop in seminarians the ability most appropriate for promotion of dialogue with people, such as a capacity to listen to other people and to open their hearts in a spirit of charity to the various circumstances of human need."[24] The seminarians are to be persons of integrity and of solid character as public persons.

The seventh section is on arranged further studies after the seminary training. The Council Fathers recommended an arranged further study program but failed to give it a curriculum and structures of operation. This has given rise to various forms of abuses and crisis in priesthood. The question then is, how are the teachings of Optatam Totius reflected in Vatican documents after it? Are the Vatican documents that came after the Optatam Totius document a follow-up or a throw-off, a support or a suppression, an encouragement or discouragement of each other?

In the first place, Cardinal Garrone pointed out that the ecclesiology of Optatam Totius is grounded in the ecclesiology of Lumen Gentium and Gaudium Et Spes, which has three new interpretations. The first new interpretation is "the Church as a communion." It means that "the communal life of the faithful" is grounded in the "mystical communion" of the Trinitarian Life of God.[25] This has a huge implication for a priest who is both a person of community and a servant-leader of the community. The second interpretation is "the Church as a people of God." It is a way of acknowledging the historicity of the Church in which case, the Church is "within not above human history." [26] By adopting the biblical phrase: "the people of God," the Council Fathers run the risk of blurring the line of distinction between the common priesthood of the faithful and the ministerial priesthood. The Council Fathers adopted the Thomistic ideology to state that "though they differ from one another in essence and not only in degree, the common priesthood of the faithful and the ministerial or hierarchical priesthood are nonetheless interrelated." [27] We will discover later on in our discussion that the claim to Thomistic ideology in this case did not do much good in saving the distinctive identities of both parties: the common priesthood of the faithful and the ministerial priesthood of the clergy.

The third interpretation of the Church is "the Church in the service to the kingdom of God." This interpretation has two big implications for the understanding of the Church at this period in history. There is an orientation of the Church towards the kingdom of God and its mission. The mission of the Church to God's kingdom "is to announce the kingdom's arrival and to prepare for God's reign, that new order of things that will bring peace, justice, and love."[28] The Church like its members – the common and the ministerial priesthood of God, has a double task to teach in the world and to learn from the Word.

The Optatam Totius is strongly reflected in Pastores Dabo Vobis (1992). Pastores Dabo Vobis made three new points about the seminary: First, a call to return to the Tridentine position that the bishop takes a direct role in directing the seminaries; Second, that Rome's general oversight on everything must not suffocate the local adaptations; and third, it calls on seminaries "to strive to overcome their isolation and enter into greater contact with the world the priests are being trained to serve."[29]

The other special contribution of Pastores Dabo Vobis is the emphasis on the four "areas" of priestly formation: the human (the capacity to relate to others); the spiritual (the capacity to live a selfless life on behalf of others); the intellectual (the capacity to integrate various fields of information and to draw lessons and learning from life); and the pastoral (the capacity to care, to recognize and affirm gifts, to work collaboratively with others).

What are the implications of this model in our understanding of the theology and spirituality of priesthood today? According to cardinal Garrone, who carried out an extensive reflection on Vatican II model and formation, one of the major problems of the Church today is the seminary system. To use biblical metaphor, it is an issue of "new wine into old wineskins."[30] The current situation in the Church with the Tredentine seminary system and the Vatican II pastoral model is just a scenario of the biblical image of "new wine into old wineskins." It is an issue of an adaptability question of the old system to "new challenges," "new problems," "new situations," "new cultures," "new peoples," "new languages," "new communities," "new Churches," etc. of today.

The real challenge here is not whether the "old system" is adaptable or not, but that the question is presumed or ignored by the Vatican II Council Fathers and those after them. Instead, there have been relentless efforts to introduce "pastoral courses and pastoral formation programs," good as they are in themselves but not enough.[31] The educational or developmental problems of life need more than just the addition of new programs to the curriculum of life or study.

This situation of a program-solution to all issues of life, Monsignor Charles M. Murphy will argue, raises a number of groundbreaking questions: Is the pastoral Council's intention to update the Church adequately addressing the new pastoral situations of today's Church? Is the "seminary system (16th century system) which predates the Council" capable enough to perform the new tasks of priestly education of the twenty-first century Church? Will the introduction of new "pastoral courses and pastoral formation programs" be an adequate substitute to transform the seminary as a "center of life of the diocese from which the candidates come?"[32] Will "propaedeutic programs provide basic evangelization of candidates and to make up for their academic deficiencies" and to be able to "actually form authentic Christians in a secularized world?"[33] Will "the seminary that still operates within the academic model of an academic year, that itself derives from bygone agricultural society in which children were needed in summer to plant and harvest the crops," be adequate to meet the needs of diversely different communities?[34] Does "the high Christology of the French School restore to the priesthood a needed dignity and respect? Or does it need to be balanced with a Christology that gives greater place to Christ's messianic role as the humble servant, exemplified in the

Letter to the Hebrews, where Christ's unique intercession is grounded in human weakness? (Heb. 5:1)"[35] Will "continued formation after ordination" often guided by seminaries, "again within the Tredentine model," make any significant or needed differences in the lives and ministries of priests and people of God? [36]

Just to maintain the status quo is not enough. The suggestion of Gabriel Marie Cardinal Garrone that the priestly formation in the seminaries follow closely the new ecclesiology of Vatican II Council is a way to move forward. According to Cardinal Garrone, the Vatican II Council fathers enumerated three forms of understanding the Church today: The first is a Church as a communion which is grounded in the mystical communion of the Trinitarian God, Father, Son and the Holy Spirit. In this sense, a seminary that perceives itself as an ecclesial communion aims at training priests who will be both the persons of communion with other priests and religious, and servant-leaders of the community of God's people in ministry.

The second is a Church as a people of God which emphasizes the historicity of the Church as one within not above human history. A seminary that perceives itself as a family of God's people forms priests who will see themselves as being called to be and to serve among the people, not above them. The third form of Vatican II's understanding of the Church is the Church in the service of God's kingdom which involves the announcing of the arrival of the kingdom and the preparation of God's reign of peace, justice and love. A seminary which perceives itself as a formation center in service of God's kingdom does not simply teach to test (to have knowledge and pass exams) but tries to form and transform candidates for priesthood to be persons and agents of peace, justice and love. It is a diversified training process that stresses all aspects of formation: The human formation that moves beyond human knowledge to skills and abilities to relate respectfully and responsibly with others. It is also a spiritual formation which inspires candidates to move beyond spiritual exercises in order to acquire the skills and abilities to live selflessly on behalf of others. It is equally an intellectual formation which shifts emphasis from intellectual knowledge to develop a capacity to integrate the diverse fields of information as to draw lessons and learning of life from them. And finally, it is a pastoral formation which is to foster the capacity to care, to recognize and affirm giftedness and work collaboratively to nurture and promote growth in all aspects of life.

## The Seminary Model of NeoCatechumenal Way

The Neocatechumenal Way was founded in Madrid by Francisco Arguello, an artist and Carmen Hermandez, a former religious sister. Both of them were living and working among poor people and were motivated to bring change of heart to isolated, ignorant parishioners who are far away from the Church's life and a change in a parish structure that is unwelcoming and non-supporting. The way they planned to meet the double needs was through a small Christian community. The Neocatechumenal Way soon gained a full support of the archbishop of Madrid in the 1960s. Not long after that, Rome recognized it and gave it one parish to administer, then many parishes. In fact, the first Neocatechumenal seminary was in Rome. According to Monsignor Charles Murphy, the author of a book, *Models of Priestly Formation,* 2006, "there are now fifty-two such seminaries from which over a thousand priests have been ordained. By 2006, there were four such seminaries in the United States in the Archdioceses of Newark, Denver, and Washington and in the diocese of Dallas."[37] I am not aware any Neocatechumenal Way seminary in Nigeria or in Africa.

The Neocatechumenal Way enjoyed papal support and encouragement beginning with Pope Paul VI, then with John Paul II who invited the leaders of the Way to his first Mass after his election as a Pope. Even Pope Benedict XVI supports the Neocatechumenal Way and sees in it a force for socializing faith and a powerful tool in winning the war against secularization and individualism in the world of today.

What is the spirituality of Neocatechumenal Way? The spirituality of Neocatechumenal Way is Scripture-based in which the "Word is learned to be lived, to be 'echoed'" and it is "intended to 'form' not just 'inform.'"[38] It is a spirituality that is community-based which serves as "the source of spiritual direction." That is, the community members serve one another as spiritual directors by helping one another to "discern God's will and how God's will is impacting their lives."[39] The Neocatechumenal Way seminary operates without spiritual directors but only confessors for the sacrament of reconciliation.

The Neocatechumenal Way spirituality is also based on God's providential care of everyone. It is related to the Transfiguration experience which depicts the sense of being "taken" to the mountain by Christ (initial reluctance or unwillingness to follow) and there

Peter exclaims: "Lord, it is good for us to be here" (Luke 9: 33) – a later realization of God's goodness and caring presence. It is equally a liturgical spirituality which is Scriptural based. It is not simply "a Bible –sharing exercise" but something deeply involving some process of self-discovery that follows some biblical patterns like God's first question to Adam and Eve: "Where are you?" (Gen. 3:9); Jesus' question to his disciples: "But who do you say that I am?" (Matt. 16:15); and Jesus' question to the disciples of John the Baptist: "What are you looking for?" (John 1: 38).

The Neocatechumenal Way liturgy is a little different from an ordinary Eucharistic celebration. Apart from the normal homily given at Holy Eucharistic celebrations, "the members of the community share their own personal experiences of the Word and their struggle to live it more fully" [40] It is often an extended liturgy lasting more than two hours. Everything about the liturgical celebrations is meant to inspire participants, not simply to entertain with songs and music accompaniments (organs or guitars).

## The Implications of this Model for the Theology and Spirituality of Priesthood

What are the implications of the Neocatechumenal Way model in our understanding of the theology and spirituality of priesthood today? The first point, and a fundamental one is the issue of small community based and community discerning process. In the Neocatechumenal Way, "everyone is a part of small Christian community" which is intimately accepted, lived, celebrated and witnessed in the daily lives of the small basic Christian community. The small basic Christian community is a way of life of the people, a way of celebrating the Word and the Eucharist, a way of being a people of God, a way of witnessing to Christ and his mission, a way of discerning vocation and fostering it. It means that "the discernment of a vocation to the priesthood therefore is a discernment by the community itself of an individual's calling."[41] The small Christian community is not a replacement but an instrument of God and the Holy Spirit in the work of salvation. There are enormous challenges here.

The forming of the small Christian community is never an easy task or a "cheap" one, especially among a highly diverse, divided people and the secularized world of today. It is even more difficult to live and foster an authentic spirit of the small Christian community. Therefore, "the community interaction is considered crucial in advancing the conversion of the individual member and growth in the faith."[42] The difference is clear. A vocation for a "typical seminarian" moves beyond a simple desire to serve the people and share the Eucharist or the sacraments with the people to be more of a transformed life of a disciple of Christ through a continual experience of conversion.

Secondly, "while a typical seminarian subconsciously may be given the impression that to be ordained he should keep as low a profile as possible during his seminary years, adhering to the regulations of the seminary in his public life while keeping his private life to himself, the seminarian who is part of the Way is very well known by the community in all aspects of his life." [43] The Neocatechumenal Way is also great in some other ways: it is a great tool for an integrated seminary formation (intimately involving the psychological, affective and human development) with its combination of Christian initiation process and the seminary formation process. It can be a powerful instrument of transformation in the lives of parishes. The Neocathecumenal Way can help us to eliminate "seminary shopping" and an attitude of a "separation from home" in our candidates for priesthood which poses serious challenge in the Church today. "Seminary shopping" and an attitude of a "separation from home" are new tendencies among seminaries and some modern priests today. During the years of seminary formation, some candidates may choose to "buy" their time in the seminary as a project of passing exams and avoiding being expelled from the seminary till priestly ordination. Their "separation from home" during seminary years is a kind of family investment to be reaped once after priestly ordination. I shall come back to this new tendency in seminary formation and its implications for priestly life later on. The Neocatechumenal Way can also foster a nurturing of a team spirit, a necessary skill for collaborative ministry. For the Neocatechumenal Way, seminary life is not counted in years but in growth through repentance and conversion of hearts.

On a less positive side, the Neocatechumenal Way has been accused of "elitism" and "exclusivism" which may be possible when the small Christian community is pushed too far. By "pushing it too far" I mean, when the members of a small basic Christian community tend towards exclusive relationships and leadership that build "walls" that divide rather than "bridges" that unite the people of God. Another concern is the issue of balance between the "external forum" ("the zone of public disclosure") and the "internal forum" ("the area of conscience and privacy"). Monsignor Murphy sees these two forums as depicting the typical seminarian and the seminarians of the Way. He explains that "while a seminarian in other seminaries might be tempted 'to tell them nothing' that might impede his ordination, seminarians of the Way are seemed required to say everything about themselves within the community sharing."[44] In short, the Neocatechmenal Way model has so much good to offer the Church and its priesthood today.

**New Foundation Model of Diocesan Seminary of Paris**

The New Foundation model of seminary formation was a child of necessity, being an organized response to the shortage of priestly vocations in Paris. It was founded in 1984 by Jean-Marie Cardinal Lustiger as a "'spiritual year' for potential candidates for the priesthood."[45] The idea of a "spiritual year" is not totally a new invention. It has been already discussed in the apostolic exhortation, *Pastores Dabo Vobis* in which it is described it as "propaedeutic period."[46] This model is not just a rescue-operation program or a filling –in of gap project but rather an education process. Cardinal Lustiger pointed out six characteristics of this program. The first is that it is a year of discernment. The second is that it should be a spiritual foundational experience. The third is that it is essentially a spiritual program, not an academic one. The fourth is that its focus is on the entire spiritual life of diocesan priests, not just for one year. The fifth is that it is oriented towards the spiritual needs of the present moment of priestly life. And the sixth characteristic is that it aims at a spiritual conversion. That is to say, it is a transformation process of dealing with personal "imperfections" and personal "obstacles" in a spiritual life and its growth processes. Finally, as a privileged time of discernment, this period may be for both the students and their supervisors an opportunity for a candid evaluation of the students' needs and their adequacies for the pastoral needs of the priesthood of Jesus Christ.

In terms of the specific qualities of the Diocesan seminary of Paris, the key and central theme is "personal conversion and the conversion particular to a person called to priesthood."[47] There is a desire to move away from "the quasi-monastic form" of old seminaries to a new form which is centered on "conversion, the total gift of self to Christ made possible by the hard spiritual work of achieving the freedom of spirit required to make such a fundamental, life-shaping decision."[48] There are some specific elements of the spirituality of this seminary of Paris model. According to Cardinal Lustiger, "the elements of such a conversion include the practice of evangelical counsels and celibacy. Its deepening and nourishment comes from immersion in Scripture, fidelity to prayer, the liturgy of the Church, and the common life."[49] Others include a spirit of adaptability, availability, disinterestedness and collaboration.

## The Implications of this Model for the Theology and Spirituality of Priesthood

The over-all aim of the Seminary of Paris model is to "de-institutionalize" the seminary system. This is in response to two prevailing challenges of the time: "the dramatic decline in the number of diocesan priests and the need for a new kind of formation for diocesan priesthood adapted to a changed kind of candidate and changing pastoral needs."[50] Cardinal Pio Laghi, the then prefect of the Vatican's Congregations for Catholic Education made some salient points here. First, he prefers the term, "period of spiritual formation" rather than "spiritual year." He contends that spiritual formation is for the whole life, not just for one year. Implicated in this observation of Cardinal Laghi is the question: "Can conversion of life be achieved within a single year?"[51] The undeniable truth is that spiritual formation, which must include human formation is not a factor of a particular time, particular institution, people, places or circumstances. It is based on a particularity of each one of them and all of them, and more.

## Priestly Formation in Nigeria

It is difficult to speak of a model of seminary formation in Nigeria. The Nigerian major seminaries (diocesan and religious groups alike) show orientation to more than one of the five models of seminary formation we discussed above. From my understanding in this study, I would like to point out that a multi-faceted seminary model in Nigeria has strong tendency toward a highly institutionalized, academic system of the Tridentine model. The Tridentine model was founded on the teaching of St. Charles Borromeo (1538-1584). For Borromeo, a priest is a "dispenser" of the Sacraments, his spirituality is ascetical and Christological, his mission is to save souls and his education is obedience to the rules, like a military training school. Some of the Tridentine's characteristics are typical of the Nigerian model.

The other model very typical of the Nigerian model is the French School model. The French School model is dominated by the teachings of Cardinal Pierre de Berulle (1575-1629), Jean Jacques Olier (1608-1657), and St Vincent de Paul (1580-1660). For the French School, a priest is a "spiritual elite," Christ's victim and representative. Its spirituality is divinization and participation in the incarnated Christ; its mission is denial of self and Eucharistic adoration; its education is relational (deeply confessor-penitent kind) like a novitiate training school. Particularly typical of the French School model is its tripartite tensions: The first tension is the human versus the divine. This tension tends to promote a primacy of intellectual knowledge as against the human sciences like psychology, sociology, anthropology. The second tension is the diocese versus the seminary. This tension fosters some conflictual relationships between the local ordinaries and the seminary authority. In some major seminaries in Nigeria, this particular tension has created some serious rifts and wounds on some parts of the Church's body and hierarchy. The third tension is the pastoral versus the clerical which tends to foster an unhealthy gap between the priests and the people, as well as various forms of clericalism.

The other model that is typical of the Nigerian seminary model is the Vatican II model. The Vatican II model is based on Vatican II documents (especially Optatam Totius, Decree on the Training of Priests, 1965; Presbyterorum Ordinis, Decree on the Ministry and Life of Priests, 1965; Gaudium Et Spes, Dogmatic Constitution of the Church in the Modern World, 1965; Lumen Gentium, Dogmatic Constitution of the Church, 1964) and the Synodal Documents (like the 1970 Synod of Bishops on Priestly Identity; 1990 Synod of Bishops on Priestly Further Formation; the Apostolic Exhortation of Pope John Paul II of 1992, Pastores Dabo Vobis; and the Post Synodal Apostolic Exhortation of 1995, Ecclesia in Africa). For Vatican II model, a priest is a ritual person of Christ, co-worker with the bishop and a servant of the people of God; Its spirituality is communion in the Church (as the people of God) and in the world. It has no clearly defined educational model. One particular characteristic from the Vatican II model is a strong tendency to program-solutions to all problems. If the seminarians are not doing well in liturgy, add more classes of liturgy. If a great number of seminarians are misbehaving, add more rules. There is a belief that more is better and a belief in big numbers.

The missionary seminary school of St. Paul at Gwagwalada in the Western part of Nigeria has a seminary model which comes close to the Neocatechumenal Way model. The Neocatechumenal Way model is based on the teachings of her founders Francisco Arguello, an artist, and Carmen Hernandez, an ex-Nun in 1960s. For the Neocatechumenal Way, a priest is a member of an evangelical, missionary community; its spirituality is "personal conversion to the Gospel way of life;"[52] its mission is evangelical community-building and collaboration; its educational model is "formative Christian community" and itinerant missionary (formation-on-the-road). The missionary seminary of St. Paul is yet to imbibe the full load of a total commitment and strict discipline of the Neocatechumenal Way model.

In all, I wish to emphasize that one of the greatest challenges to priesthood in the Catholic Church today is a poor attention given to human and spiritual formation in our seminary schools. This has inevitably created huge relational problems in all parts of the world within and outside of the Church. The poor human and spiritual development in seminary education is one of the root causes, if not the key root cause, of crisis in the priesthood in the world over. Whether we define the crisis like Richard Sipe as a *sexual crisis* or like Donald Cozzens as a *crisis of soul* or like Alan Abernethy as a *crisis of frustration* or like Michael Rose as a *cultural crisis* or like Andrew Greeley as *a calling in crisis* or like Roderick Strange as a *crisis of discipleship (an identity crisis),* human and spiritual development has a stake in each case. When we speak of human development as human formation in regard to priestly life and ministry, what are we talking about? The answer to this question will occupy our attention in the next chapter, chapter three.

1   "Ex opere operato" – a Latin phrase which literally means "From the work done." This Scholastic term, "ex opere operato" was coined to express "how a sacrament achieves its effects: not because of the faith of the recipient and / or the worthiness of the minister but because of the power of Christ who acts within and through it."(Richard P. McBrien, (1994) Catholicism, New York: HarperSanFrancisco, p. 1239).

2   Bunson, Matthew (1995) Our Sunday Visitor's Encyclopedia of Catholic History, Huntington, Indiana: Our Sunday Visitor Inc. p. 629

3   Murphy, Charles M. (2006) Models of Priestly Formation: Past, Present and Future, New York: A Herder and Herder Book, p. 15

4   Concilium Trendentinum, Session 23, De Reformatione, in Murphy, Charles M. (2006) Ibid., p. 17

5   Murphy, Charles M. (2006) Ibid., p. 16

6   Murphy, Charles M. (2006) Ibid., p. 18

7   Ibid., p.22

8   Murphy, Charles M. (2006) Ibid., p. 25

9   Ibid., p. 27

10   Ibid.

11   Lipsky, David (2003) Absolutely American: Four Years at West Point, Boston: Houghton Mifflin, quoted in Murphy, Charles M. (2006) Ibid., p. 27

12   Murphy, Charles M. (2006) Ibid., p. 30

13   Ibid.

14   Murphy, Charles M. (2006) Ibid., p. 32

15   Murphy, Charles M. (2006) Ibid., p. 38

16   Murphy, Charles M. (2006) Ibid., p. 39

17   Congar, Yves, (1967) A Gospel Priesthood, Transl. P.J. Hepburne-Scott, New York: Herder and Herder, p. 204 quoted in Murphy, Charles M. (2006) Ibid., p. 39

18   The Evaluation Process is adopted in the structure and pattern of Clinical Pastoral Education program, especially its certification process. Clinical Pastoral Education Program (CPE) is set up by U.S. Conference of Catholic Bishops and the Commission on Certification and Accreditation (USCCB/CCA) to provide comprehensive, spiritually based pastoral education program to qualified students of all religious backgrounds, beliefs and affiliation to develop and promote caring and sharing communities of people who may reach out to the sick, poor, aged, abused and wounded ones in different institutions (like hospitals, nursing homes, Assisted living homes, etc.

19   Murphy, Charles M. (2006) Ibid., p. 43

20   Abbott, Walter M. ed. (1989) Optatam Totius, Decree on Priestly Formation: The Documents of Vatican II, chapter 4, #8, p. 444

21  Abbott, Walter M. ed. (1989) Ibid., #12 pp.448-449

22  Ibid.

23  Ibid., p. 453

24  Ibid., p. 455

25  Murphy, Charles M. (2006) Ibid., p. 44

26  Ibid., p. 45

27  Abbott, Walter M. (1989) Lumen Gentium, no.10

28  Murphy, Charles, M. (2006) ibid., pp. 46-7

29  Ibid., p. 47

30  Mark 2:22 (Revised Standard Version, Catholic Edition)

31  Murphy, Charles M. (2006) Ibid., p. 55

32  Ibid.

33  Ibid.

34  Ibid., p.56

35  Ibid.

36  Ibid.

37  Murphy, Charles M. (2006) Ibid., p. 60

38  Ibid., p. 65

39  Ibid.

40  Ibid., p. 66

41  Ibid., p. 67

42  Ibid.

43  Ibid.

44  Murphy, Charles M. (2006) Ibid., p. 70

45  Ibid., p. 75

46  Pastores Dabo Vobis no. 62

47  Murphy, Charles M. (2006) Ibid., p. 80

48  Ibid.

49  Ibid., p. 81

50  Ibid., p. 82

51  Ibid., p. 83

52  Murphy, Charles M. (2006) Ibid., p. 86

# CHAPTER THREE: THE DIMENSIONS OF PRIESTLY/ HUMAN FORMATION

## Priesthood and Human Development

In chapter two, we explored the five known models of priestly formation in the Catholic world and their implications for priestly life, theology and spirituality as to their relation to the Nigerian context. Chapter two revealed that the five models of priestly education practiced in the Catholic Church today were close to the ones practiced in the old Tridentine seminary system (the sixteenth century seminary system). It is just like the biblical analogy of "new wines" in an "old wineskin." The Tridentine system prized intellectual knowledge against human development. There is need then to raise the question: Should human development be an issue of concern in the priestly formation, life and ministry in the Catholic Church?

Before the Second Vatican Council and even after it, the emphasis in the training of candidates for priesthood and religious life was on "denial" rather than on "development" of human nature. The French school seminary model which influenced the seminary system in the Catholic Church up to the Vatican II Council and beyond, demanded that "Christians and the priests most of all, must disown the 'flesh' and lived entirely on the plane of the spirit."[1] A number of factors contributed to this scenario. The most outstanding factor was the "cold feet" attitude of the Catholic Church with regard to human and social sciences like psychology and sociology. This was due to the harsh criticism of religion by the founding fathers of these social sciences, Sigmund Freud (1856-1939) and Karl Marx (1818-1883) respectively.

Sigmund Freud described religion as a "crutch." He claimed that "it gets in the way of people's ability to walk on their own two feet. It gets in the way of their taking responsibility for their lives, making hard decisions, growing up to a maturity that can handle the knocks of life with strength and resilience."[2] What Freud is inadvertently pointing to is a deep human need to "grow up to maturity" and to be responsible. The stand of Freud as an atheist is always there, however, a positive reading of his writings cannot be ignored. It is only wise to look at the whole picture without ignoring any part of it.

Karl Marx, on his own part, called religion an "opium." Marx explained that "like a drug administered by the doctor, religion puts people to sleep or desensitizes them so the doctor can perform all kinds of painful procedures without the patient feeling anything."[3] In a similar manner, what Marx is inadvertently emphasizing is a deep social need to grow up respectfully and responsibly in our interactions with one another. It is always helpful to develop a positive reading of things of life in a discriminatory, discerning spirit. A person may not believe in what we believe and still may have some good messages for the people of God. The challenge not to make religion into a "crutch" or an "opium" is a living issue of everyday life. It is a daily challenge "to be," "to live," and "to work" respectfully and responsibly in community. Over the years, in the life of the Church, especially with the event of the Second Vatican Council, there has been a growing emphasis on the need for an all-round formation of candidates for the priesthood in the Catholic Church. However, the operative structures to make this kind of an all round formation to happen in many seminary schools are not yet in place. In many seminary schools, what we have is more of an academic study than a formation process. There are two needs here: first, a need for full academic study and a need for an all-round formation process. To pretend that the two needs are the same and that the two needs (study and Formation) can be met with the same structures of education are part of the problem.

The seminary education system in the Catholic world today is in line with the high-school or the graduate education system of many countries where it operates. It is essentially an academic structure of education. There is a need for an additional structure of formation in our seminary schools in line with the Neocatechumenal Way model and/or the New Foundation model of Paris. It may mean restructuring the seminary education system to bring in a full weight of the formation education process like the added spiritual year formation process, now in practice in some dioceses in the world. The idea of adding more subjects to an academic structure of education will produce more academic results, not formation results. We need an added formation structure of education to produce some formation results. To keep on doing the same thing we have been doing and to expect different results is at best self-deceptive. The need, then, for an additional structure of formation to the existing academic structure of education in our seminary schools cannot be overemphasized. It is a genuine necessity.

During my senior seminary studies in the 70s and 80s in Nigeria, the human sciences like psychology and sociology were part of the seminary curriculum. There is no doubt that students were learning from these human sciences, but how much does one expect in an academic structure of education? The challenge is even more today than ever with the cultural/political upheaval of the 60s and the religious terrorism of the 90s. The cultural upheaval of the 60s was a political reaction against the teachings of the Fathers of the Second Vatican Council and their aftermaths; while the religious terrorism of the 90s was some fanatic interpretation and applications of some religious beliefs against other people's religious beliefs and practices. These conflicting issues and some attitude of stereotyping that went with them affected the people's lives and expectations in very dynamic ways.

Benedict Groeschel in his book: *Spiritual Passages: The Psychology of Spiritual Development (1983)* hinted on some forms of religious and cultural stereotyping in the understanding of human development in today's society. He wrote:

> Until very recently, many genuinely religious young people, especially those who enter the seminary or religious life, were fitted into a mold, a static and basically uncreative psychological frame of reference. Indeed, this static view also pervaded secular education. Often, a person was expected to practice mature virtues by means of liturgical ceremony or act of public commitment. A high level of maturity was expected as soon as a habit was put on or marriage vows exchanged. Such a view did not consider the individual's past or future potentials. Young people were expected to conform at once to a precise model of behavior and were thought ill-intentioned if they did not.[4]

What Benedict Groeschel is describing as "fitted into a mold" mentality is a practice whereby some months or weeks of rote education classes on prayers and Church doctrines with a liturgical ceremony of white gown and lighted candles, some young people are often treated as adults in the Catholic Church, knowing what is right or wrong. S/he is expected to "conform at once to a precise model of behavior" of an adult faithful and when s/he fails to measure up, (which inevitably will happen) s/he is blamed and punished. A Sixteen or eighteen year old (teenagers yet to deal with identity issues, not to talk of intimacy matters) who exchanges marriage vows is expected to "conform at once to a precise model of behavior" of a Christian mother or a Christian father in the Church. When they fail, they are labeled as "fallen Christians." A Twenty-five or thirty year old who receives a religious habit or priestly ordination is expected to "conform at once to a precise model of behavior" not only as Christian mother or father but also as a community leader of Church institutions and offices.

Here again we face a failed-case of a presumption that an academic structure of education will adequately meet the needs of a formation structure of education. Definitely, some questions need to be raised at this juncture: How founded is this cultural expectation of a stable adulthood which is attained once and for all in a religious ceremony in the Church in the light of human developmental research studies today? What do we see? What is happening? How tenable is this cultural expectation of a stable adulthood in real life situations and lived experiences in today's society? Would the crisis in priesthood today be considered a function of this cultural expectation? What would the documented researches on human development recommend in this matter? These are some of the issues I will address in this chapter.

## Human Development in General

The human questions: who are we? How do we grow and develop? What changes and what does not change as we grow and develop? These are not simple classroom questions. They are life-questions we face in daily human encounters and relationships. The human question is a lifelong question. It is an open-ended question because there is no conclusive answer to it. Richard P. McBrien, in his book: *Catholicism (1994),* describes the human question as "unique." McBrien explains that "what makes the anthropological question unique is that we are at once the questioner and the questioned. Consequently, our answers are always inadequate. They can only lead to further questions and further attempts at answers." [5] McBrien also teaches that the anthropological question is not only "unique," it is also "multifaceted." He claims that "our understanding of ourselves is possible only if we use a variety of approaches: biology, ethnology, sociology, economics, politics, psychology, literature, philosophy, and theology." [6] There is no one approach to human questions that has all the answers to human problems.

There is then no comprehensive model of studying human development. Every model of human study offers us a perspective view of our humanity. The psychosocial developmental theory of Erik Erikson which I adopted to use in this study is one among many other theories of human development. The focus of our study here is on human formation and the crisis in priesthood today. It is not necessarily on the analysis of different theories on human development, even though Erik Erikson's psychosocial development theory will be used as a guide-model in this study.

As we shall soon discover, Erikson will insist that we grow throughout our lifespan. Erikson describes his stages of growth as a "dilemma" or a "crisis." For Erikson, "to develop a complete, stable identity, the individual must move through and successfully resolve eight 'crises' or 'dilemmas' over the course of the lifetime." [7] One important question to be raised here once more is: Would it be correct to state that the crisis in priesthood today is a function of human development? This is a very critical question for this work. Before we delve into this question of the relationship between crisis and development in regard to priesthood, let us first explore Erikson's psychosocial theory of human development. I would like to reemphasize that Erik Erikson's psychosocial theory of human development serves as a structural "map" for our understanding of human development. A map is only a "structural guide" not the "thing" it represents. It is important that we bear this point of a "map" or a "model" in mind as we move forward in exploring the Erikson's theory and its implications for priestly life and ministry in today's Church community.

Erik Erikson understands human development as "the epigenetic principle of development." Erikson teaches "that anything that grows has a ground plan, and that out of this ground plan the parts arise, each part having its time of special ascendancy, until all parts have arisen to form a functioning whole." [8] That is to say, psychosocial forces push us through a series of growth-challenges at different stages in life. Evelyn and James Whitehead who coauthored a book, *Christian Life Patterns: The Psychological Challenges and Religious Invitations of Adult Life* (1979) named some four key identity-questions that each life event raises for us as: "who am I? Who am I with? What should I do? What does it all mean?"[9] Viktor Frankl , a German psychologist speaks of "a triangle of meaning." The "triangle of meaning" according to Frankl, symbolizes the three ways of finding meaning in life: 1. "What I give to life through my **creativity** (creative gifts); 2. What I receive from life through **experiences** (experiential gifts); and 3. The stance I take toward life through my **attitude** (attitudinal values)."[10] Let us now turn our attention to Erikson's theory of human development as a structural guidepost for human formation and development in a life journey.

## Erik Erikson (1902-1994) and Human development

Erik Erikson (1902-1994) was a German born American psychiatrist. Erikson was a disciple of Sigmund Freud (1856-1939), the founder of psychoanalysis and the stages of psychosexual development. In the place of Freud's psychosexual development, Erikson presented psychosocial development which he called the *epigenetic principle*. This theory is based on a principle that "we are both all alike, and all different."[11] Erikson's development plan "consists of two elements: that personality develops according to maturational determined steps and that each society is structured to encourage challenges that arise during these stages."[12] That is to say, at each stage in a growth process, there is a defined maturity step to be taken and there is also a society-structured challenge to be accomplished.

The point of this project here is that this two-point structure of growth process: a defined maturity step to be taken at each stage of maturity and a society-structured challenge to be accomplished, offers us some raw materials for a structure for the human educational formation. That is to say, the formation process is to guide people through their growth process. The formation structure of education should be an addition to academic structure of education, not a replacement. Let us now look at the message of Erik Erikson's developmental theory:

Each individual proceeds through eight stages of development from cradle to grave. Each stage presents to the individual with a crisis. If a particular crisis is handled well, a positive outcome ensures. If it is not handled well, the resulting outcome is negative. Few people emerge from a particular stage with entirely positive or negative outcome. In fact, Erikson argues that a healthy balance is to be struck between the two poles. However, the outcome should tend towards the positive side of the scale. Although people can reexperience these crises during a life change, by and large the crises take place at particular times in life. The resolution of one stage lays the foundation for negotiating the challenges of the next stage. [13]

The key point of Erikson's theory is that in each stage of human development, there is a definition by a pair of opposing possibilities that may tend to the optimum outcome of that dilemma or to the potential negative or less healthy outcome. There is also the potential strength to be gained from a healthy resolution of each dilemma.

The first stage is the infancy stage (0-1years) of *trust versus mistrust.* Erikson teaches that from the time a child is born to year one, the child is faced with a task of developing loving, trusting relationships with the caregivers and thus gains the strength of *hope.* Otherwise, the child will settle down with a persisting sense of mistrust in relationships. [14]

The second stage is the toddler stage (2-3years) of *autonomy versus shame and doubt.* At this time, a child learns to take control by developing the physical skills like walking and toilet training, and therefore s/he acquires the strength of the *will.* When this does not happen, the child may tend toward shame and doubt.[15] The third stage is the preschooler stage (4-5years) of *initiative versus guilt.* Here, the preschooler learns to be assertive, to take initiative as to develop the sense of *purpose.* S/he may otherwise be too forceful as to harm others and thus settle down to guilt feeling. The fourth stage is the school-aged child (6-12 years) of *industry versus inferiority.* The school-aged child is now to develop complex skills for the new challenges of school works, so as to gain the strength of *competence.* In alternative, s/he will feel inferior to others. This is a challenging time to deal with ever-increasing expectations of work and academic life or to succumb to fear of inadequacy in handling tasks.[16]

The fifth stage, according to Erikson, is the teenager stage (13-18 years) of *identity versus role confusion.* This is a teenage period of self definition in both levels – who am I? and what should I be? - in many areas of life including work life, social life, religious life and political life.

The challenge here is for the teenager to move beyond the socialization schema of childhood years to a more stable sense of self, to gain the strength of fidelity. In alternative, s/he is reduced to settle with role confusion or diffusion. Erikson considers the above five stages as the childhood and adolescent developmental stages. The next three stages of development are the adulthood ones. However, the fifth stage is perceived as the foundation stage for an adult life.

The sixth stage is the young adult stage (19-25 years) of *intimacy versus isolation*. The young adult has to decide how to share him/herself in intimate relationships or to remain isolated. The virtue of this stage is love. The seventh stage is the midlife stage (25-65 years) of *generativity versus self absorption and stagnation*. This is the age of finding meaning in life through a productive life of "parenthood, creative work and fulfilling social relationships – instead of settling into complacency and self-absorption."[17] The virtue of this stage is caring. The eighth and last stage (65+) is *Ego integrity versus despair*. The older adult faces the fact of aging process and approaching death with a pursuit of "wisdom and satisfaction with life's accomplishments rather than longing and regret."[18]

In the light of Erikson's theory (structured map) of human development, we now look constructively at the key questions or concerns of this work (as we noted above): How would Erikson's theory of human development inform the on-going formation of priestly life and ministry today? Would Erikson's theory help to form a structural guideline for an on-going formation of priesthood in the Catholic Church? Would it be correct to state that the crisis in priesthood today is a function of human development? To answer these fundamental questions, there is need to make clear distinctions on the relationships among following key terms: "change," "growth," "development" and "crisis" in human formation. Let us begin with enlisting the dictionary meanings of these terms before we address their distinctive interrelationships in human formation.

The English word, "change," according to the Webster's College Dictionary means: "1. to make different in form; 2. to transform; 3. to exchange for another or other; 4. to give and take reciprocally; 5. to transfer from one (conveyance) to another; 6. to give or get small money in exchange for; 7. to give or get foreign money in exchange for; etc."[19] In regards to human formation, numbers one and two meanings are relevant to us here: "to make different in form" and "to transform." The dictionary meaning of the word, to grow is: "1. to increase in size by a natural process of development; 2. to come into being and develop; 3. to form and increase in size by a process of inorganic accretion, as in crystallization; 4. to arise or issue as a natural development; 5. to increase gradually in size, amount, etc." [20] From the meaning of the word, to grow, we get the idea that growth may imply development but not in all cases. Maybe the meaning of development will throw more light in the interconnection between growth and development.

The dictionary meaning of the English word, to develop is: 1. to bring out the possibilities; bring to a more advanced, effective, or usable state; 2. to cause to grow or expand; 3. to bring into being or activity, produce; 4. to generate or acquire, as by natural growth or internal processes; 5. to elaborate or expand in detail; etc." [21] Looking at the meaning of the word development in contrast to the word, growth, I would like to point out two things: First, growth specifically implies increase in size and expansion in space (more in quantity). Second, while the word, development implies growth in its specifications, and also, it implies further specifications of possibilities, advancement, effectiveness, usability, and valuability (more in quantity as well as in quality). Also, the dictionary meaning of the word, crisis is: "1. a turning point, as in a sequence of events, for better or for worse; 2. a condition of instability; 3. a personal tragedy, emotional upheaval, or the like; 4. a. the point in the course of a serious disease at which a decisive change occurs, leading to recovery or to death; b. the change itself; etc." [22] Looking at the dictionary meanings of the four words: to change, to grow, to develop and crisis, we notice some interconnection and relatedness: to change means at least to make a difference; to grow means at least to increase in size and space (to increase in quantity); to develop means at least to bring out the possibilities (to increase in quality); and crisis means at least a turning point. It is evident from this analysis that whether we speak of "to increase in size and space" (growth) or "to bring out the possibilities" (development) or "a turning point" (crisis), it always involves "to make a difference" (change). Among the four variables, change is the constant variable. Another point to note here is, while growth may be visible most of the time, development may not be visible sometimes.

The most critical point to make here is the relationships between crisis and growth or development. At this juncture, I bring in "Erikson's distinction between a developmental crisis and a neurotic crisis." [23] Erikson teaches that "while ambiguity and disorientation may occur in both, a neurotic crisis is recognized by its dissipation of energy and its tendency toward isolation. A developmental or 'normative' crisis, on the other hand, is energizing and leads, however confusingly, to growth and further integration of the personality." [24] To the question: Is the crisis in priesthood today a function of human development? From Erikson's distinction between developmental crisis and neurotic crisis, the answer is "yes" with a distinction. What Erikson describes as the developmental crisis is a direct function of human development. The neurotic crisis is an indirect function of human development, which David Shapiro describes as "neurotic functioning." Erikson teaches that whether as a child or as an adult, we move through and resolve a series of life-dilemmas or crises at various stages in one's lifespan. We don't choose the life-dilemmas, the life-dilemmas choose us. He explains that "each person is pushed through this sequence of dilemmas by biological maturation, by social pressures, and by the demands of the roles one takes on"[25] in a life journey. On the other hand, David Shapiro, in explaining "neurotic styles" said, "by 'neurotic styles' I mean those modes of functioning that seem characteristic, respectively, of the various neurotic conditions. I shall consider here, particularly, ways of thinking and perceiving, ways of experiencing emotion, modes of subjective experience in general, and most of activity that are associated with various pathologies." [26]

In terms of crisis and development, there are two key issues to keep in mind: "linked identity" and "balance and boundaries." According to Erikson and those who followed after him in stage development (like James Marcia, 1980 or Alan Waterman and Sally Archer, 1990) "the teenager or young adult must develop several linked identities: an occupational identity (What work should I do?), a gender or a gender role identity (How do I go about being a man or a woman?), and political and religious identities (What do I believe in?)." [27] Erikson teaches that "if these identities are not worked out, then the young person suffers from a sense of confusion, a sense of not knowing what or who s/he is." [28] That is to say, the young person lives with a crisis of a confused identity (neurosis condition) of what should s/he do in life? How should s/he be with others? And what should s/he believe in politics and in religion?

The second issue to be noted here in regard to crisis and development is "balance and boundaries." The young person's "linked identity" is not worked out once and for all in life. One's life identity is not built on "rock." It is built on a "balance and boundaries." Erikson teaches that each one of us moves through eight dilemmas or stages at different intervals in a lifespan. As we saw above, "each dilemma or stage is defined by a pair of opposing possibilities, one of which describes the optimum outcome of that dilemma, the other, the potential negative or less healthy outcome, such as trust versus mistrust (in 0-1 year child) or integrity versus despair (in 65+ older adult)." [29] This means that one little thing in life can upset this balance and creates a renegotiation of new boundaries. For instance, a mother's lack of attention to a crying baby or a quarrel at a work place for a working adult will call for a reworking of the balance in life issues and a renegotiation of new boundaries.

The other aspect of balance is the issue of a "healthy resolution" of a dilemma or a stage in a life process. Our life is lived in a continuum, a journey in a continuum. Life is not just a choice of trust against mistrust, or intimacy against isolation. We do not simply "pick up" a life of trust or a life of intimacy, rather we move towards more positive trust and more positive intimacy in a continuum. Helen Bee explains that "'healthy resolution,' however, does not mean moving totally to the apparently positive end of any one of the continua Erikson describes. An infant can have too much trust, too much industriousness can lead to narrow virtuosity, too much identity cohesion in adolescence can result in fanaticism. The best resolution, in this view, is some balance in between." [30] In all levels of life, balance is critical and a committed respect for boundaries is a constant challenge. At this juncture, we take time to look at Erikson's teaching on adult life development and how such teaching will impact priestly life and ministry today.

## Human Development and Priestly Life and Ministry

Priesthood is not just an ordination. Priesthood is more than a priestly ordination. There are at least four essential aspects of the priesthood of Jesus Christ. First, we speak of the priesthood of Christ as an "institution" which has a long tradition of history that began with Christ, but has important shadows in Old Testament period. Second, we speak of the priesthood of Christ as "a way of life" (a vocation) which we are invited to share through the divine/human call. This vocation or a way of life must be lived fully and truly humanly and spiritually. Third, we speak of the priesthood of Christ as a "Sacrament," which is celebrated in the priestly ordinations. And fourth, we speak of the priesthood of Christ as a "witness," which is lived in priestly mission and ministries with other faithful in the world, not away from the world. An authentic priest in the manner of Jesus Christ is not one or two of these four aspects of Christ's priesthood, but all of the four aspects held in a healthy balance, fully and truly in complete humanness and spirituality. Priesthood is then more than priestly ordination. To equate the priesthood with a priestly ordination is like to equate a tree with one of its fruits. A fruit is from a tree but a tree is more than its fruits.

Over the years, the overwhelming emphasis on priestly ordination has led to two forms of reductionism: the priesthood with a presumed or denied human self and the priesthood without a Spiritual self (rather we have the priesthood with spiritual exercises). In this chapter, we concentrate on the human person of the priesthood. The next chapter (chapter four) will focus on the spiritual self or spirituality of the priesthood. Meanwhile, let us look at how an understanding of human development will impact the priestly life and ministry today: 1) Ordination and Growing up (Intimacy issues); 2) Ordination and Professional training (skill development issues); and 3) Ordination and Community leadership (community leadership issues).

**Ordination and the Task of Growing Up (Intimacy Issues)**

The task of growing up is not a day's journey. It is a lifelong process. The understanding of a lifelong growth process is against a cultural belief that adulthood is a "stable" state in life and that it is attained "once and for all" at a point in life. Our study of human development in priesthood, especially in the light of the epigenetic principle of Erik Erikson has shown that we have not only stages of development, but that there are also developmental challenges and psychological risks or crises to be addressed in the process. According Erikson, the task of life of a young adult between the ages of 19 and 25 is primarily to develop a capacity for "intimacy" or "isolation" in relationships. That is, how does a young adult handle "an overlapping of space" in intimate relationships (social maturity). Also, s/he must develop a personal capacity and "a willingness to be influenced and openness to the possibility of change (emotional maturity)." [31]

It is presumed that before this period, the young adult must have developed a well integrated "linked identity: an occupational identity (what work should I do?), a gender or gender role identity (how do I go about being a man or woman?), and a political and religious identities (what do I believe in?). [32] The grace of ordination may not accomplish this for us. We know very well that God works with us but not for us. The Gospel message is clear: "for with God nothing will be impossible." [33]

Karl Albrecht, in his book, *Social Intelligence: the New Science of Success (2005),* defines five needed social skills for young adults in his definition of social intelligence "with an acronym 'S.P.A.C.E.' – 1) Situation awareness, 2) Presence, 3) Authenticity, 4) Clarity, and 5) Empathy."[34] On the other hand, Daniel Goleman, another sociologist, is of the view that Emotional Intelligence deals with "a wide array of competencies and skills that drive leadership performance" which includes: "1) Self-awareness – the ability to read one's emotion and recognize their impact while using your gut feelings to guide decisions. 2) Self-management – involves controlling one's emotions and impulses and adapting to changing circumstances. 3) Social awareness – the ability to sense, understand, and react to others' emotions while comprehending social networks. 4) Relationship management – the ability to inspire, influence, and dialogue with others while managing conflict."[35] These are the initial challenges of growing up as an adult in the community. How do all these growth challenges apply to a "just ordained" Catholic priest?

The canonical age for priestly ordination in the Catholic Church is 25. [36] Before this time, many seminarians spend their lives in a secluded, strictly regimented seminary community where all decisions are ready-made by the voice of the bell interpreted as the Voice of God. Out of the seminary and during holidays, he spends most of his time with little children teaching catechism. Where is the opportunity for growth in emotional and social maturity? The grace of priestly ordination makes all the difference, but it is never an answer for emotional and social maturity. Society perceives the situation differently as observed by Benedict Groeschel. Groeschel pointed out that "a high level of maturity was expected as soon as a habit was put on or marriage vows exchanged."[37] Definitely, ordination makes one a priest but it will not guarantee his maturity.

Growing up is not just a task of knowledge or a gift of grace alone, but much more of mutuality in nurturing relationships. Growing up involves a lot of reworking, reshaping, reforming, transforming and integration processes. Maturity at this time, according to Erikson, involves not only an ability to define in relationships "who am I with?" and "how am I with people?" (intimacy versus isolation). It also involves "what can I do?" "what should I do?" (generativity versus stagnation) and "what does it all mean?" (personal integrity versus despair). The challenge is for the individual to be an integrated person as to live above one's roles. Bob Biehl in his book, *Why You Do What You Do: Answering to Your Most Puzzling Emotional Mysteries (1993)* reminds us that we have not one self but three selves. 1) *a public self* (our image) – the flawless, perfect self which is presented to everyone; 2) *a private self* (our roles) – the self played out by our roles as father, mother, teacher, priest, brother, sister, uncle etc.; and 3) *a personal self* (our person) - known to the person alone and to God.[38]

The point of Biehl's analysis of self is that growth in maturity is a process of self-integration, otherwise the person settles down to live a divided life of hiding from oneself, playing the roles and wearing a "mask" of public self. This can be a big risk or source of crisis for priests who fail to get the needed opportunity and support systems for emotional and social maturity during seminary school years and after priestly ordination. The truth of the matter is that the present seminary school system does not offer this opportunity (of emotional and social maturity) and the "role-playing" of priestly ministry after ordination helps so little. We have real crisis on our hands here.

## Ordination and Professional Training (Skill development Issues)

An academic degree in medicine alone does not make a person a medical doctor. There is more to be a medical doctor than just acquiring an academic degree in medicine. An academic degree in education alone does not make a person a school teacher. There is more to being a school teacher than just obtaining an academic degree in education. An academic degree in law alone does not make one a lawyer. There is more to being a lawyer than just possessing a degree certificate in law. In a like manner, an academic degree in philosophy and theology with the grace of ordination will not transform a person into a "professional" leader, counselor, administrator, and a supervisor of the office of a pastor in a local Church. Professional training and well-streamlined orientation processes are a necessity for each of these leadership roles. Even five or more years of helping out in a parish as a co-pastor may not substitute for the required professional training in pastoral functionaries. A number of years in priesthood do not amount to the same number of years in an integrated experience.

Priesthood is by no means a profession. Priesthood is neither a job nor a career. Priesthood is more than a profession, more than a career or a job. But then, the professional training and appropriate preparation for the duties and responsibilities of a pastor are not to be trusted to the inspiration of the Holy Spirit alone. It is said that heaven helps those who help themselves, and it is true. God works **with** His priests and the lay people, not **for** them. God will not do for us, that, which He trusts us with His gifts to do for ourselves. Grace does not replace nature, rather grace works with nature.

Applying here again Erikson's psychosocial developmental theory, Erikson teaches that between the ages of 25 and 65, every human person faces the life-developmental challenges to be generative – to develop appropriate skills on how to support and care for the next generation of people. The alternative option, according to Erikson is "self-absorption" or "stagnation."[39] The practice of adding one or two new programs to the existing system will make little or no difference. Here again, the possibility of another form of crisis – "occupational incompetence" (to use Lawrence J. Peter's phrase) is a real challenge to many of us.

**Ordination and Community Leadership**

Leaders are not born, they are made. Leadership is not a power to impose laws, to demand obedience and punish offenders. A leader is not simply someone who gets "things" done, a taskmaster. Leadership is more than doing things. Leadership is more of leading oneself and influencing others. A leader is more a person of wisdom than just of knowledge.

According to the psychosocial development of Erik Erikson, wisdom is the virtue of good leadership which is manifested in a life of "integrity" or otherwise, "despair." Everyone is a leader in one way or another. But there is a stage in life in which leadership becomes a primary task of life. This is within the age of 65 and above, according to Erikson's theory. Leadership at this period of life is not by "doing" but by "being." This level of life has a different form of a growth process – a growth in contemplation not in competition. Benedict Groeschel puts it this way:

> Instead of competing with the young, one supports them, equally content whether this support is appreciated, taken for granted, or ignored. The experience of futility and failure which comes to almost all older people is now transformed into the humble prayer of St. Francis, "Let us begin now." One learns to accept one's shortcomings.[40]

According to Groeschel, priests and people who are 65 and above have come to a stage in life where they can offer great gifts of wisdom to the young without minding how they are received. The contentment of this age group is that the gifts of wisdom are giving to the young "now" which may be received later on. One thing to remember is that people in old age have a tremendous gift of time and wisdom that waits to be harvested and celebrated with thanksgiving. The challenge of development at this last stage of life is: what do we do with old age? Do we work till we drop dead or do we retire and wait to die? What kinds of life-support do people in old age need and what kinds of life-support can old people offer? What life-support systems and structures help to nurture and nourish life in retirement years? These are not intellectual questions and they demand more than intellectual answers. I know one Monsignor in my diocese who retired twice and then, he died in active service. What does this scenario tell us? There is some unaddressed "fears" in the system that is begging for attention.

Structuring a comprehensive plan for retirement years in the Catholic Church and providing the leadership it entails is more than having some insured money for retired priests like the "opus securitatis" program. Money is important but it is not everything. Putting up a home for the elderly is not the whole answer to the issue. The lack of or limited emotional and social support to people in old age can cause great havoc. A good understanding and the skills of caring for the person of a priest, the support systems, human connections and affirmations cannot be purchased by money. Compassionate presence is more than a paid job.

## Priest as a Human Person (the Human Self)

If priests must take adequate care of themselves and others, the needed knowledge and skills are sine qua non. Each priest must understand clearly who he is as a person and what it is all about in relationships and leadership. A priest with a confused sense of self is a danger not only to himself but more so to people in his life and leadership.

The word, "person" goes back to its Latin root, *"persona (personare, to sound through)* and the Greek root, *thropoton* (face, actor's mask)."[41] Having said this, I have no intention of dabbling into the philosophical controversy over these terms and what they should or should not signify, an issue Pope John Paul II once described as a "'mistaken anthropology,' that is, on some mistake about what it is to be a human person."[42] I would like to explore the theological and moral understanding of a human person as it applies to a Catholic Christian person and then, to a Catholic priest.

It is acclaimed that Tertullian was the first to use the term, person in early Christian period in his reflection on the Trinity and the Incarnation. But then, it is the Roman jurists who defined the term, person as, "*Persona est sui iuris et alteri incommunicabilis,* 'A person is a being of its own and does not have its being in common with any other.'"[43] This definition is important in emphasizing the "incommunicability" and the "unrepeatability" of each one of us, our uniqueness as a person. Boethius, a sixth-century Roman philosopher, also toed a similar line of thought in his own definition of person, "Persona est substantia individua naturae rationalis: A person is an individual substance having a rational nature."[44]

Boethius's idea of a person prevailed throughout the medieval period with little modifications. Such modifications are evident especially in the works of "Thomas Aquinas, Richard of St. Victor, and Duns Scotus. The modification can be discovered also in modern theological thought, such as in Karl Rahner's encyclopedia, *Sacramentum Mundi.*"[45] In this document, Karl Rahner states that: "the actual unique reality of a spiritual being, an undivided whole existing independently and not interchangeable with any other ... belong to itself and ... therefore its own end in itself ... [with an] inviolable dignity."[46] The emphasis on a person's incommunicability, unrepeatability and inviolability is to stress that each person is a "subject of rights" and responsibilities.

This claim holds a ground against an unpopular "philosophy of a society known as collectivism" (as found in socialism). This form of socialism tends to absorb "individual human beings into society in such a way as to disregard them as ends in themselves, as beings of their own, and that it thus depersonalizes them."[47] In this regard, a priest is to insist and to foster in his person and in the persons of others the "subject of rights" and authentic human connections and affirmations at various levels of community life. Stressing the implications on the issue of subjects of rights, Pope John Paul II said in *Centesimus Annus, The Hundredth Year of Rerum Novarum,* "A person who is deprived of something he can call 'his own,' and of the possibility of earning a living through his own initiative, comes to depend on a social machine and on those who control it. This makes it much harder for him to recognize his dignity as a person, and hinders progress toward the building up of an authentic human community."[48]

A subtle sense of one's person is critical not only for the person but also for other people and for the community. A human person is incommunicable, unrepeatable, and inviolable in the sense that the individual can neither be replaced by another person nor be separated from oneself; therefore, a belief that one size fits all is seriously misleading. This fact poses serious questions on the "fitting-into-mold" system of education now operative in most Catholic seminary schools. A person of a priest or a Christian person is self conscious or has the interiority of self. This is not to say that a person is simply consciousness, as to claim that "without consciousness there is no personal life and acting."[49] This is one extreme case in this scenario. The other is to deny the need to develop one's interiority or consciousness and remain dormant. There is need to be aware of the difference between "the being of a person" and "the conscious acting of the person." It has much to do with "self presence and the self possession of the persons, thereby exploring personal being from within."[50] The aspect of an interior life of a person of the priesthood in the Catholic Church will be explored further in the next chapter.

The human person is equally a person of freedom and truth. As the Scripture says, "You will know the truth, and the truth will set you free." [51] Any freedom which is not rooted in truth is a double bondage. It is not freedom at all. Stressing the importance of authentic religious freedom, the Fathers of Vatican II Council stated: "If human beings are to be treated as persons, they must be allowed to decide on their own about Christ and his Church; but if they are coerced into professing Christ, then they are violated as persons and their profession is worth little." [52] A priest must not only exercise his freedom in truth, but he is to encourage and influence other people to live and grow in freedom and truth. Having highlighted these basic issues of a person of the priesthood, we may shift our attention to a priest as a person-in-relations.

## Priest as a Person-in-Relations and a Person-in-leadership

Over the years, most Catholic documents and doctrines on priesthood are all about priest as a minister. In many ways, the general impression is that a priest is what he does. Even the seminary system and educational structures focus mainly on what to do and how to obey. The root factor to this mentality is the medieval principle: "ex opere operato." The Latin principle, "ex opere operato" literally means "From the work done." A mere literal understanding of this principle may lead to undue emphasis on "work done" or what to do, even though, the principle teaches something else.

The principle, "ex opere operato" teaches that the effects of the Sacraments do not depend only on the faith of the recipient or on the worthiness of the minister but on the power of Jesus Christ who acts within and through them. In other words, the efficacy of the sacraments depend on the work of Christ already fully achieved through His suffering, death and the resurrection, not just on the worthiness of a minister or the faith of a recipient. Apart from the danger of literal understanding of this principle, there is a possibility of abuse which may be "good news" or "bad news" for the community of God's people. It is good news when priests and people see through this principle their utter dependency on God for salvation and learn to be humble and to give thanks in all things. It is bad news when priests and people see through the principle an opportunity to be reckless and irresponsible in life, especially, in spiritual matters.

The biblical injunction "to deny oneself" is taken literally by many Christians to mean "to reject" rather than to "surrender" one's life to Christ. To speak of a priest as a person-in-relations will make little meaning to most people.

Recently, there is a noticeable shift in this understanding of the life and ministry of priests. In 1970, there was a Synod of Bishops in Rome on priestly identity. It is a universal acknowledgement that a priest is not simply what he does, he is also his relationships. This point is well acclaimed by Christopher Ruddy in his book, *Tested in Every Way: The Catholic Priesthood in Today's Church (2006)*, where he writes:

> The conversation that emerged from the conference focused more on the priestly identity and relationships than on ministry and structures; who the priest *is* took precedence over what he *does*. While there clearly can be no separation of priestly identity and ministry, as the priest's ministry shapes his personal identity, nonetheless the participants mainly shared the conviction that the key issues facing priests today are relational ones: the priest *is* his relationships. [53]

It is true Ruddy is speaking from an American background, but the observation he made about the issue of relationships in the Catholic priesthood is not simply American. It is a truth that concerns the Catholic priesthood everywhere. The irony of the whole situation is that what people are experiencing and expressing in life is directly opposite to what they are getting in preparation years in the seminary schools. There are mixed up messages here. There is both a lack in the system and structure of seminary formation. The Church seems to have known only one way of solving human problems: add new and more programs. If it doesn't work, add more programs. There is a belief that every problem can be solved by adding new programs. The truth is that if a "house" has a broken foundation, adding more weight (more programs) will only pull it down faster.

The big challenge here is that a lot is taken for granted or presumed in the seminary school system. In my seminary school days in the 70s and early 80s, all that was taught in human relationships was about morality and sins – definitions and analysis of sins to be avoided. We are taught what we should not do, not how we are to live respectfully and responsibly as authentic human beings. Mistakes are punished (sometimes with expulsion) rather than corrected. A seminarian as a person-in-relation is a "game" of survival of the fittest. It is simply a struggle to avoid expulsion. The teaching staff is focused on fishing out persons to be expelled. The seminarians are "hiding" from being expelled. So, it is more of a "game" than a life in a community in many ways. A priest as a person-in-relationships in many ways, is a "news" to some priests after their ordination. In preparation for this work, I visited my old seminary schools and some new ones. The old seminary system and structures of activities and education had not changed much. The obvious changes I noticed clearly were some new programs, new buildings, some new faces in the domestic and academic staffs, every other thing seemed to be almost the same as I left them some two decades ago. It is amazing.

A priest is not just in relationships with others. "A priest is his relationships" as Christopher Ruddy wants us to understand. This statement says it all. It is an onerous task of life. It can be a messy one when there is poor sense of self awareness, wounded self esteem, blurred boundaries and confused sense of balanced identities in life. Speaking on the messy task of emotional involvement in this scenario, Eugene Kennedy and Sara C. Charles write:

> Stress is a reality – like love or electricity – unmistakable in experience yet difficult to define. However, stress touches everybody sooner or later, and for members of certain occupations it is a daily companion. A person whose chief business is to help others is the most vulnerable to its effects because, unlike other professionals who can at least turn to the stable world of balance sheets or test tubes once in a while, helpers actually work in the presence of the greatest stress-producers we know – other people. And ordinarily the helping person is alone in this situation, sometimes out of range of supportive colleagues or reference books exactly when they would be most useful. Stress seems to be a dignified burden

for the dedicated person, something he or she discounts as part of the personal price of serving others; often it is shrugged off or even denied altogether. After all, does not the goal of assisting others justify emotional sacrifices?[54]

The person of a priest-in-relationship is touched beyond what our ordinary eyes can see. Something deep and important is happening inside a priest-in-relation which demands his attention that cannot be ignored without dangerous consequences. In the above passage, Kennedy and Charles label what is happening to persons-in-relationships as "stress" and they tell us how we are affected in the process. The reality here is not how much we are coping to survive or the kinds of maneuvers we adopted. The question is: Do we have what it takes to live through such situations of stress and accomplish our goals effectively without compromising ourselves or others? Kennedy and Charles suggest that first, we need a balanced sense of self, we also need some guiding principles and skills to navigate our ways through life.

A balanced sense of self has much to do with an appreciative understanding of what Walter Conn, in his book, *The Desiring Self (1998)*, describes as "the Self-as-subject" and "the Self-as-object." Adopting William James' analysis, Conn explains that "the Self-as-subject" involves a subjective self-presence which has two aspects: "in the first instance there is clearly the presence of some object ('whatever') to a subject ('I'). But in the second it is not clear whether there is the presence of an object ('myself') to a subject ('I') or the presence of a subject ('I') to itself."[55] In other words, as "the Self-as-subject," I am, on the one hand, a *"Conscious Knowing I"* - as a "conscious intentionality" and on the other hand, a *"Reflective Knowing I"* - as an "intentionality consciousness."[56] For instance, I watch a football game on TV; this is a conscious knowing act. Then, I can also reflect on the football game I watched on TV as a reflective knowing act. In the first instance, I am present as a subject to some object (the football game on TV – a "cognitive" presence). In the second instance, I am present as a subject to myself as the object (my memory of the game on TV – a "cognitive" and "constitutive" presence), therefore, a double experience of the "I" and the "me" of myself as one subject. The point of William James' analysis is to highlight the degree of awareness and involvement in the interiority of the self-presence. Some people are present without any sense of awareness of what they are present to and how they are present in such situations. The high point of "the self-as-subject" according to Walter Conn is that "while the "I" is distinct from the "me" in the duplex self, it is never separate from it; the self is one."[57]

On the other hand, Conn equally explains that "the self-as-object" according to William James, consists of the "three dimensions of 'me': the material 'me,' the social 'me,' and the spiritual ('me')."[58] The material ("me") are the persons and things I may identify as "mine," for instance, my family, my parents, my friends, my wife, my children, my clothes, my car, my house etc. The social ("me") "consists of the recognition we get from those who matter to us."[59] They are our social selves. Any damage or disruption in any of them is damage in our selves. A priest who is in charge of a whole town or a bishop who has jurisdiction over a diocese covering so many cities has increasing vulnerability in his social selves. This kind of awareness on the part of a priest will help in appreciation of how issues touch him and the degree of his involvement in the concerns of others in relationship and leadership roles.

The spiritual ("me") according to William James is the "core and nucleus" of our inner sacred space of our lives, the sanctuary of our lives. Our inner sacred space or our inner sanctuary can be distracted by what James calls "feelings of the self" which includes "self-appreciation" and "self-seeking." Self-appreciation has also two parts: "self-complacency (self-esteem, but also pride, conceit, vanity, arrogance) and self-dissatisfaction (confusion, shame, mortification, but also despair)."[60]

The other part is self-seeking, in which case, we seek everything at the three dimensions of the self-as-the object: On the level of the material ("me"), we seek to be admired, love of influence and power. On the level of the social ("me"), we seek bodily beauty, nice clothes, and all kinds of possessions. And on the spiritual ("me"), we also seek fellowship with saints, goodness, and the presence of God. The point of the whole analysis is that a priest-in-relationship is very involved at diverse levels of activities and commitments that escape the notice of an ordinary eye. There is much more to human relationships than what happens at the external levels. Life-events or life-issues have depth in themselves that may not be ignored without dangerous consequences. Every life-event therefore invites us to an inner journey of self-awareness and interiority of spiritual life, the task of the next chapter, chapter four. Before we move to chapter four, I would like to explore the perception of human development in African/Nigerian Catholic Church, in fact among the Igbo community in the South-Eastern part of Nigeria.

## Human Development in African/Nigerian Church and Its Implications for Priesthood

One of the best things that happened in African Church is the 1994 Synod of Bishops, Special Assembly for Africa.[61] What motivated the calling together of the Special Assembly for Africa was as important as what it achieved. The key motivating factor was an issue of human relationships among the African Catholic Christians which was played out most profoundly in the Rwanda crisis and the Nigerian/Biafran civil war. Why did we single out these two civil unrests among others in Africa at that period in history? In both cases, it was a war of the Christians slaughtering fellow Christians in cold blood in thousands. In the case of 1994 Rwanda crisis, the conflict was between the Hutus and the Tutsis who were predominantly Catholics. In the case of Nigerian civil war of 1967 to 1970, the leaders and the majority of the people of the two warring groups were Christians, General Gowon leading the Northern and the Western people of Nigeria as one group and Lt. Con. Chukwuemeka Odimegwu Ojukwu leading the Eastern people of Nigeria (the Biafrans) as the other group. Reflecting on the challenging questions of the senseless massacre of Christians by fellow Christians, the Catholic Bishops' Conference of Nigeria writes:

> Both Hutus and Tutsis were well represented in the Rwandan Catholic Church. The question, then was: "How could Catholics do this to one another?" That led to a more fundamental question: "How deeply had the Christian faith penetrated into the hearts and minds of people who would slaughter their fellow human beings in cold blood for whatever reason?" Further questions were raised: What really is the worth of Christian Baptism for an African? It seemed that as far as an African was concerned, blood was thicker than the water of Baptism. That could probably explain the propensity of many of an African in times of crisis to place ethnic considerations much above and ahead of the demands of his Christian faith for universal charity. Could that have been the reason that Hutu Catholics in Rwanda failed to see Tutsis Catholic as their brothers and sisters, and went ahead to massacre them in their thousands. Back home, could the Nigeria civil war have taken place if we understood ourselves as sisters and brothers, children of the same one family of God?[62]

As I said earlier, the best and the worst happened in the African Church with the event of Synod of Bishops, Special Assembly for Africa. The best is that the synod helped the African Church to rediscover itself as a family of God, at least in name. The worst is that the Synod fathers omitted or ignored a critical issue (marriage in African Church) which would have opened a road to a rediscovery of the African Church as a family of God. There is no family without marriage (in principle or in fact). As we Africans know, marriage is one of the most provocative issues in African Church and culture. Until the African priests and people alike openly and honestly deal comprehensively the fundamental issue of marriage in African Church and culture, the founding of the African Church as a family of God is a made-believe.

One critical issue about the Church in Africa/Nigeria is the neglect of what Jesus called "the least of these" in the Kingdom of God. Jesus said and repeated: "Truly, I say to you, as you did it to one of the least of these my brethren, you did it to me."[63] "The Least of these" in African Church are the children, women and the poor. The "Least of these" will always define and determine whether the African Church becomes a Church of God or something else. In the words of Cheryl J. Sanders, "None of us can feed every hungry person, or give clothes to all the needy, or provide home to all the homeless, or minister healing to all the sick, or give justice to all who are imprisoned. The Lord has not called us to eliminate poverty, or sickness or injustice, but we are called to be responsive to their effect in people's lives. ... Our response to human need is the test of our fitness of our salvation and our holiness."[64] If the Christian Church, indeed the Catholic Church is to be truly and fully a people's church in Africa, the shortest road to it is the Church's response to the human and spiritual needs of "the least of these" – the children, women and the poor, the marginalized ones in African culture. The needed transformative ministry for the African Church (the African people) is what Cheryl J. Sanders called the "ministry at the margins, the prophetic mission of women, youth, and the poor."[65] It has its own agenda and process.

The Gospel of Jesus Christ is yet to be given a chance in African countries and among the African people. The African people are yet to receive the undiluted Gospel of Jesus Christ, a True Gospel unmixed with Western civilization and culture. The Christian Church in Africa, in many ways, is a colonial church and it still remains a colonial church to date. A colonial church carries out a colonial agenda of the "Colonizers," not the agenda of the Gospel of Jesus Christ. A colonial agenda perpetuates a further colonialization of the African people and the African culture. The African people feel alienated, estranged and disillusioned on their own land, in their own churches, among their own people and their own priests.

An agenda defines a meeting and gives it some sense of focus and direction. To pretend to be the African Church while we still continue with colonial agendas is self-deception. To replace White priests with Black priests while retaining the old agenda makes little or no difference. Reverend Lawrence Lucas described this kind of scenario as "Black priest, White Church." He stated, "Basically, Lord, it's all racism!" [66] Cheryl Sanders suggests that the "ministry at the margins" which I propose as the ministry of the African Church has its own agenda, focus, direction and approach. She breaks down the agenda into four parts: The first part is "the Ethics of the Gospel" which includes "accountability: the fear of the Lord; compassion: the kingdom mandate; and empathy: the golden rule."[67] The other three parts are: part II, "the prophetic ministry of women;" part III, "the ministry at the margins: children and Youth; and part IV, "breaking down barriers: a challenge to the Church" which consists of: "the children's bread, reconciliation and ministry and mission in multicultural perspective."[68] The whole process is quite interesting, it begins with recognition of persons and their gifts, empowerment, acknowledgement of wounds and barriers, nurturing relationships, reconciliation and celebration of differences as gifts to be shared, not as threats to fear and fight.

Sanders is not suggesting a change of the Gospel or a change of the Christian doctrines but to be true to the Gospel of Jesus Christ and to follow Jesus' way, the way of the kingdom of God. The Gospel Church of Jesus Christ is not a church of the powerful, the rich and the majority. The Gospel Church of Jesus Christ is the Church of "the least of these," the poor, the marginalized, the neglected women, etc. It is a Church of "the least of these," a Church where we leave the majority (99 sheep) to look for the least one (the lost sheep); it is a Church where we don't join the powerful men to stone the weak, sinful woman (caught in the very act of adultery) but help her to reconcile and live; it is a Church where we don't sell the poor debtor with his/her family and children to pay his/her debt or deny him/her funeral rites, but cancel the debts and support him/her to move forward in life.

The colonial Church reads the Gospel from the point of view of the rich, the powerful and the majority. The true Church of Africa, a family of God, must read from the perspective of "the least of these" – the poor, the women (especially the widows) and the children. This is the perspective of Jesus Christ who began his mission this way:

> And Jesus came to Nazareth, where he had been brought up; and he went to the synagogue, as his custom was, on the Sabbath day. And he stood up to read; and there was given to him the book of the prophet Isaiah. He opened the book and found a place where it was written,"The Spirit of the Lord is upon me, because he has anointed me to preach good news to the poor. He has sent me to proclaim release to the captives and recovery of sight to the blind, to set at liberty those who are oppressed, to proclaim the acceptable year of the Lord." And he closed the book, and gave it back to the attendant, and sat down; and the eyes of all in the synagogue were fixed on him. And he began to say to them, "Today this scripture has been fulfilled in your hearing." [69]

Every priest, indeed every Christian in the African Church must truly and sincerely say to every distressed woman, to every child, to every poor one in the Church and the world, "Today this scripture has been fulfilled in your hearing," not once in a while but all the times, even many times in a day. We don't stop at pronouncing it with our mouths, we follow it up with our lives, actions, prayers and sacrifices to see it accomplished. Like Christ, He did not stop at proclaiming his mission at Nazareth, he followed up with his life, actions, words, feeding, healing and his whole self up to the cross at Calvary and beyond to the throne of God in heaven through resurrection and ascension. This is how to be a Church which is a "family of God." It is a Church which is a community and a communion of brothers and sisters in Jesus Christ. It is indeed a Church where everyone is welcome, received, supported and cared for with reverence, respect and dignity.

## Catholic Priesthood and Nigerian Church (the Igbo Church in the South Eastern Nigeria)

Everything that has been discussed above in the African Church applies equally to the Nigerian Church. I chose to begin the discussion with the turning-point event of the Synod of Bishops, Special Assembly for Africa. I made the choice because I consider the synod the most significant event in the history of Christianity in Africa. In line with that I commend the efforts of the Catholic Bishops' Conference of Nigeria (CBCN) in following up on that synod with two works: *The Church in Nigeria: Family of God on Mission (2004)* and *I Chose You: The Nigerian Priest in the Third Millennium (2004)*. In these two documents there are sincere efforts to name and address the current problems of today's priests and the Church as they are. Every priest, in fact every Christian should endeavor to read those two documents prayerfully and meditatively.

In preparation for this work, I circulated questionnaires and conducted interviews among priests and bishops in the Catholic dioceses in the Eastern part of Nigeria (among the Igbo people). I gave out about 450 questionnaires and about 220 were returned, about 50 per cent of what was distributed. The interesting thing about the questionnaire is that those who responded made substantial, sincere contributions. The respondents cautioned against three factors of an emerging subculture among some priests in Nigerian Church and they also made some valuable recommendations. The three factors of an emerging subculture (or some questionable attitudinal changes among some priests) in Nigerian Church today are: First, the priesthood is perceived by some as a personal achievement (an attitude of "I have arrived" or "I have made it"). Second, the priesthood is looked upon by some people as a family investment (an attitude of "Now, we've our own 'share' in the Church"). And third, the priesthood is appreciated by some priests as an accomplished social status (an attitude of "I'm above all," "I know it all," "I can do whatever I like."). A possible root-cause of these tendencies may be from an understanding of seminary formation as a 14 or 16 years of passing examinations and avoiding expulsion.

The central theme for both the questionnaire and the interview is on relationship experiences: priests' experience in the seminaries and its lessons for today's seminarians, rector and staff; priests' experience in ministry and its lessons for bishop/priests relationships, priest/priest relationships and priest/laity relationships. It is all about priests looking critically and evaluatively on themselves, their relationships and experiences. The age bracket of the respondents is between 28 and 74 years old.

**Summary**

In this chapter we looked at the human development in Catholic priesthood. Following from the conclusions of the earlier chapter (chapter two), it became clear that human development was yet to be taken seriously in seminary training and in secular education. The priests and the lay people live in the world of today but our systems and structures of education are those of Medieval and post medieval periods. There are some disturbing factors of the old system that call for our immediate attention.

Benedict Groeschel describes it as a "fitting-into-the-mold" model of education in which everything is automatic and permanently stable in life. Evelyn and James Whitehead perceive it as a form of "blindness" to a cultural shift from an "implicit cultural expectation" which promotes a belief in a stable adulthood that is achieved once and for all to a different one promoted by modern human sciences. Anne Wilson Shaef, on her part, sees an "addictive" cultural system of education in which life is denied, not developed; truths are covered up, not discovered; gifts are shamed, not shared; problems are dismissed, not discussed. In this way, the system reinforces and maintains itself in a vicious cycle of denial, control and violence.

We employed the services of the psychosocial theory of Erik Erikson to demonstrate a need to take human development seriously in the formation of priests in and outside the seminary schools in the Catholic Church. We explored the challenges of human growth and development in relation to the three fundamental questions of adult's "life of love:" Who am I with and how?; "a Life of work" - What can I or should do?; And " a meaning in life" - What does it all mean?; as they apply to priests and the lay people. The seminary schools must prepare candidates beyond ordination to live full lives in the community. A priest is a Self-in-relation both as a Self-as-subject and as a Self-as-object, not simply as a minister of the sacraments but more so as a responsible, living person and a community leader. The African Church as the family of God remains a dream except there is a fundamental shift from a colonial agenda to a Gospel agenda in ministry and a reorientation of leadership from the powerful to "the least of these" in the Church and society. In the next chapter (chapter four), we will explore a priestly spirituality that is both developmental and formative. A parish pastor with a monastic spirituality of religious exercises is a problem, not a solution.

1   Murphy, Charles M. (2006) Models of Priestly Formation: Past, Present, and Future, New York: A Herder and Herder Book, p. 30

2   Hill, Brennan R. et al (1997) Faith, Religion and Theology: A Contemporary Introduction, Revised &Expanded, Connecticut: Twenty-third Publications, p. 137

3   Hill, Brennan R. et al (1997) Ibid. p. 141

4   Groeschel, Benedict J. (1983) Spiritual Passages: The Psychology of Spiritual Development, "For Those Who Seek", New York: Crossroad, pp. 39-40

5   McBrien, Richard P. (1994) Catholicism, New Edition, New York: Harper SanFrancisco, p. 100

6   McBrien, Richard P. (1994) Ibid., p. 101

7   Bee, Ann V. (1996) The Journey of Adulthood, Third Edition, New Jersey: Prentice-Hall Inc. p. 54

8   Muuss, Rolf E. (1996) Theories of Adolescence, Sixth Edition, New York: The McGraw-Hill Companies, Inc. p. 43

9   Whitehead, Evelyn E. and James D. (1979) Christian Life Patterns: The Psychological Challenges and Religious Invitations of Adult Life, New York: The Crossroad Publishing Company, p. 27

10  Graber, Ann V. (2003) Viktor Frankl's Logotherapy: Method of Choice in Ecumenical Pastoral Psychology

11  Bee, Helen L. (1996) The Journey of Adulthood, Third Edition, New Jersey: Prentice-Hall Inc. p. 53

12  Kaplan, Paul S. (1988) The Human Odyssey: Life-Span Development, Second Edition, New York: West Publishing Company, p. 30

13  Ibid.

14  Ibid.

15  Ibid, p.24

16  Kaplan, Paul S. (1993) The Human Odyssey: Life-Span Development, Second Edition, New York: West Publishing Company, p. 25

17  Kaplan, Paul S. (1993) Ibid., p. 318

18  Kaplan, Paul S. (1993) Ibid, p. 321

19  Random House Webster's College Dictionary, (1999) New York: Random House Inc. p. 220

20  Ibid., pp. 578-9

21  Ibid., p. 362

22  Ibid., p. 315

23  Whitehead, Evelyn E. and James D. (1979) Christian Life Patterns: The Psychological Challenges and Religious Invitations of Adult Life, New York: Crossroad, p. 49

24  Ibid., pp. 49-50

25  Bee, Helen L. (1996) Ibid., p. 58

26  Shapiro, David (1965)Neurotic Styles, Los Angeles, California: Basic Books, p. 1

27  Bee, Helen L. (1996) Ibid., p. 57

28  Ibid.

29  Bee, Helen L. (1996) Ibid., p. 55

30  Bee, Helen L. (1996) Ibid., pp. 55-6

31  Whitehead, Evelyn E. and Charles D. (1979) Ibid., p. 74

32  Bee, Helen L. (1996) Ibid., p. 57

33  Luke 1: 37 (RSV, Catholic Edition).

34  Wikipedia Encyclopedia on the Internet, http://en.wikipedia.org/wiki/social_
    intelligence on December 27, 2008

35  Wikipedia Encyclopedia, in the Internet, http://en.wikipedia.org/wiki/
    Emotional_intelligence on December 27, 2008

36  Canon 1031 # 1

37  Groeschel, Benedict J. (1983) Ibid., p. 40

38  Biehl, Bob. (1993) Why You Do What You Do: Answering to Your Most Puzzling
    Mysteries, Nashville, Tennessee: Thomas Nelson Publishers, p. 8

39  Bee, Helen L. (1996) The Journey of Adulthood, Third Edition, New Jersey:
    Prince-Hall Inc. p. 56

40  Groeschel, Benedict J. (1983) Ibid., p. 63

41  Conn, Walter E. (1998) The Desiring Self: Rooting Pastoral Counseling and
    Spiritual Direction in Self-Transcendence, New York: Paulist Press, p. 39

42  Crosby, John F. "Human Person" in Our Sunday Visitor's Encyclopedia of
    Catholic Doctrine, edited by Russell Shaw (1997) Huntington, Indiana: Our
    Sunday Visitor Publishing, Our Sunday Visitor Inc. p. 307

43  Ibid.

44  Ibid.

45  Conn, Walter E. (1998) Ibid., p. 39

46  M. Miller and A. Halder, "Person" in Sacramentum Mundi, ed. K. Rahner et al,
    New York: Herder, 1969, 6: 404

47  Crosby, John F. "Human Person," Ibid, p. 307

48  Miller, Michael, (1996) The Encyclicals of John Paul II, Huntington, Indiana:
    Our Sunday Visitor Publishing, Our Sunday Visitor Inc. p. 601

49  Crosby, John F. "Human Person," Ibid., p. 308

50  Ibid.

51  John 8: 32 (RSV, Catholic Edition)

52  Vatican II Council, Declaration on Religious Freedom, Dignitatis Humanae, in
    Crosby John F. "Human Person" Ibid., p. 308

53 Ruddy, Christopher (2006) Tested in Every Way: The Catholic Priesthood in Today's Church, New York: A herder & Herder Book, pp. 5-6

54 Kennedy, E. and Charles, Sara C. (1998) On Becoming a Counselor: A Basic Guide to Nonprofessional Counselors, New Expanded Edition, New York: Crossroad, p. 23

55 Conn, Walter E. (1998) Ibid., p. 47

56 Conn, Walter E. (1998) Ibid., p.48

57 Conn, Walter E. (1998) Ibid., p. 52

58 Conn, Walter E. (1998) Ibid., p. 53

59 Ibid.

60 Ibid.

61 It may appear to the reader that the Church in Africa began with the 1992 Synod of Bishops. It may be perceived that way but that is not my intention. I chose to begin with the Synod event because I consider it a turning point event in African Church, therefore a good starting point. Anyone who is interest in the history of faith in Africa can refer to the bibliography especially John Baurs' book: 2000 Years of Christianity in Africa (1994), and Chancellor Williams, The Destruction of Black Civilization (1987).

62 Catholic Bishops' Conference of Nigeria, (2004) The Church in Nigeria: Family of God on Mission, Enugu, Nigeria: CIDJAP Press, p. 26-27

63 Matthew 25: 40, 45 (RSV, Catholic Edition)

64 Sanders, Cheryl J. (1997) Ministry at the Margins: The Prophetic Mission of Women, Youth & the Poor, Downers Grove, Illinois: InterVarsity Press, p. 33

65 Sanders, Cheryl J. (1997) Ibid., p. 3

66 Lucas, Lawrence (1970) Black Priest, White Church: Catholics and Racism, New York: Random House, p. 1

67 Sanders, Cheryl J. (1997) Ibid., p. 7

68 Ibid.

69 Luke 4: 16-21(RSV, Catholic Edition)

# Chapter Four: The Dimensions of Spiritual Formation

## Spiritual Life and Relationship Questions

In chapter three, we saw that a priest is a human being called to a way of life and ministry of God. It is a call to a life and ministry of the incarnate God. This call demands constant human and spiritual development and formation. We explored the demands and implications of human development of candidates for the priesthood in chapter three. Now we explore the demands and implications of spiritual development and formation in the priesthood. First, we will discuss the general meaning of a priestly spirituality. Second, we will focus our attention on the living of a priestly spirituality at two levels: a) Discerning one's spiritual roots to the inner center; and b) Structures and disciplines of spirituality. Third, we will explore the priestly life and spiritual formation, which will include: a) Lifestyles of priests; b) Moral formation; c) Affective formation; d) Cognitive formation; and e) Religious formation. Fourth and finally, we explore the priesthood and a crisis of spiritual abuse. Here again, we discuss: a) The Church community and spiritual abuse; b) Spiritual neglects; and c) Religion and spiritual abuse. At the end, we conclude with the some highlights from the preparatory questionnaires' respondents: the respondents' observation and recommendations for mature, pastoral priesthood.

## Meaning of Priestly Spirituality

Spirituality is a daily consecration in the truth of the Gospel and in the paschal mystery of Jesus Christ in the Holy Trinity. The phrase, "a daily consecration in the truth of the Gospel and in the paschal mystery" means that spirituality is much more about a daily witnessing of the holiness of God in the truth of the Gospel by continually dying to sin and rising with Christ in the new life of the resurrection, in communion with the Holy Trinity. It is more than a daily exercise of some spiritual practices or the knowledge of some institutional theories of spirituality. Spirituality then, is essentially "a living process," not just "a knowing process" or "a doing process." Ernest E. Larkin, in one of his papers on Priestly spirituality claims that "priestly spirituality would unfold as lived experience in answer to a challenge rather than as a ready-made program of spiritual exercises." [1] It is a spirituality of a "lived experience" in the paschal mystery in honoring and serving the challenges of life. William H. Shannan, in the book, *The Spirituality of the Diocesan Priest (1997)* believes that spirituality adds a "dimension of depths and interiority" to who we are and what we do or say in life. He writes:

> Interiority, then, is at the heart of any true spirituality, whether we are talking about a lay person, a religious or, as in this chapter, the priest. Taking time to live on the inside will not only mean that the priest will find his own identity in God and his communion with other faithful; it will also unify his own life. It will give him an inner center, an inner core, from which his actions will proceed. Because he has an unclouded sense of who he is and a clearer vision of what the things are that really matter, he will have a more accurate insight into life and the priorities he needs to set for himself. This inner unity will strengthen him to do better whatever it is he has to do. For he will really be there in the doing. That inner unity will give us a consciousness of authentic freedom. The priest whose life is lived from inside out will be able to stand on his own feet and make decisions of conscience that are his own and not vicarious decisions made for him by someone else. Inner unity brings inner calm. We come to learn that many of the things that once unsettled us, we are now able to take in stride. Whatever directions our lives and ministries may lead us in, we will always know that there is a center that roots our lives, like the center of the spokes of a wheel. [2]

Spirituality is not what we do but it is what gives meaning and purpose to what we do. Spirituality is not what we pursue in life, it is what gives direction to what we pursue in life. Spirituality is who we are and what we grow to be in God. Spirituality is not simply a life but it is more than a life. It is holiness but more than holiness. Therefore, "these understandings of spirituality take us beyond the notion that spirituality is not reducible to holiness, though holiness remains an essential and fundamental component of spirituality. We have come to understand spirituality as encompassing the whole of one's life in relationship to that which is ultimate. In the life of the Christian, it is the daily dying and rising, the daily experience of communion and alienation, of virtue and sin, that constitute our redeemed lives in Christ." [3] Until we discover and are fully and truly established and live authentically from "a center that roots our lives and ministries," we are just like pieces of papers floating about in a whirling wind or rolling stones in a desert land. How does one begin to articulate this journey to one's inner Center or inner Core of life in the Spirit?

## Discerning One's Root to the Inner Center

The limitlessness and interiority of one's spirituality is enormously encompassing and all involving that one can only speak of it as a "center" of one's formative growth and development in life. There is then no one way but different ways to our spiritual Center or interiority. Yet, each person must discern his or her appropriate and authentic way to a God's Center in him or herself. In his book, *Spiritual Passages: The Psychology of Spiritual Development (1983),* Benedict Groeschel acknowledges that "the center of Christian spirituality is the Incarnate Word of God." He explains that "Jesus is the center, not as a point of gravity, but as a single source of light in an utterly dark and lifeless universe, just as He is the source of light and life to the material creation ("Through Him all things came to be," Jn. 1:3)." [4] We hear and respond to the Incarnate Word of God differently. Groeschel points out four different Basic perceptions or approaches to God as the "Center" and Source of our spirituality: The first approach is "God as One." Groeschel explains that "God is known as the One, the Supreme, and Living Unity will attract a person whose life is an intellectual and emotional pursuit of integration." [5] In other words, your life's tendencies help to define your "root" to your spiritual Center. An example of a person who adopted this approach in history is St. Catherine of Genoa, a fifteenth century mystic. The danger for people who approach God as One is how to handle the growing awareness of "internal contradiction or opposing forces which threaten to tear the self apart."[6] The challenge is an issue of balance for a healthy, effective functioning human being. God is to be accepted (by a self surrender to the call of God) as the source of unity in a chaotic world. It is then a continual choice to "surrender to the call of God or fall apart." It is a challenge of living and learning to accept a life of self surrendering not to fight it.

The second approach or perception is "God as True." This applies to "such people (who) feel called by God as he is the Ultimate reality, Truth itself, unlimited Being, that which simply is."[7] An example of someone who adopted this approach in history is Thomas Aquinas. The challenge for those who approach God as the Truth is "not that they will turn aside," but "that they will tarry on the way, getting involved with this side road or that." [8] Groeschel draws the message home by pointing out some occasions in history where truth is tarried in some dangerous ways. A case in point in history was the "modern scholarship, with its great number of published theories, many of them of some interest and merit, offer a labyrinth of ideas wherein to hide from the Living Truth." The other occasion, indeed, an unfortunate one, was "the institutional Church with its profound insight into the unity of philosophical, theological, and revealed truth, had accidentally provided the leisure not only for academic study but also for intellectualization which dulled the voice of Living Truth."[9] That is to say that the living truth must be proclaimed, witnessed, and lived in concrete life, not just known intellectually. In the words of St. Francis of Assisi, "I wish to know You (God) so that I may come to love You." The knowledge of truth must lead to works of truth in love, the works of forgiveness, justice and peace.

The third approach is "God as Good." According to Groeschel, the people who seek God as Good "are at once the most beloved and affectionate of human beings;" and therefore they "are usually cheerful, compassionate and gregarious." [10] An example of someone who adopted this approach in history is St. Francis of Assisi, whom St. Bonaventure referred to as "generous, cheerful, and compassionate as a youth." [11] The challenge of the seekers of the good is that they may be very vulnerable to "betrayal, manipulation" or abuse. This scenario may often lead to "a kind of stunned disillusionment" and a tendency to "run away" or to "comfortably settle for less than the Absolute and hide from all that is ugly and damaged." [12] This may mean a desire to acknowledge the Christ of Easter Sunday while ignoring or even denying the Christ of Good Friday.

The fourth approach is "God as Beautiful." We remember that the ancient philosopher, "Plato taught, we find unfailing and infinite beauty only if we pass from transitory beauties to essential beauty." [13] In connection to Plato's stand, Groeschel points out that "since beauty and pleasure, however, are the two sides of the same experience, there is always the temptation for the seekers of Divine Beauty to settle for the less." [14] Some examples of people who seek God as Beauty are St. Augustine, Michelangelo and Oscar Wilde. St. Augustine, for instance, wrote in the *Confessions*: "But what is that I love when I love you? Not the beauty of any bodily thing, nor the order of seasons, not the brightness of light that rejoices the eye, nor the sweet melodies of songs, nor the sweet fragrance of flowers and ointments and spices; not manna or honey, not the limbs that carnal love embraces. None of these things do I love in loving my God. Yet in a sense I do love light and melody and fragrance and food and embrace when I love my God." [15] The challenge of this approach (God as Beauty), like the other three approaches (God as One, God as True, and God as Good) is not to settle for anything less than the One, the True, the Good and the Beautiful God. No one approach is better than the other. It is the same God we seek and find in and through each of the approaches.

**Structures of Spirituality**

The other area of spirituality to be considered here is the structures of spirituality. We "build" our lives every day (every minute) humanly and spiritually or we "tear" them down. Like all building, having designed the foundation (our inner Center or inner Core), now, we look into the structures of the "body" of the Christian spirituality. John Bradshaw would like us to keep in mind that "the spiritual quest is not some added benefit to our life, something you embark on if you have the time and inclination."[16] No, spirituality is not something for us to choose to be or not to be. Bradshaw makes it abundantly clear that "we are spiritual beings on an earthly journey. Our spirituality makes up our beingness. We are the kind of spiritual beings who, in order to adequately be spirit, need a body. We are not earthly beings trying to get spiritual. We are essentially spiritual." [17] To be deeply spiritual is to be truly and authentically our very selves.

Richard J. Foster and Emilie Griffin speak of the three "ways to grow closer to God and to act according to God's will." [18] They are the three structures of spiritual disciplines, namely: the Inward spiritual disciplines; the Outward spiritual disciplines; and the Corporate spiritual disciplines. There are twelve spiritual disciplines that are practiced under these three ways of spiritual growth. The first way of spiritual growth is the Inward spiritual disciplines. The inward spiritual disciplines include: meditation, prayer, fasting and study. This is the sphere of interiority or inner transformation (the intra-transformation or self-transcendence). The second way of spiritual growth is "the outward spiritual discipline." It includes: simplicity, solitude, submission and service. The outward spiritual disciplines invite us to solidarity and collaborative mission to peace and justice. This is the area of interrelationships (the extra-transformation). And finally, the third way of spiritual growth is the corporate spiritual disciplines. The corporate spiritual disciplines are: confession, worship, guidance, and celebration. This is the area of social justice, the challenge of "linking faith to justice."

The spiritual disciplines are ways to spiritual formation or self-transcendence, transformation and social justice (linking faith to justice). They are not the cause of spiritual formation, transformation or self-transcendence. What transforms us is God's grace that comes to us through these disciplines. Stressing on this point, Foster and Griffin write:

> The spiritual disciplines are pointed toward spiritual formation – and transformation. Spiritual formation involves a fundamental choice. Choosing to live for Jesus Christ may mean adopting a certain style of life, or perhaps more properly, a rule of life. We take on a series of spiritual practices that will open us to God's work in our lives. At the same time we need to remember that spiritual transformation is a work of grace. It is what God does in us. What we do counts, because we must choose to enter into, and pursue, our friendship with Jesus Christ. This choice, which we hope will become more and more pure and single-hearted, may have to be made over and over again. Readings from the spiritual classics, then, are pointed toward a warming of our hearts, a deepening of our friendship with Jesus Christ. Yet we always want to remember that the power of God undergirds our efforts and lead us along the way.
>
> Perhaps we could think of spiritual formation as a pattern, a series of concrete actions that will gently move us toward transformation in Christ. The disciplines themselves, however, are not transformative. The transformation in us is God's work. It is a work of grace. That deeply transformative grace comes to us not through our own doing but as pure gift.
>
> And yet something is demanded from us: the free gift of

ourselves, our submission, our willingness to change, our assent to God's grace. In the end our yes is what's required. In our own words and in our own way, we need to say, "Speak, Lord, your servant is listening." We need to say, "Be it done to me according to your will."

One more thing to remember: spiritual formation is ongoing. We need not be impatient; we need to take no measurements. As we build a history with God, others may notice from time to time the good ways that God is working with us. The effects of such spiritual formation will be observed, not in terms of abrupt changes, but as a continuous flow. [19]

I cannot but say a profound "yes" to every aspect of the above quotation. It is what spiritual formation is all about. Spiritual formation has its own approaches: God as One, God as True, God as Good and God as Beauty (the four voices of God, to use Groeschel's words). There is no one approach which is the best approach to God. There is no one approach which is the "whole" of all the approaches, like the system theory which states that the whole is greater than the sum of all the parts. God is greater than all the approaches put together. God is more than all the approaches to Him. In the words of Benedict Groeschel: "we are led by the divine and by one, or perhaps two, of the four voices of God, although the others are never entirely absent. The danger always is settling for less. We seek Heaven, but we play with things which will ultimately lead us either downward and away from our eternal destiny, or at best suspended between Heaven and Hell. That is, after all, the description of Purgatory." [20] Spiritual life involves being led by the Divine to the Divine. We must never settle for anything less than the Divine.

As Foster and Griffin point out, the spiritual disciplines themselves are not transformative. The spiritual disciplines alone cannot transform us. The grace of God transforms us. And this grace is a free gift. At the same time, we are not simply "containers" of God's graces. Definitely, "something is demanded from us: the free gift of ourselves, our submission, our willingness to change, our assent to God's grace." [21] The free gift of the self that is truly owned (not aimed), willing to change and cooperate with God's graces (through total self-surrender to God in all things, not necessarily self-control) is one of the key challenges of spiritual formation.

The purpose of spiritual formation is not transformation. In the words of Foster and Griffin, "spiritual formation involves a fundamental choice. Choosing to live for Jesus Christ may mean adopting a certain style of life, or perhaps more properly, a rule of life. ... In our own words and in our own way, we need to say, 'Speak, Lord, your servant is listening;' or to say, 'Be it done to me according to your will.'" [22] We need not only to say "it" but also to live and witness "it" always in words and deeds. What developmental tasks help to foster the spiritual formation and transformation of a priestly life and ministry in the three structured ways - the inward, the outward and the corporate ways are our next concern in this work. How are these three ways structured in an ongoing life of a priest?

## Priestly Life and Spiritual formation (A Moment of Truth)

Spirituality is not what we do. It is what gives meaning and purpose to what we do. Spirituality is not what we pursue, have or achieve. It is who we are and to grow to be fully in God. I have mentioned earlier that one of the great tragedies of our time is a belief that spirituality is something we do. It is not some religious exercises we perform at one time or the other. A general parish priest who thinks he is spiritual because he is maintaining the status quo of monastic spirituality: praying the daily **B**reviary and meditation, the daily **M**ass and communion and the daily **R**osary and works of mercy (the "**BMR**" priests/people) may be living the "yesterday spirituality" in today's world. It is good but not enough. The truth remains that people may go through these activities for many years without their Selves; that is, they remain the same old persons (unchanged persons) inside. They do the DUTY without living the LIFE.

The two thousand years old spiritual exercises promoted by the monastic spirituality may have served them then, but may not adequately meet the spiritual needs of the priests and people of the 21st century Church. We live in a very different world, a very mundane world. The world we live in is not only different and difficult, but it is also confused and confusing in many ways. Anne Wilson Schaef in her book, *When Society Becomes an Addict,* states that "our society is deteriorating at an alarming rate. As we watch the news and read the newspapers, we are increasingly made aware of corruption in the high places, financial collapse, and lack of morality in settings ranging from preschools to meat packing plants."[23] There seems to be some form of "spiritual bankruptcy" and moral malaise in our society today. The world is in a crisis of spiritual bankruptcy. For John Bradshaw, it is a society growing in a lifestyle of "compulsivity". He explains it this way:

> The most crucial aspect of any compulsivity is the *life-damaging aspect of it.* Life-damaging means that the compulsive/addictive behavior causes personal dysfunction. Compulsivity of any sort blocks us from getting our needs met through our own basic human powers. The compulsivity takes up all our energy. Our choices are narrowed. Our freedom is lost. Our will is disabled. Compulsivity is a state of inner barrenness. We are totally externalized, without any self-reflection and interior life. How can we have an inner life when we feel flawed and defective as human beings? This shame core keeps the addict from going inward. The true self hides behind a masked false self.
>
> Compulsivity is also about bad habits that become vicious over a period of time. Philosophers speak of habits as second natures. Good habits are virtues, which are strengths added to our personhood. Bad habits are vices and have the power to control our lives and take it over. Bad habits are a very dominant part of the euphoric type of mood alterers such as drugs, sugar and sex. Drugs and food also have the added factor of having their own intrinsic chemical power. These chemicals are in themselves addicting.[24]

Bradshaw pushes his points beyond doubt with a graphic detail of how all-involving and widespread the menace of compulsivity is in today's society. He sees a pattern of three factors reinforcing each other to create a compulsive living in our society: 1) A rule-controlled life (overt and covert rules), 2) The poisonous pedagogy, and 3) A shame-based person/people. Bradshaw explains that "the overt rules that create dysfunctionality are the rules of the poisonous pedagogy."[25]

The poisonous pedagogy, according to Alice Miller, is "a form of parenting that violates the rights of children, (it "exalts obedience as its highest value"). Such violation is then reenacted when these children became parents."[26] The pedagogy is "poisonous because it institutionalizes violation of rights as a way of parental education and as a tradition of "adult children." Bradshaw points out that the poisonous pedagogy is further reinforced and promoted by three other forces: Co-dependency, denial, cultural and subcultural boundaries. The co-dependency, according to Bradshaw, is "the core outcome of a dysfunctional family system" and it is "a dis-ease of self-esteem." He teaches that "people who are co-dependent no longer have their own feelings, needs and wants. They react to family distress and play out a rigid role."[27] In the process, the rigid role becomes a self to the person (a false self). The real self is suppressed or denied for the sake of playing the rigid role. Bradshaw explains that the "rigid roles are ways to survive the intolerable situation in a dysfunctional family" or community (some kinds of "ego defenses" or "fantasy bond" or "vital lies"). [28]

Denial, according to Bradshaw, is a significant characteristic nature of a dysfunctional family or community. The denial consists of "shared secrets" and "shared denial." Bradshaw explains that "the denial forces members to keep believing the myths and vital lies in spite of the facts, or to keep expecting that the same behaviors will have different outcomes."[29] The possibility of change is very remote unless strongly empowered (not controlled) from the outside.

The third reinforcing factor of the poisonous pedagogy is the cultural and subcultural boundaries. The co-dependency helps the individual person in the family to develop a rigid ego boundary in the belief that the role is his/her self. The family fantasy bond, denial, helps to maintain the family "vital lies" or "shared secrets" that keep the "intrafamily boundaries" rigid and closed.

The keeping of healthy, flexible boundaries is helpful, but when boundaries become rigid and close systems, they block and imprison people. John Bradshaw teaches that tribal or ethnic groups, "nationalities and religious affiliations are the strongest factors in this type of boundary. Italians, Greeks, the Irish, etc. have their own special rules and 'vital lies,' likewise with Pentecostalists, Catholics, Baptists, Mormons, Jews, etc. These subculture boundaries control the flow of information coming into and going out of the family."[30] It is not only the flow of information and knowledge that the subcultural boundaries control, they also control entitlements, offices, positions and memberships – who belongs and who does not belong, who are strangers or foreigners. The "special rules" of the cultural and subcultural boundaries help to keep alive the poisonous pedagogy from one generation to the other. John Bradshaw explains how the "erroneous rules" operate in the closed, dysfunctional family system to propagate dysfunctionality in endless generations:

> The overt rules that create dysfunctionality are the rules of the poisonous pedagogy. The parents are dysfunctioned as a result of

these erroneous rules, which they carry within their own psyches. The parents parent themselves with these rules. Without critically questioning and updating them, they pass them on to their children. Thus, parents become unintentional carriers of a virus. [31]

John Bradshaw names eight of the "erroneous rules" as follows: The first rule is the "rule of control." Bradshaw believes that the rule of control is "a cardinal rule in all dysfunctional, shame-based family systems." [32] The effort is to control "all interactions, feelings and personal behaviors at all times." The big price the members of the family pay is a loss of "spontaneity" and a "sincere disability of the will."[33] The members lose the sense of the will-power to rise up to daily challenges with spontaneity and decisiveness.

The second rule of the poisonous pedagogy is the "rule of perfectionism." John Bradshaw calls it a "tyranny of being right" in everything. Perfectionism promotes a competitive spirit of "better-than-others" which leads to a feeling of shame among the members of the family (a shame-based people). The frustration, "fear and avoidance of making mistakes" creates in members a feeling of hopelessness in the inhuman task of seeking for perfection.

The third rule of the poisonous pedagogy is the "rule of blame." The game of blaming others is a way to cover up for the shame of perfectionism. The perfectionist prefers to deny his/her shame rather than to feel shame, to accept that we are weak and vulnerable. A feeling of vulnerability is a danger to be avoided at all cost. The way out of feeling of shame is to project it to others, or to blame others for one's weakness or mistakes. The fourth rule is the "rule of no freedom." Virginia Satir speaks of five types of human freedom as: the freedom to perceive what we see or hear; the freedom to think what we think; the freedom to feel what we feel; the freedom to ask what we want; and the freedom to take risks on our behalf. When we live as if we needed permission before we do any of these activities of life, then we are not exercising our freedom according to Virginia Satir.[34]

The fifth rule of poisonous pedagogy is "the no-talk rule." It is a follow up from a fundamental dysfunctional belief of "shared secrets" and "shared denial" to keep their intolerable sense of insecurity manageable or controlled. The sixth rule is "the no-listen rule," which is also part of the "shared denial" of a dysfunctional, closed family system. We prefer to deny than to listen. The seventh rule is the "incompletion rule." The dysfunctional family prefers constant tension in a relaxed atmosphere. They like to keep the fights and disagreements on at all times. According John Bradshaw, "the family has either conflict or confluence, but never contact. They have rigid boundaries (divided by solid "walls") or they are totally enmeshed with each other. The eighth rule of poisonous pedagogy is the "unreliability rule." In a dysfunctional, closed family, there is no reliability or trust because the members have enmeshed boundaries or walled boundaries. They fear independence and responsibility. The sense of self is buried in the roles that have become their false selves. The need "to be" is replaced by a need "to do." That is, the true self is denied to keep and maintain a false self of playing rigid roles.

The enduring medieval spirituality of doing religious exercises may find a fertile ground in the culture of playing rigid roles. If priesthood is understood as playing roles, the danger of spiritual abuse is inevitable. The sense of self is in danger of total loss and an abuse of the parishioners is a real concern. This means that without an authentic, growing sense of self, life is mainly abusive humanly and spiritually. Glenn P. Zaepfel makes this point clearly by stating: "From a practical perspective, to earnestly desire a psychologically and spiritually healthy relationship with my mate and others, I must be willing to develop, pursue, and refine my relationship with God while understanding and developing my inner self as a consequence of this primary relationship. For any chance of spiritual depth and growth in my relationship with my mate, I must develop and maintain commitment and growth in my personal walk with Christ and let Christ grow and mature me from my innermost being."[35] Glenn P. Zaepfel believes that "the person is growing triunely: in the knowledge of God, in the understanding of self, and in the relationship with others."[36] The first level of growth in spirituality then, is knowledge of God. The second level of growth and development is the understanding of self. And the third level of growth and development is relationship with others. Glenn Zaepfel teaches that the understanding of self is a function of the knowledge of God. And the relationship with others is a function of the understanding of self and knowledge of God. A healthy spiritual growth of a priest or a Christian demands an integration of the three levels of growth and development.

## Spirituality and the Lifestyles of Priests

Our spirituality defines our person and determines how we live, relate and work as Christians and as priests of God. Abraham Maslow is quoted as having said: "The spiritual life is ... part of the human essence. It is a defining characteristic of human nature, without which human nature is not fully human."[37] A person with an unhealthy spiritual life will find it hard to live a healthy life and to maintain healthy relationships with others. I mentioned above that a healthy spiritual life has at least three important components: the knowledge of God (which is more than knowing about God — mere information about God); the understanding of the self; and a growing, appreciated relationship with others.

We may speak of three different lifestyles of a priest: a lifestyle of a "soldier," a lifestyle of a "slave," and a lifestyle of a "servant." These terms, soldier, slave, servant, signify the personality or personhood of a priest in relation to Christ, to God and to the people of God. When we are not sure or aware of how we are related to Christ (to God), a lot of things may go wrong. Even Jesus has to question his disciples directly: "What about you?" Jesus asked them. "Who do you say I am?"[38] We are not only to know who Jesus is, but also who we are in Jesus? Whether as the lay faithful or as the priests of God we are deeply and truly spiritual human beings. This point makes a great difference in all we are and in all we do or say in life. Elaborating on the spiritual dimension of our lives at all time and space, Kenneth C. Haugk writes:

> Everyone's life has a spiritual dimension. God persists in revealing this dimension wherever and whenever he can, despite society's continual efforts to thwart him. As one who seeks to care for others as a Christian, you need to be ready to relate to the deep spiritual needs of others. Your readiness to do so will be communicated to others by the climate of acceptance and encouragement you create, by your sensitivity to opportunities to raise the issue, and by your willingness to take whatever time is necessary. [39]

It is critical to bear in mind that our spirituality is highly implicated in how we use or misuse, honor or dishonor, respect or disrespect, celebrate or desecrate our times and our spaces. Time and space are sacred realities we share with God and with others in life. We keep them alive or dead, helpful or harmful, peaceful or poisoned, etc. It is a choice. Jesus calls his disciples to a servanthood ministry, not servitude or soldier. When we live and work merely as slaves or soldiers in their worldly sense, we desecrate ourselves, our space and time. Jesus Christ is very clear in this matter, for He declared, "the Son of man came not to be served but to serve."[40] In servanthood, there is a freedom to serve in wholeness and holiness. Emphasizing the difference in the lifestyle between servanthood and servitude, Kenneth Haugk states:

> You are called to freedom as a Christian – to freedom from the coercive obligation to serve and from irresponsible apathy, but more importantly, to the freedom to serve. Few aspects of Christianity are more subject to misgivings and misunderstanding than the call to servanthood. Guilt, anger, and miscommunication are often associated with it – all traceable to a basic confusion of servanthood with servitude. Servitude connotes bondage, slavery, and involuntary labor. Servanthood, on the other hand, incorporates the ideas of willingness, choice, and voluntary commitment. There is a world of difference between servanthood and servitude. At best, the person snared by servitude acts out of a sense of duty and fear, but the person living in servanthood acts out of a sense of commitment and love.[41]

The personality and spirituality that flow from the understanding of servanthood as opposed to servitude or soldier are quite different. The challenges they entail are equally different and diverse. The different spirit of service connotes different spiritual energies: the spiritual energy of a soldier connotes a sense of force, control, domination and intimidation; that of the servitude signifies "bondage, slavery and involuntary labor;" and the servanthood, on its part, implies "willingness, choice and voluntary commitment." How the spirituality of one's lifestyle is played out in a priestly ministry is quite informative.

A priest who has a shallow spirituality that is based mainly on a shallow knowledge of God, tends to "play God" by bullying and controlling parishioners. He will identify more as a "soldier of Christ" in a literal sense of the word, "soldier." His style of ministry is fight-to-win, a ministry of cut-throat *competition* and *control*. He interprets the laws strictly and maintains rigid boundaries in relationships with others. For priests who are dominantly this way, the priesthood is an achievement. Priestly life or ministry is either a "reward" to be received or a "punishment" to be given.

On the other hand, a priest who is weak or has a wounded spirituality with a weak or wounded sense of self, tends to see himself as a "slave" of

Christ. He understands humility as humiliation and lives it out that way. He exercises a ministry of *compensation*. With this form of ministry, he feels overwhelmingly needy. He has a strong tendency to be compensated in everything; and/or a compulsion to obey in anything without reasoning or questioning. He never questions but complains a lot and grudges.

On a different note, if a priest has an in-depth knowledge of God and a good understanding of himself in a daily deepening of spirituality, he will see himself more as a "servant of Christ." To a "servant of God" priest, it is a ministry of compassion, a mutuality of care and support to everyone in need. Here, needs are important as to give direction and attention to mission. Ministry is mission and mission is selfless service to all.

A word of caution here. The three lifestyles of priests I have just described are not parallel groupings. They are on a continuum whereby a priest as a soldier of Christ's lifestyle and a priest as a slave of Christ are at the two extremes on a continuum, while a priest as a servant of God is at the center. We are on a developmental continuum. No one is all the time living a lifestyle of a soldier of Christ or all the time witnessing as a slave of Christ. Events, crises, situations and circumstances can move one in either direction. However, there may be some developed patterns and dominant tendency towards one direction or another on the continuum.

The key question of this work is what is the relationship between human crisis and spiritual formation? Dr. Glenn P. Zaepfel would like us to believe that spiritual formation involves three variables: knowledge of God (level 1), understanding of self (level 2), and relationship with others (level 3). He teaches that the understanding of self (level 2) is a function of the knowledge of God (level 1). The relationship with others is the function of the understanding of self (level 2) and the knowledge of God (level 1). Glenn P. Zaepfel also insists that "level 2 increases in growth and appreciation of level 1. And level 3 increases in growth and appreciation of levels 1 and 2."[42] The point Glenn Zaepfel wants to stress is that level 1 (the knowledge of God) is the constant variable among the three variables: levels 1, 2, and 3. That is to say, the understanding of the Self (level 2) offers the ground for an understanding of the knowledge of God (level 1). In a similar manner, a good relationship with others grows on the foundation of a balanced understanding of the Self in knowing and serving God. In simple language, we grow in God. God does not need to grow, we, human beings do. The emphasis here is on "being" deeply in God and with other people, not just on "doing" ministry.

The idea of growing spiritually in a lifestyle of servanthood may be illustrated with a metaphor of an ocean and a container. The bigger the container, the more water it collects from the ocean, and not vice versa. We assume that the "container" is the human person and the "Ocean" is God. If the container is cracked or broken (that is, in crisis), the possibility of retaining the Ocean water will be remote, if not impossible. Therefore, the size and the condition of the container affect drastically how much water from the Ocean it can hold or retain in itself, as well as how much it can share with others. It follows then, that a person's (whether a priest or a lay faithful) sense of true self and understanding of self is critical to spiritual formation. What is the understanding of True Self in spiritual formation?

## Understanding of the True Self as a Key Condition in Spiritual Formation

Going back to our metaphor of the Ocean and the container, the container may be floating on the Ocean without retaining some water in itself. To say that we are spiritual beings does not mean we are growing spiritually. Spiritual formation is a "journey within." John Bradshaw explains it this way:

> Moving within is the journey of unfolding spirituality. Since we humans are essentially spiritual, there is no other way to discover our essential selves except through deepening awareness. My soul as my ultimate identity lies in a realm beyond my family or culture. But paradoxically, I can only discover it through my family and culture.[43]

Spiritual formation requires a developed true self in good relationship with others. It is always in relationship with the family, the Church, and the culture or society. The spiritual formation may be described as "conversion" or in the words of Walter Conn, "the inner transformation." Conn teaches that the Christian conversion as an inner transformation is "not just a matter of believing something new, of affirming a new faith, of adopting a new story. Conversion is not just a change of content, a switching over from one faith story to another. But much more importantly, Christian conversion is the introduction of a new kind of story into one's life, a story with its intrinsic requirements for moral, affective, cognitive, and religious transformation."[44] Let us now look at the four parts of a spiritual formation process: the moral conversion, the affective conversion, the cognitive conversion and the religious conversion.

## Basic Moral Conversion (A Transformed Way of Living)

The word, conversion, implies both an act and a process in regard to change or reorientation in life. Conversion as an act implies one-time-event issue, while conversion as a process denotes a continuity, sequentiality and/or orderliness of many issues or events. Conversion as a Christian experience is that one not only is a Christian; one is constantly becoming a Christian. Conversion to the Gospel is both an act and a process. Accordingly, Christian existence moves between the polarities of principle and process, of being and becoming, of essence and existence, of the universal and the particular, of conviction and risk, of substance and form. But these are not mutually opposed; the one requires and includes the other. Principles are at once products of experience and shapers of experience. Catholic moral theology is concerned with principles and process alike.[45]

Moral conversion is not just changing our actions, but more of changing the source of the choice of our actions and behaviors. It is transforming our desires, not only our action. To attain inner transformation is not to take some purging or cleansing herbs or drugs. It is rather a transformative awareness from a crisis of identity to a consolidation of identity. To live a divided-life is to be morally unconverted, a person who manifests different selves at different situations and commitments, a person of many faces. A morally converted person has one true Self that responds appropriately to the needs of different situations and commitments. He or she has a personality that may put on different "aprons" (uniforms) to serve different needs and commitments. The apron or uniform is not the Self, but a way of appropriate response to some particular needs and/or commitments. It is a process of integrating one's identities.

As children, our life process may be characterized as having the quality of "sameness and continuity." At puberty, we face the first shock that everything is not the same and continuous. Then, we continue till we come to the defining period between adolescence and adulthood. It is a time to choose my true self or to lose it, to define my inner center of decision and direction or to condemn myself to be a mere follower of other's decisions and directions in life. This is the period at which each one of us redefines, reclaims and reintegrates one's earlier identities to form an inner center of authority and authenticity. Analyzing the challenges of this reintegration of different identities, Walter Conn writes:

> Adolescents, "faced with this physiological revolution within them and with tangible adult tasks ahead of them, are now primarily concerned with what they appear to be in the eyes of others as compared with what they feel they are, and with the question of how to connect the roles and skills cultivated earlier with the occupational prototypes of the day" (Erikson, *Childhood and Society*, (1963), p. 261). Above all, adolescence is a "moratorium for the integration of the identity elements" specific to the earlier stages, an integration which must be realized in the new, larger, and more demanding context of society. As the infant needed to establish trust in itself and others, the adolescent needs to find people and ideas to have faith in, to be dedicated to. As the toddler knew itself as what it could freely will, the adolescent must now freely decide on the avenue of duty and service. As young child flourished in imaginative play, the adolescent seeks "peers and leading, or misleading elders who will give imaginative, if not illusory, scope to his aspirations ..." As the school-age child desired to make something work well, the adolescent finds that the "choice of an occupation assumes a significance beyond the question of remuneration and status." Though always difficult, this period of identity integration will be less stormy for those adolescents whose gifts and training allow them easy access to the economic and technological world.[46]

This task of identity integration is different to different persons depending on the person's social awareness, personal gifts and training. For priests who move from junior seminary schools to senior or major seminary colleges, most of these identity integration tasks may remain unresolved until after ordination in the pastoral ministry. No wonder then, many priests face tough identity challenges within their first five or ten years of ministry after priestly ordination.

Erik Erikson teaches that a balanced resolution of identity challenges results in a development of the virtue of fidelity. He defines fidelity as "the ability to sustain loyalties freely pledged in spite of the inevitable contradictions of value systems." According to Erikson, fidelity offers us the "opportunity to fulfill personal potentialities (including erotic vitality or its sublimation) in a context which permits the young person to be true to himself (herself) and true to significant others."[47] Erikson believes that the issue of attaining an inner transformation of growing from a crisis of identity to a consolidation of identity can be seen and evaluated. Some evidences of a faithful (a person of fidelity) are "a high sense of duty, accuracy, and veracity in the rendering of reality; the sentiment of truthfulness, as in sincerity and conviction; the quality of genuineness, as in authenticity; the trait of loyalty, of 'being true'; fairness to the rules of the game; and finally all that is implied in devotion – a freely given but binding vow, with the fateful implication for a curse befalling traitors."[48] Whatever may be lacking in the competencies of a person of fidelity are areas of further spiritual growth to be met with compassionate support and encouragement, not with criticism, blame or punishment. This is a serious challenge to spiritual companions (the spiritual directors and formators) in families, schools and churches.

## Affective Conversion (A Transformed Way of Loving)

Human beings are relational by nature. In deciding "who am I?" (the identity issues), I am at the same time faced with the question of "who am I with?"(the affective issues). Moral conversion is not just an identity issue. It is more of a conversion "to value (which) calls us to move beyond the self; it is more of a challenge than an achievement; it discloses the gap between the self we are and the self we should be. The challenge to close that gap is the challenge to move beyond ourselves not only in our knowledge but also in our decision and action – the challenge to make our action consistent with our judgment of what we should do and should be."[49] Moral conversion is then a constant challenge to live morally in all its authenticity. It is a continuous challenge of reconciling "the yet" and "the not-yet" of our lives, decisions and actions in consistent moral uprightness.

In similar manner, affective conversion has to do with "falling-in-love" to become "beings-in-love." To be authentically beings-in-love, we need to be "more or less secure in our own identity" to be capable to "risk that identity by falling in love."[50] In this regard, Bernard Lonergan "has suggested that a person is affectively self-transcendent when the isolation of the individual is broken and he or she spontaneously acts not just for self but for others as well. Further, when a person falls in love, his or her love is embodied not just in this or that act or even in any series of acts, but in a dynamic state of being-in-love. Such being-in-love is the concrete first principle from which a person's affective life flows: one's desires and fears, one's joys and sorrows, one's discernment of values, one's decisions and deeds."[51]

If a person is not transformed totally or "embodied" to be "a being-in-love", he or she may become "a beast-in-love". To be "a beast-in-love" or "an abuse-in-love" is to turn love into "something to get" or "something to use." God is love. To be an "abuse-in-love" is to make God or his people a "thing" to use or a "thing" to possess. The seminary policy of no personal friendship is indeed a disaster for an authentic self-transcendence in affective conversion. It is simply a "moral impotence" because no one can develop intimacy with a crowd. What may not be healthy among seminarians is a closed friendship that ignores or blurs the boundaries. Personal friendship is healthy provided the boundaries and balance are respected and fostered in the process (the work of a spiritual companions (spiritual directors and formators). It is critical then to bear in mind that "affective conversion is a transformation of desire: a turning from desire for possession to desire for generosity. It is a reorientation from the possessiveness rooted in obsessive concern for one's needs to self-giving in intimate love for others."[52] The affective conversion is a constant challenge (not an achievement) of becoming a being-in-love with others. Being-in-love has nothing to do with lust or sexual promiscuity. It is rather an ongoing generous self-giving in intimate love for others. Affective conversion constantly calls for "more expansive generosity and ever deeper forgiveness" of oneself and others. The spiritual companions (spiritual directors and formators) should target the areas of expansive generosity and a deepening spirit of sincere forgiveness as focus for spiritual growth and maturity at all levels in life.

## Cognitive Conversion (A Transformed Way of Knowing)

Cognitive conversion is growing in the awareness and full acceptance that we may know much, but we never know all. Only God knows all. Even, when we know something well, there is still a lot we don't know about it. It is a humbling experience, hence, cognitive conversion is a constant challenge of growing out of arrogance (self-centeredness) to humility as a knower. Seen from the point of view of Piaget's cognitive development, it is a transition from "the infant's geocentrism to the adult's dialectical realism, (which) is fundamental not only to one's understanding of the world, but also to self-understanding."[53]

Cognitive conversion is more than cognitive development. Cognitive conversion, according to Walter Conn, is "the critical recognition of the constitutive and normative role of one's own judgment in knowing reality and therefore value." And it is "rooted in the discovery of one's reality as a critical knower that it leads not to arrogance but to humility."[54] When knowledge is for knowledge's sake, it is empty. When knowledge is transformed to become care and compassion for the known, it is meaningful and purposeful. That is to say, cognitive conversion implies generous care and compassion. Conn explains it this way: "Caring is the active expression of empathy, the ability to understand and feel with the needs of others, to share and experience their perspectives as vividly as our own. But if empathy, the cognitive root of compassion, is a realistic understanding of others, its 'flip side' is humility, a realistic view of ourselves."[55] The cognitive conversion is a continuous challenge, not an achievement. To know is to know that we don't know, therefore, to be more humble. And also to be constantly aware that whatever power, possession, prestige or position we have, we still need help, and therefore, to be compassionate to all. When people claim to know but never come to this awareness, their knowledge is their imprisonment and an enslavement to others. The spiritual companions (spiritual directors and formators) will do well in accompanying their clients (seminarians) in these two critical areas of cognitive spiritual growth or conversion.

## Religious Conversion (A Transformed Way of Being)

Life is a journey. It is either we are *going out* or *coming home.* To be overloaded with other things other than life, is to allow oneself to be *pulled back* or to be *pushed down.* It is a choice. Some psychologists, particularly the Swiss psychologist, Carl G. Jung speak of "the second half of life as a special time for interior exploration about the ultimate meaning of life."[56] For Carl Jung, it is an "individuation" process, an inner movement to become a totally, unique, whole person, to become "the Self, which is the whole personality and which functions like our inmost Center."[57] It is an inner call to grow in personal ways to one's unique wholeness and holiness of life in all its diversity.

Relating Carl Jung's view to conversion process, Seward Hiltner states that "at mid-life, conversion means life or death. After devoting the first half of life to external affairs of family and livelihood, one must now face the interior depths. The existential clock is ticking. One either reflects at this point, or regresses. Now it is either conversion or the catastrophe of denial and mediocrity."[58] Religious conversion is a strategic turning point in a person's life whereby one is challenged to commence what John Sanford describes as an inner "journey to wholeness." This inner journey to wholeness, John Sanford defines as an "individuation (which) is a search for and discovery of meaning, not a meaning we consciously devise, but the meaning embedded in life itself."[59]

The inner journey to wholeness is a self-discovering process, a kind of "self-actualization." It is a process of "becoming whole (which) does not mean being perfect, but being completed. It does not necessarily mean happiness, but growth. It is often painful, but, fortunately, it is never boring. It is not getting out of life what we think we want, but it is the development and purification of the soul."[60] A great danger in an institutionalized, systematized religion is that we often lose our sense of selves to an institution or to a system. One's sense of self is lost in the institutionalized self or in the systematized self. One's sense of faith may also suffer a similar loss of personal faith to a collective faith due to overemphasis or highly systematized, formalized, ritualized celebrations. In such a situation, a religious conversion may turn out to be a conversion to a religious institution, not to a personal God. A personal faith may mean faith in a religious institution, not a personal faith in a personal God. This is a real challenge to priests who are schooled and trained to live, work, define, and identify with different institutions at different stages of life. Emphasizing the enormous challenges of this scenario to the vital need for authentic religious conversion, Walter Conn writes:

> Religious conversion is not just a process of becoming "religious," but a totally radical reorientation of one's entire life, of one's very Self. One turns to God, not to religion, in such a conversion; one allows God to move to the center of one's life, to take over and direct it. Indeed, both persons with, as well as those without, a religious perspective are eligible candidates for a religious conversion in this radical sense. For the former, such an ultimate conversion may be best understood, perhaps, as a conversion from religion to God. When religious conversion is seen from the traditional Christian perspective of self-surrender, the relativization of human autonomy is stressed. Properly understood, one surrenders not oneself or one's personal moral autonomy, but one's deepest (though unadmitted) pretense to absolute autonomy. But such total surrender is rare, and possible only for those who have totally fallen in love with a mysterious, uncomprehended God, for the person who has been grasped by an other-worldly love and completely transformed into a being-in-love. Now one's very being – indeed, all of reality – is seen as gifts.[61]

What is at stake in religious conversion is an invitation to surrender "one's deepest (though unadmitted) pretense to absolute autonomy" to gain one's authentic personal moral autonomy (an inner center of authority in which human spirit is in union with God's Spirit). It is very important to bear in mind, that religious conversion, like all the other conversions is not an achievement which is attained once and for all. No, it is a challenge which is reviewed and renewed at every point of decisions and actions throughout a lifetime. Otherwise, the human autonomy (the human spirit) assumes an absolute autonomy by false self-identification with some ungodly absolute power on the one hand, and on the other hand, by a false self-identification with the religious institution or the religious system. Life is lived in a circle. At each point on the circle of life, one is either moving in a **direction of the circle** or in a **diversion off the circle** of life. It is either one follows a **direction of life** or a **diversion off life** at each point of decision and action in a life journey. In a situation whereby a **diversion off life** becomes a way of living, a "spiritual abuse" of oneself and of others (the parishioners) becomes a way of life and ministry. Then, a lifestyle of spiritual abuse is enthroned, institutionalized and systematized with time into different forms of abuse: spiritual abuse of self, others, offices, positions, language, rituals, creed, codes or laws etc. The issue of spiritual abuse will be explored more later on.

There are three important points to note here: First, the religious conversion, like the other three conversions we discussed above (moral, affective, and cognitive conversions) or any forms of spiritual conversion, is never an achievement which is attained once and for all. No, conversion is always a challenge. In other words, no human person, priests or the lay faithful alike, has achieved moral conversion as to be permanently a person of fidelity in all commitments and of careful respect to others in all aspects, such that he or she may never betray any trust or disrespect others in life. No human person has achieved affective conversion as to have gained permanent expansive generosity and a deepened spirit of forgiveness to all, such that there are no more neglects or quarrels in his or her relationships with others. No human person has achieved cognitive conversion as to have attained complete humility about oneself and a total compassion toward others that he or she is never proud or unfairly critical or condemnatory of others in life. No human being has achieved religious conversion as to have acquired permanent personal moral autonomy and a strong spirit of justice, balance and boundaries in all aspects of life and work. No, we all are in constant need of conversion in all its forms until we breathe the last breath in death. This is why the principle of reward and punishment (the "poisonous pedagogy," to use John Bradshaw's term) is not only wicked and negative, it is also immoral and spiritually abusive. It is a generative source of crisis in life and in work, in the family, the Church, the society and the world.

The second point to note here is that conversion is a lifelong process. Conversion has no established order of sequence in life. The order in which I discussed it here has no hard and fast rule about it. It is just a way I choose to approach the topic. However, the four aspects of a Christian conversion constitute the integral components of a common road to a disciplined, moral Christian life. That is to say, the four aspects of conversion process (moral, affective, cognitive and religious conversions) are the spiritual agenda for wholeness and holiness of life as a disciplined disciple of Jesus Christ. One conversion question raises the other conversion questions. By constantly and completely resolving the conversion questions of inner spiritual journey to wholeness and holiness, one develops a pattern of spiritual strength in life, otherwise it is a pattern of spiritual weakness or spiritual abuse.

The third point to note here is that in this project, I choose to use the term, "spiritual companion" instead of "spiritual director" for one reason. Based on the principle that life is a journey, we are all pilgrims on a spiritual journey to God. We are companions to one another, not directors. Stressing on the great depth and richness of the metaphor of "companioning" as different from "directing" Dr. Alan Wolfelt writes:

> Companioning is about walking alongside; it is not about leading. Companioning is about learning from others; it is not about teaching them. Companioning is being present to another person's pain; it is not about taking away or relieving the pain. Companioning is about discovering the gifts of silence; it is not about filling every moment with talk. Companioning is about listening with the heart; it is not about analyzing with the head. Companioning is about bearing witness to the struggles of others; it is not about judging or directing those struggles. Companioning is about going to the wilderness of the soul with another human being; it is not about thinking you are responsible for finding the way out.[62]

Dr. Alan Wolfelt wants to emphasize that the notion of "directing" takes the energy away from the actual mission of spiritual journey which is all about "companioning." Wolfelt likes to drive the message home that spiritual journeying with another person is about walking with, not leading; about learning from others, not teaching them; about being present to another, not directing spiritual exercises; about discovering gifts of silence together, not talking all the time; about listening with the heart, not analyzing with the head; about witnessing to the struggles, not judging or directing them; about experiencing the desert together, not rescuing one from it. Definitely, Wolfelt's analysis may serve as a checklist for some seminary spiritual directors who understand spiritual direction as a work of giving pieces of advice and spiritual exercises.

The fact remains that we are all in a spiritual journey. If we are not growing spiritually through the conversion process, we are stocked in spiritual bankruptcy. John Bradshaw describes people stocked in spiritual bankruptcy as "adult children." An "adult child" is an abused and abusive person. Spiritual bankruptcy is an issue of great concern in the Church and society today. John Bradshaw explains how much our people and our community are affected by this scenario. For him, it is a big crisis.

Once a child's inner self is flawed by shame, the experience of self is painful. To compensate, the child develops a *false self* in order to survive. The false self forms a defensive mask, distracting the true self from its pain and inner loneliness. After years of acting, performing and pretending, the child loses contact with the true self. That true self is numbed out. The false self cover-up makes it impossible to develop self-esteem.

The crisis is far worse than is generally known because adults who parent their children badly cover up their shame-based inner selves. So the crisis is not just about how we raise our children; it's about a large number of people who look like adults, talk and dress like adults, but who are actually adult children. These adult children often run our schools, our churches and our government. They also create families. ... the crisis in the family today (is) – the crisis of adult children raising children who will become adult children.[63]

John Bradshaw is making a case that there are adult children who "run" not only our families, schools, and our government, but also our churches. The claim by Bradshaw that there may be some adult children in our Churches is an issue of concern. A greater concern is that the problem of adult children is rooted in spiritual abuse. John Bradshaw believes that "we are essentially spiritual." He then argues that "if we humans are essentially spiritual, then when we are abandoned, abused or enmeshed, we are spiritually violated. Indeed, when our caretakers acted shamelessly, they were playing God."[64] Spiritual abuse is an issue of great concern for the wholeness and holiness of the Church and her faithful today.

## Priesthood and the Crisis of Spiritual Abuse

Spiritual abuse is an unfortunate phenomenon in the Church today. John Bradshaw defines spiritual abuse simply as what happens "when our caretakers acted shamelessly, they were playing God."[65] "To play God" is to make God an idol. Spiritual abuse may happen by what we do or fail to do, by who we try to be or fail to be in life, work and relationships. It is not simply a priesthood issue, anyone who acts as a caretaker shamelessly creates spiritual abuse of some kind. But our focus here is on priesthood and spiritual abuse.

What may be regarded as the New Testament definition of priesthood is: "For every high priest chosen from among men (people) is appointed to act on behalf of men (the people) in relation to God, to offer gifts and sacrifices for sins."[66] Priests are called "to act on behalf of (the people) in relation to God," not to play God. A priest may play God by neglect, action or by false self. I have already explored the different ways a priest may put himself in a scenario of spiritual abuse by neglecting his spiritual conversion process (the moral, the affective, the cognitive and the religious conversion). Now I would like to highlight how spiritual abuse may affect the life, relationships and ministry of priests.

## Church Community and Spiritual Abuse

Spiritual neglect is at the root of spiritual abuse. Every abuse begins with some form of neglect, neglect of oneself or others or their genuine needs. If a priest neglects his spiritual needs for conversion and growth, he is spiritually abused and he is likely to be abusive in relationships with others. Spiritual neglect, therefore, is a red flag of spiritual abuses at different levels and depths. A community that is neglected in different ways is an abused community and may be abusive in relationships. An abused and abusive community is "a closed community." John Bradshaw calls it "a closed system." He explains:

> A closed system sees any other system that is different from it as the enemy. This is the cause of wars and the violent destruction that goes with it. ... Closed systems are extremely dangerous because they deself their members and deprive them of self-esteem. Closed systems are dangerous because they allow no feedback. When no new information can be integrated into a system, it feeds on itself and becomes an absolutizing agent. (It plays God). Its own beliefs become sacred laws; its own rules infallible; its own leaders all-powerful. This is exactly the problem with monarchial patriarchy and the poisonous pedagogy it spawns.[67]

All forms of spiritual neglect are factors of spiritual abuse. We now highlight some forms of spiritual neglect.

## Neglecting Spiritual Growth

A principal factor of spiritual neglect is a neglect of spiritual growth. As human beings, we are constantly growing and/or decaying (dying). It is always true both on the human level and on the spiritual level. To grow, we need more than a healthy self, we need food. What helps us to maintain a spiritual healthy self or healthy spirit is spiritual conversion (moral, affective, cognitive and religious conversions). The spiritual food for spiritual growth is the spiritual disciplines. The spiritual disciplines are in three categories as we discussed above: 1) Inward disciplines (meditation, prayer, fasting and study); 2) Outward disciplines (simplicity, solitude, submission, and service); and 3) Corporate disciplines (confession, worship, guidance, and celebration). A person can be spiritually sick or weak due to a lack of spiritual conversion. Or, he or she may be spiritually malnourished due to lack of or insufficient spiritual disciplines. In either case, the person is in spiritual neglect, is spiritually abused and may be abusive in relationships.

## Neglecting Family Violence

The family is the nucleus of the society and the bedrock of our lives as human beings. What happens to the family happens to all of us, because we all belong to the same family of God whether we believe it or not. A neglect of the family is a great neglect and the neglect of family violence is a dangerous neglect. We all come from a family. We all bear some patterns or wounds of our family. Efforts to improve the family are efforts to improve the society and the people. Virginia Satir believes strongly in the power of the family to change the world. She writes:

> Giving ourselves full permission to make the family a place to develop people who are more truly human will reflect itself in a safer and more humanly responsible world. We can make the family a real place for developing real people. Each of us is a discovery, and each of us makes a difference. Everyone who holds a position of power or influence in the world was once an infant. How he or she uses power of influence depends largely on what that person learned in the family while growing up. When we help troubled families become nurturing – and nurturing ones become even more nurturing – each person's increased humanity will filter out into government, schools, businesses, religions and other institutions that contribute to the quality of our lives.[68]

A neglect of the family is an abuse of the family. It is not just the family that is abused but also the government, the schools, the churches, the society, and above all, all of us, the people of God. A lot may go wrong if we are spiritually "blind" or weak in fostering a growing healthy, nurturing family life and relationships.

## Neglecting Stewardship

The life and ministry of priesthood is a life and ministry of service or stewardship. To neglect stewardship is to neglect Jesus Christ and His priesthood. Jesus made it clear in His Gospel message:

> But Jesus called them to him and said, "You know that the rulers of the Gentiles lord it over them, and their great men exercise authority over them. It shall not be so among you; but whoever would be great among you must be your servant, and whoever would be first among you must be your slave; even as the Son of man came not to be served but to serve, and to give his life as a ransom for many."[69]

Jesus did not only command stewardship, He lived it to its fullness. Jesus witnessed it in the lives of his disciples by washing their feet.[70] Jesus witnessed it in leadership among the people by not insisting on his privileges, prerogatives or entitlements. [71] Again, Jesus witnessed stewardship among the people (in the society) in refusing a cheap popularity or grandiose celebrity of being crowned a king by public opinion. [72] Priests who sincerely commit themselves to follow the footsteps of Jesus Christ, the Eternal High Priest must take these points seriously.

Stewardship is more than performing some acts of service once in a while or even all the time. Stewardship is not simply acting out (just doing things or having some active bodies). Jesus did not only perform some acts of service, His "whole being is defined by servanthood. The ultimate act of service is, of course, his death and his self-gift to his disciples in the coming of the Holy Spirit" and the Holy Communion (the Holy Eucharist). [73] A priest is not only to live his entire life as a self-gift to God and his people, but he must also discern and foster the self-gift of others for the enrichment of the community. A priest must be "it," witness "it" and lead "it" in his life and ministry ("it" meaning a lifestyle of stewardship).

## Neglecting Inclusive Spirituality

From the point of faith, spirituality may be defined as a life of faith or a lived faith as a way of life. We live our lives in faith. There are both commonalities and differences in our lives of faith. Faith, according to Paul Tillich, is "ultimate concern."[74] By this definition, Tillich teaches that "faith believes that there is an ultimate source of all existence, as well as a goal for life." The Christians name the "Ultimate Source" as God, the Jews call him Elohim, the Moslems call him Allah, the Hindus name him Brahman. Each faith group has its own spirituality. There is a lot to be learned and shared among different faith-groups and among different individuals' lives of faith if a spirit of mutual respect, living truth in love, justice, education and dialogue is maintained and fostered in all levels of relationships.

An inclusive spirituality does not stop with interfaith and interreligious recognition and respect. It must also foster a culture of inclusive language in liturgy, a politics of give and take, a government of empowerment and service to all without discrimination, a shared community life that honors and celebrates differences as gifts to all.

## Neglecting Social Justice

Peter J. Henriot et al. wrote a book in 1985 (the Centenary edition was published in 1999), captioned: *Catholic Social Teaching: Our Best Kept Secret.* In it, they claim that "the Church has a developed body of teaching on social, economic, political, and cultural matters and what that body says seem to have been forgotten – or have never been known – by a majority of the Roman Catholic community. ..." [75] Peter Henriot and his colleagues are focusing on the Catholic community in the United States of America, but the issue they raised about the neglected social teaching and social justice is a worldwide problem. Peter J. Henriot et al. began this book with a chapter on "An Evolving Social Message: From Pope Leo XIII to the Second Vatican Council." They claim that "the Church's social teaching in the modern period dates from 1891, when Pope Leo XIII in the encyclical letter, *The condition of Labor (Rerum Novarum),* spoke out against inhuman conditions, which were the normal plights of working people in industrial societies."[76] It is important to pay attention to the focus of each of these encyclicals and their main teachings on social justice.

At the fortieth years of *The Condition of Labor,* in 1931, Pope Pius XI published the next encyclical, *The Reconstruction of the Social Order (Quadragesimo Anno).* In it, Pope Pius XI condemned what may be called the "dictatorship of the proletariat." He strongly criticized the "unregulated competition" of capitalism and the "promotion of class struggle and the narrow reliance for leadership on the working class" of communism. [77] The leadership of Pope Pius XI helped in the formation of United Nations and later on, under his successor, Pope John XXIII, we have the launching of the United Nations' *Universal Declaration of human Rights* in 1948.

On the thirtieth anniversary of Pope Pius XI's Quadragesimo Anno, Pope John XXIII launched the encyclical: *In Christianity and Social Progress (Mater et Magistra, 1961);* and two years after, in 1963, he published his second social encyclical, *Peace on Earth (Pacem in Terris, 1963).* In these encyclicals, Pope John XXIII "set forth a number of principles to guide both Christians and policy makers in addressing the gap between rich and poor nations and the threat to world peace." He emphasized the need for all to work together to "create local, national, and global institutions which would both respect human dignity and promote justice and peace."[78] In October 1962, Pope John XXIII took a step forward to add actions to words by convening the Second Vatican Council which helped to structure a "world" Church (the nature and mission of the Church to and in the world). The most important three documents of the Second Vatican Council in structuring a "world Church" are: *The Church as the Light of the World (Lumen Gentium); The Church in the Modern World (Gaudium et Spes, 1965)* and *On Religious Freedom (Dignitatis Humanae, 1965).* The Catholic Church will be best served if all (priests and lay faithful alike) will honestly commit themselves to a good reading and understanding of the documents of the Second Vatican Council.

The Second Vatican Council is not just one of the twenty-one ecumenical councils in the Catholic Church. It is a turning-point event that defines very profoundly "the end of one era and the beginning of a new era." Peter Henriot et al. put it this way:

> In many respects, Vatican II represented the end of one era and the beginning of a new era. The enthusiasm and energies of the Age of Enlightenment had been spent. This philosophical movement of the eighteenth century, marked by a rejection of traditional social, religious and political ideas and an emphasis on rationalism, had culminated in the holocaust in Europe and in a world sharply divided. These events had dashed hopes that our secular society, based on human reason severed from religious faith, would lead to unending progress. Instead a misguided rationalism had unleashed forces which threatened to destroy the world. The Church had turned inward in reaction to a rationalistic

age which demeaned religious belief. Religion, more and more defined as a "private" affair between the individual and God, was relegated to a marginal role in secular society. At the same time, the Church channeled its energies outward to evangelize the "mission lands" of Africa, Asia, and Latin America. During Vatican II, the Council leaders rejected that marginal role in society as inconsistent with the unique religious mission which Christ had given to his Church.[79]

The Council leaders' agenda of re-evangelizing the evangelized Western world was not well-received or understood by the priests and the lay faithful in the Church, especially in the Western world. This confusion of misunderstood or misconceived agenda of the Second Vatican Council is still an issue in the Catholic Church and in the Catholic priesthood today. It created a mild rift in the hierarchy, some sense of suspicion among the bishops and priests in some parts of Catholic world that is yet to be healed. The ongoing crisis in the priesthood today is widening the rift rather than healing it.

The evolving social message of the Church leadership after the Second Vatican Council continued to address the social issues of the people of God. For instance, in 1967, Pope Paul VI published an encyclical letter, *The Development of Peoples (Populorum Progressio)*. In it, he addressed the "structural dimensions of global injustice" in regard to world's poor and hungry people. Pope Paul VI "appealed to both rich and poor nations to work together in a spirit of solidarity to establish an order of justice and bring about the renewal of the temporal order." [80]

At the eightieth anniversary of Pope Leo XIII's *The Condition of Labor,* Pope Paul VI launched his second social encyclical letter, *A Call to Action (Octogesima Adveniens, 1971)*. In it, Pope Paul VI affirmed the difficulty of trying to transform the social order from the global level and the role of the local Christian communities in meeting this challenge. He urged the Christians to engage the Gospel in an "ongoing incarnational process which involves three separate moments: 1. Evaluation and analysis of their contemporary situation. 2. Prayer, discernment, and reflection, bringing the light of the Gospel and the teachings of the Church to bear on the situation. 3. Pastoral action which fights injustices and works for the transformation of society, thus laboring to make the 'reign' of God a reality."[81]

In 1975, Pope Paul VI published his third social encyclical letter, *Evangelization in the Modern World (Evangelii Nuntiandi)*. In this letter, Pope Paul VI "emphasized that preaching the Gospel would be incomplete if it did not take into account human rights and the themes of family life, life in society, peace, justice and development,"(including liberation at its spiritual and temporal levels). [82] What Pope Paul VI teaches in these three encyclical letters (*The Development of Peoples, Populorum Progressio, 1967; A Call to Action, Octogesima Adveniens, 1971;* and *Evangelization in the Modern World, Evangelii Nunciandi, 1975)* is that the Second Vatican Council is a turning-point event that marks an end of the old era and a beginning of a new era. With his first encyclical letter, *Populorum Progressio 1967,* Pope Paul VI invites the Church to take up an agenda of the "world" Church by focusing on developing **DOCTRINES** to the development of **PEOPLES** in a united "spirit of **solidarity** to establish an order of justice and bring about the renewal of the temporal order." Keep in mind that "a world Church" is not simply "a worldly Church." A worldly church is interested in control of power, position, possession and popularity. A world Church as opposed to a worldly Church is a Church that lives and witnesses its mission and ministry in the world for the good of all and the glory of God.

With his second encyclical letter, *A Call to Action, Octogesima Adveniens 1971,* Pope Paul VI calls on the entire Church to shift from "the difficulties inherent in establishing a just social order" from the top down to "the role of local Christian community in meeting this responsibility."[83] The new methodical principle that will aid the local Christian community in this task is an "ongoing incarnational process which involves three separate moments of evaluation and analysis; prayer, discernment and reflection; and pastoral action. With his third encyclical letter, *Evangelization in the Modern World, Evangelii Nuntiandi 1975,* Pope Paul VI calls for a shift from a form of evangelization that imposes the Gospel on the people to the preaching of the Gospel that "take into account human rights and the themes of family life, life in society, peace, justice, and development." It must include "liberation – in both spiritual and temporal senses" as well as "the plan of the redemption (that) includes combating injustice."[84]

The tradition of linking the Gospel and social justice through a shift of emphasis and method was continued by Pope John Paul II in many of his social encyclical letters. The first is *Redeemer of Humankind (Redemptor Hominis, 1979).* Here, Pope John Paul II teaches "that when we put the human at the center then we see contemporary society in need of redemption." [85] In 1980, Pope John Paul II launched his second social encyclical letter, *Rich in Mercy (Dives Misericordiae)*. In it, he presented mercy as a social love that links to justice, while challenging the "disrespect of the environment and an uncritical stance toward technological advance."[86] In his third social encyclical teaching, *On Human Work (Laborem Exercens, 1981)*, John Paul II stressed "the priority of labor over capital" and its centrality in creating a just society. He also highlighted the dangers of "economism which would reduce humans to mere instruments of production." [87] Many African countries including Nigeria are in danger of the evils of western economism today. John Paul II also called for greater solidarity as against liberal capitalism and collectivist socialism.

In 1990, Pope John Paul II published his fourth social encyclical letter, *The Missionary Activity of the Church (Redemptoris Missio)*. Here, he stressed "the necessity of proclaiming Christ as a means of restoring human dignity" and the importance of "inculturation, liberation, ecumenical activity, human rights, and the value of witnessing to the Gospel."[88] And finally, on the one hundred years' anniversary of Pope Leo XIII's *The Condition of Labor (Rerum Novarum 1891)*, Pope John Paul II launched his fifth social encyclical letter, *One Hundred Years (Centesimus Annus, 1991)*. In it, he emphasizes that the social teaching itself is an "essential part of the Church missionary activity."[89] Remember, these are rich documents that should not be reduced to simple statements without some serious damage to their enormous vital meanings and messages. I am doing this kind of intensive summarization of these vital social justice documents as an invitation to a more integrative, meditative study by all.

The important point of all this analysis is that there is a great teaching but not much learning in the whole process. When teachings happen without much learning, the message is yet to be received. The point is that when the social order is neglected, it affects everyone in the community, priests and the lay faithful alike. There is a terrible danger to life in general where inhuman conditions are left unquestioned, where the plights of the working people are compromised, where unregulated competition of capitalism sets up the poor for a price in the community, where human dignity is disrespected and the need for justice and peace is ignored. The neglect of social justice study in the Church is not just a problem, it is a crisis.

## Religion and Spiritual Abuse

Spiritual abuse happens everywhere, even in religion. When spirituality is confused with religion, we create room for spiritual abuse. There are some areas of relatedness and differences between spirituality and religion. However, it is misleading to assume that spirituality is synonymous with religion. The dictionary meaning of religion is "a set of beliefs concerning the causes, nature, and purpose of the universe, especially when considered as the creation of a superhuman agency or agencies, usually involving devotional and ritual observances, and often containing a moral code for the conduct of human affairs."[90] Modern theologians speak of religion as "what counts most in life" which is based on four factors (the 4Cs): Creed (the set of beliefs); Code (the rules of life); Ceremony (the rituals or celebrations of life); and Community (the people of similar or same faith). Paul Tillich, one of the leading Protestant theologians of the twentieth century claims that "religion is made up of whatever is one's 'Ultimate concern.'" He defines religion as "the state of being grasped by an ultimate concern, a concern which qualifies all other concerns as preliminary and which itself contains the answer to the question of the meaning of life."[91] In essence then, religion "consists of what we want to do in life and why we want to do it. 'What' and 'why' or 'behavior' and 'belief' feed into each other and determine each other."[92] If religion has to do with behavior and belief or acting and thinking or praxis and theory or doing and understanding, then religion deals with the "content" of life and its meaning.

Spirituality, as we defined earlier in this project is living the paschal life of Christ in the Spirit of God. The dictionary meaning of "spirit" is "the animating principle of life, especially, of humans; vital essence."[93] The dictionary also defines "spiritual" as "pertaining to the spirit or soul, as distinguished from the physical nature," and "spirituality" as "the quality or fact of being spiritual, incorporeal or immaterial nature."[94] Spirituality then, has to do with life and the quality of life (the animating quality of life itself). Spirituality as life and its animating quality is based on What John Mostyn calls the "Grid" principle, that "God is at work in our lives."[95] This principle has "four elements: 1) the *intrapersonal,* 2) the *interpersonal,* 3) the *structural,* and 4) the *environmental* aspects of life."[96] It means that God is at work in my intrapersonal, interpersonal, structural and environmental aspects of life as the supreme vital essence of all that is. What happens when religion is pushed up to mean the same thing with spirituality? Confusion!

This is a tragedy of history, what John Bradshaw describes as spiritual bankruptcy, the tendency to presume that religion is spirituality. The "body" (the content of life) is religion and the Life itself (the Vital Essence) with its animating quality (the context of life) is spirituality. When religion is assumed to be spirituality, we are left with "the body" or "the content" of life, religion. Religion, we mentioned earlier, has four aspects: the Creed (set of beliefs); the Code (rules of life); the Ceremony (rituals of life); and the Community (the people of similar or same faith). When "the body" (religion) is severed from "the Spirit" (spirituality), the possibility of corruption is most probable. When religion loses its spirituality, it becomes its own God. When religion loses its living spirit of reformation, it grows into a deadly spirit of deformity. The four elements of religion (creed, code, ceremony and community) stand the danger of being "absolutisized" or "divinized" "so that the religion becomes just as important as (or even more important) than the Ultimate Mystery of God."[97] Brennan R. Hill et al describe this tendency as different "viruses" that attack the body of religion (a corruption of religion).

The first virus, according to Brennan Hill and others, is "the virus of idolatry (which) infects the body of religion mainly through its creeds or belief system."[98] Brennan Hill et al are of the view that "a statue of the divinity is not necessarily an idol, for, strictly speaking, an idol is not something that represents God but something that takes the place of or limits God."[99] Viewed from this perspective, there may be a great need to reconsider very critically what was started by the missionaries and continued to this day, the unwholesome condemnation of the African/Igbo traditional religious symbolism as paganism and idolatry. Often times, the real idolatry is left unnamed and unchallenged. Brennan Hill et al explain it this way:

> Religious leaders, for example, (theologians too) invest their teachings, and sometimes even themselves, with a power or authority that is supposed to belong only to God. This usually happens subtly, perhaps without the religious leaders clearly realizing what they are doing. Their word is identified with God's Word; or their authority is made to be the only avenue to "sure knowledge" of God's will. In this way, religion itself becomes an idol. Or, in an image from Buddhism, the finger that is supposed to point to the moon takes the place of the moon. This is one of the most frequently found forms of corruption within religion.[100]

This is a situation of an abused religion that becomes abusive to its adherents. Spiritual abuse becomes a way of life and ministry in such a situation or circumstances. It doesn't get better. It gets worse. The second form of corruption that will follow is legalism. This is a religious virus that shows up mainly in the religious code. It is a situation where the Church laws are so absolutized that human beings and their genuine needs are sacrificed or denied to keep the laws at all costs. Everything and everybody are read and interpreted from the laws:

> It leads religious believers or their leaders to define religion as primarily a matter of obeying the law, the ethical-legal system that the community has agreed upon. A good Christian, therefore, is someone who obeys the law and goes to church every Sunday. Being religious is mainly a question of do's and don'ts, of a certain form of conduct.[101]

When we become what we do, we settle down to a terrible crisis of identity (Phariseeism). We cease from being subjects of actions to become objects of actions or means to other ends. The abuses of all kinds are possible in this scenario. This situation will create room for further corruption of religion, setting the ground for a third religious virus of superstition.

The corruption of superstition infects religion mainly from its rituals or cults. Here, there is a disproportionate emphasis on the externals of rituals. The proliferation of healing ministries and healing houses or centers is a real concern here. The confusion is the difficulty in "distinguishing healthy ritual from debilitating superstition." Brennan Hill et al. explain thus:

> Authentic ritual, therefore, is a coming together of a personal faith experience and some external ritual. In superstition, the external action takes on central importance. Everything depends on doing something and doing it right. In ritual or liturgy, one makes use of a symbol in order to express and deepen faith. In superstition or magic (another name for superstition), one "presses a button," as it were, in order to get a certain result. "Do this to get that" might express the attitude behind superstition. Superstition, therefore, is based on the belief that God or the supernatural powers can be cajoled to grant certain favors through certain actions.[102]

The sale of indulgences is a case in history. We may think of other questionable religious practices or devotions like the burying of the statue of Saint Joseph in houses on sale or distributing copies of novena prayer pamphlets of St. Jude at Churches to gain special favors. Some healing institutions promote the sales of some religious objects or articles as conditions for being "healing" in their prayer-grounds. One popular healing center in the 80s and 90s in Nigeria made a fortune in a sale of a sticker that was purported to have a miraculous power of preventing items from being stolen and houses/stores from being vandalized. This sale is still going on today in Nigeria. Whatever way superstition takes place, there is some form of over-externalization of actions from faith in God, the source of all goodness, graces and gifts of life. Such unhealthy separation leads to a loss of authenticity and focus in life.

The virus of ideology is a fundamental virus, the fourth and the final virus in the order of our discussion here. Once we get to this level, everything is a loss. While it is true that the virus of idolatry attacks the creed, the virus of legalism corrupts the code, and the virus of superstition corrodes the rituals or ceremonies, they are all an attack on the object of religion. The virus of ideology destroys the human community, the subjects of religion. This is a fundamental loss and the devastating, divisive effects are deep and widespread in many ways. Brennan Hill et al. explain:

> We are dealing with ideology when religion is turned into a tool to serve one's own benefit, or that of one's group, before all else. The benefit can be one of money, power, or prestige. Religion is used as a means of manipulation. Religious believers are manipulated or drugged, usually by their religious leaders, to contribute to the wealth of others, or to accept their own exploited position as God's will, or to spill their blood in fighting against outsiders who are presented as the enemies of religion. Perhaps this is the most devastating and disgusting corruption of religion, for it transforms one of the essential purposes of religion – to foster the sense of interrelatedness and unity of all persons – into a tool for aggrandizing self and exploiting others.[103]

What Brennan Hill and others are analyzing is not too unfamiliar to us. It is all around us in some ways or another. In preparation for this project, I interviewed priests and bishops from the South-Eastern States of Nigeria. The issue of the ostentatious, sometimes scandalous lifestyle of priests (especially in regard to personal cars, money and women) came up very prominently in the discussions. Even some outstanding faithful raised similar concern. The point to note is that most of the parishes in this part of the country are rural and poor. The inevitable question then is: how are priests to be maintained in high-class lifestyles in poor and rural parishes? Apart from the economic hardship that such a scenario may impose on the poor parishioners, the Gospel and the priestly ministry may be highly compromised.

As evident from above, spiritual abuses are perpetuated in many ways in the system. That is to say, the virus of ideology is promoted a lot in many more dubious ways and means in the Church and in the priesthood. Heart C. Ogu, in his book, *Oh! Weep Not My Country (2005)* reported a statement by Rev. Lasunkanmi Bolaji, the Vicar of St. John Anglican Church, Ilaro, Ogun State, Nigeria as having said: "... instead of rebuking evil, Church leaders are seen to be encouraging evil."[104] Heart C. Ogu noted also "the Oputa Panel Report-Executive Summary and Recommendation as published by the Civil Societies Forum No 96 on what's role for Religion in Nigerian Politics." The panel writes:

> One of the missing links in Nigerian politics has been in determining and reaching a consensus on the exact role and place of religion. The country has remained in the firm grip of so-called believers of the two Abrahamic Religion: Islam and Christianity. ... Religious bodies ought to have much more than they did in the struggle against human rights violations, especially during the dark days of the late Abacha Regime. On the whole, the politicization of religion has undermined religion. [105]

A corruption of religion has tremendous devastative, divisive effects even beyond the religious group and beyond the nations. Corruption destroys more than eyes can see, hands can touch, and minds can imagine. There is such a colossal loss for all that it is better prevented than managed.

Brennan Hill et al. raised an important question here: "Just why does this happen?" And they quickly point out in an attempt to answer the question: "That question has no neat answer. Some attribute such corruptions to what they call "the demonic" element within all religions. But what is the demonic? And how does it work? To venture an answer: whatever "the demonic" may be, it seems to work primarily through the interplay of two human weaknesses – the inordinate desire for *security* and the inordinate desire for *wealth or power*."[106] So, for Brennan Hill and his colleagues, there are two points to note here: the first is the fact of human weakness; and the second is the issue of misplacement of identity, turning religion into what it is not. All gifts come from God alone. Religion is not God. Religion then, "is not meant to give us absolute security, nor is it meant to make us rich and powerful. When it is used for such purposes, it becomes the abode of 'the demonic' rather than of 'the divine.'"[107]

Religion is in constant need of reform and renewal, just as human beings are in continuous need of growth and renewal humanly and spiritually. When we lose our spiritual growth and renewal, we corrupt religion and mess up life with all forms of crisis. Spiritual growth is more than receiving the initiation sacraments (Baptism, Holy Eucharist, Confirmation, Matrimony or Ordination/Religious Profession) and spiritual exercises (the spiritual disciplines). The spiritual disciplines, we noted earlier, are of three categories: the Inward disciplines (meditation, prayer, fasting and study); the Outward disciplines (simplicity, solitude, submission, and service); and the Corporate discipline (confession, worship, guidance, and celebration). We mentioned also that these spiritual disciplines are not by themselves transformative. What transforms us spiritually is God's grace. The spiritual disciplines are channels of God's grace. St. Augustine said that the God who created you without you may not save you without you. We are saved both humanly and spiritually, none is to be neglected without consequences.

## Summary

The central message in this project is that spiritual abuse is at the root of all human crises. Because we are not human beings on a spiritual journey, we are spiritual beings on a human journey. At the root of every spiritual abuse is some form/s of spiritual neglect. Spiritual neglect is a denial or rejection of individual or community growth and developmental needs humanly and spiritually. These needs may be moral, affective, cognitive, and/or religious. The crisis in priesthood today is not simply a human problem to be solved or just criminal acts to be prosecuted. It is fundamentally a spiritual invitation to a neglected inner human and spiritual growth and developmental challenge/s.

This project explores the structures of crisis in the priesthood and the Catholic Church, and suggests a structural process of dealing with the crisis. The structural process has three phases: the educational process; the human formation process and the spiritual formation process. On the educational issue, this project makes a case that it is a structured crisis to keep using the sixteen century model of education to educate the twenty-first century candidates for priesthood. Adding new programs to an old model may harm more than they help. It is like building a storey house on a bungalow foundation. It takes only time to crash and crumble. It is simply a structured crisis. The educational training of priests of today must emphasize the human and spiritual formation of priests and people of today's Church in today's world.

On the human and spiritual formation issue, this project declares that to neglect the human and spiritual formation process is to become an adult child, a lifestyle of a structured crisis. An adult child is an abused and an abusive person. It is a lifestyle of spiritual abuse. To approach the crisis in priesthood simply as a crime to be prosecuted is to miss the point. It is like a physician offering "first aid" as a treatment of a sickness instead of a way to clear a space for effective diagnosis. To treat a patient before diagnosis is to put a cart before the horse. It doesn't work.

The crisis in the priesthood is a structured crisis. As a structured crisis, it affects every part and persons of the structure. This project then has double focus: broad and narrow focus. The broad focus is on priesthood in the Catholic Church, while the narrow focus is on the priesthood in a particular Church, the Igbo Church in South-East of Nigeria. The preparatory interviews and questionnaires on this project focused on this particular audience: the bishops and priests of Igbo Catholic community in the South-Eastern part of Nigeria. The interviews and questionnaires dwell heavily on the challenges of relationships between bishops and priests; priests and parishioners; rector and seminary staffs; seminary staff and seminarians, etc.

There are two important highlights of the questionnaires that I wish to stress here: 1) A three-point **observation** on the priesthood of today; and 2) Some pointed **recommendations** on the personalities of the priesthood. The respondents of the questionnaire noted a three-point observation of some developing tendencies in the Catholic priesthood of today: First, the Catholic priesthood is often perceived and appreciated in the world of today as a "personal achievement." For such people, priesthood is something to use for personal aggrandizement. Here, there is a developing attitude or a tendency to undermine the priesthood of Christ as a vocation to selfless service to God and to his people to become a self-serving profession. Second, the priesthood is perceived as a "family investment." And third, the priesthood is seen as an "accomplished social status." For people in these two categories, priesthood is a "business" or "means" of acquiring wealth or positions of honor in the society. This scenario is a fallout of a lopsided emphasis on priesthood as a ministry (power to perform rituals) and as an institution (power to control others or impose dry doctrines). It is a tragedy of a structured crisis of neglected sound educational root, human formation root and spiritual formation root. A response to the structured crisis in priesthood will be our concern in the next chapter in this project, chapter five. The other highlight of the questionnaires is the pointed recommendations on the personalities of the priesthood which I wish to list below as a final point in this summary.

## Recommendations for More Friendly and Pastoral Relationships in the Priesthood

### Bishops/ Religious Superiors

- Foster friendly relationships with all priests/people, not just with those that flock around you.
- Stop paying attention to flatteries.
- Be kind and considerate.
- Lead with pastoral care and concern.
- Be effable and relate as fathers with priests/people.
- Avoid selective treatment.
- Be Good Shepherds in the manner of Jesus Christ.
- Be more committed and involved in forming future collaborators.
- Witness kindness
- Give everyone his/her dues.
- Be less power conscious and be with the people.
- Don't be vindictive.
- Learn to be fatherly to everyone.
- Call the erring ones to dialogue and correction.
- Nothing from physical/personal point of view.
- Be more humane.
- Listen to formators who recommend conditions to the priesthood.
- Treat the priests humanely and with brotherly love.
- Form the diocese/congregation as a family.

- Avoid being bossy and power drunk.
- Consider priests more as collaborators rather than as subjects.
- Reach out to silent priests and be available
- Manifest simplicity.
- Accept that all can make mistakes.
- Respect and foster individual gifts and talents.
- Give assignments based on individual abilities, spirituality and competence.
- Be a symbol of order, peace and unity, and like it, live it.

## Priests/ Religious

- Be less materialistic.
- Offer selfless service.
- Be more mature and respectful in relationships with people.
- Avoid calumny.
- Stop running down fellow priests before the lay people.
- Be Christlike.
- Be committed to and foster a spirit of collaboration and solidarity.
- Strive after the mind (holiness) of Jesus Christ, the Eternal High Priest.
- Eschew all worldliness.
- Shun being too independent and individualistic.
- Show more solidarity and mutual support.
- Be fraternal to everyone.
- Be ever on the watch and alert.
- Live and witness the life of faith and service in the Church and the world.
- Bring fulfillment to the priesthood and behave yourselves accordingly.
- Keep your ecclesiastical and evangelical vows with dignity.
- Give less problems to the bishops/superiors.
- Be committed to your duties and be readily available.
- Be humble and kind to all.
- Don't view your superior/bishop with suspicion.
- Cherish your vocation and protect it.

- Work as a team to achieve maximum results (be a team-player).
- Forge ahead and keep up your faith.
- Always recall why Christ called us to the priesthood and act accordingly.
- Listen to the voice of Christ and not the society.
- Don't allow your lives as priests to be dictated by the people around you.
- Be convinced of the option you have made as priests of God and live up to it.
- Make more efforts in spite of difficulties to respond better to your priestly callings.
- Be good shepherds, not businessmen.
- Cultivate a caring attitude.
- Form seminarians by the good examples of your lives.
- Be energetic, not authoritarian.
- Be aware of the temporality and limitedness of your superiors' position and responsibilities as to be prudent and wise.
- Don't be too conservative.
- Be a moderator, not a taskmaster.
- Manifest simplicity and spiritual righteousness.

## Rectors/ Seminary Staff

- Teach by example.
- Avoid unhealthy wrangling and discriminations.
- Be inclusive.
- Be available and objective.
- Insist on good morals.
- Give seminarians time to discern their call.
- Be patient enough to teach properly.
- Be diligent.
- Be ready to learn more as you teach more.
- Maintain a united front.
- Insist on the rules and play by the rules.
- Be close to seminarians to hear their unspoken words, not too close to intimidate them.

- Treat seminarians as junior brothers with Christlike love and care.
- Be and maintain a team spirit in the seminary family.
- Keep the flag high and hoisted.
- Teach more with your personal lives than with the words of the mouth.
- See seminarians as uncooked eggs and handle them with care.
- Be friendly and encouraging to all (no favoritism).
- Be awake and spiritual while discerning and discovering people's vocation to the priesthood.
- Keep and respect the boundaries and foster them.
- Regard less the externals and focus more on the interior quality of seminarians.

## Seminarians

- Follow by good examples.
- Give in more to your human and spiritual formation.
- Be less worldly.
- Shun hypocriticism and formalism.
- Be open to the Holy Spirit and learning all the time.
- Don't be lured by the shiny aspects of the priesthood.
- Take your formation seriously.
- Take time to be cultivated and cultured in learning, sanctity and skills.
- Be docile.
- Be more practical.
- Imbibe the rules, don't just follow them.
- Make good use of opportunities available, they are not there forever.
- Live a balanced life.
- Be more spiritual than being materialistic and academicians.
- Be serious with every aspect of the seminary training and follow through.
- See the formation and all it entails as a way to be mature and sound.
- Aim to be a fulfilled priest after the mind of Christ.

- Be sincere and honest.
- Be wise and obedient.
- Be your brothers' keeper, not your brothers' killer.
- Learn to be disciplined and prayerful.
- Learn to be more open to formators for a better direction.

1   Larkin, E. E. and Broccolo G. T. eds., (1972) Spiritual Renewal of the American Priesthood, Washington, D.C.: USCC Publishing Office. P. 279

2   Shannan, William H. "Priestly Spirituality: Speaking Out for the Inside," in Cozzens, Donald B. ed.(1997) The Spirituality of the Diocesan Priest, Collegeville, Minnesota: The Liturgical Press, p. 91

3   Cozzens, Donald B. "Tenders of the Words" in Cozzens D. B. ed. (1997) Ibid., p. 43

4   Groeschel, Benedict J. (1983) Spiritual Passages: The Psychology of Spiritual Development, New York: The Crossroad Publishing Company, p. 17

5   Groeschel, Benedict J. (1983) Ibid., p. 6

6   Ibid.

7   Groeschel, Benedict J. (1983) Ibid., p. 8

8   Ibid.

9   Groeschel, Benedict J. (1983) Ibid., p. 8

10   Groeschel, Benedict J. (1983) Ibid., p. 9

11   Bonaventure, The Soul's Journey into God, The Tree of Life,The Tree of St. Francis, trans. E. Cousins, Classics of Western Spirituality (New York: Paulist Press, 1979), p. 185-90, quoted by Groeschel, Benedict J. (1983) Ibid., p. 9

12   Groeschel, Benedict J. (1983) Ibid., p. 9

13   Plato, Symposium, 211, in The Dialogues, trans. B. Jowett, 4th ed. (Oxford: Clarendon Press, 1953) quoted by Groeschel, Benedict J. (1983) Ibid., p. 9

14   Groeschel, Benedict J. (1983) Ibid., p. 9

15   Augustine, Confessions, trans. F. Sheed (New York: Sheed & Ward, 1965), X, vi, quoted by Groeschel, Benedict J. (1983) Ibid., 10

16   Bradshaw, J. (1996) The Family: A New Way of Creating Solid Self-Esteem, Revised Edition, Deerfield Beach, Florida: Health Communications, Inc. p. 247

17   Ibid.

18   Foster, R.J. and Griffin, E. eds. (2000) Spiritual Classics: Selected Readings for Individuals and Groups on the Twelve Spiritual Disciplines, New York: HarperSanFrancisco, p. xi

19   Foster, R. J. & Griffin, E. eds. (2000) Ibid., pp. xiii-xiv

20   Groeschel, B. J. (1983) Ibid., p. 11

21   Foster, R. J. & Griffin, E. eds. (2000) Ibid., p. xiii

22   Ibid., pp. xiii-xiv

23   Schaef, A. W. (1987) When Society Becomes an Addict, San Francisco: Harper & Row, Publishers, p. 3

24   Bradshaw, John (1996) The Family: A New Way of Creating Solid Self-Esteem, Revised Edition, Deerfield Beach, Florida: Health Communications, Inc., p. 111

25   Bradshaw, J. (1996) Ibid., p. 90

26   Bradshaw, J. (1996) Ibid., p. 7

*Paul Uche Nwobi*

27 Bradshaw, J. (1996) Ibid., p. 88
28 Ibid.
29 Ibid.
30 Bradshaw, J. (1996) Ibid., p. 89
31 Bradshaw, J. (1996) Ibid., p. 90
32 Ibid.
33 Ibid.
34 Satir, V. (1976) Making Contact, Millbrae, California: Celestial Arts, p. 19 quoted by John Bradshaw, The Family: A New way of Creating Solid Self-Esteem, Revised Edition, Florida: Health Communications, Inc., p. 53
35 Zaepfel, G. P. (1994) He Wins, She Wins: Turn the Battle for Control in Your Marriage into A "Win-Win" Partnership, Nashville, Tennessee: Thomas Nelson Inc. pp. 132-3
36 Ibid., p. 33
37 Bradshaw, J. (1996) Ibid., p. 245
38 Matthew 16:15 (Good News Bible, GNB)
39 Haugk, K. C. (1984) Christian Caregiving: A Way of Life, Minneapolis: Augsburg Publishing House, p. 60
40 Matthew 20:28 (GNB)
41 Haugk, K. C. (1984) Ibid., p. 71
42 Zaepfel, G. P. (1994) Ibid, p. 137
43 Bradshaw, J. (1996) Ibid., p. 250
44 Conn, W. E. (1998) Ibid, pp. 117-8
45 McBrien, R. P. (1994) Catholicism, Completely Revised and Updated, New York: Harper SanFrancisco, p. 1019
46 Conn, W. E. (1998) Ibid., p. 96
47 Erikson, E. (1964) Insight and Responsibility, p. 125 quoted in Conn, Walter E. (1998) Ibid., pp. 96-7
48 Conn, W. E. (1998) Ibid., p. 97
49 Conn, W. E. (1998) Ibid., p. 120
50 Conn, W. E. (1998) Ibid., p. 121
51 LOnergan, B. (1995) Method in Theology, p. 105 quoted in Conn, W. E. (1998) Ibid., p. 121
52 Conn, W. E. (1998) Ibid., p. 121
53 Conn, W. E. (1998) Ibid., pp. 122-3
54 Conn, W. E. (1998) Ibid., p. 123
55 Ibid.
56 Conn, W. E. (1998) Ibid, p. 126
57 Sanford, J. A. (1977) Healing and Wholeness, New York: Paulist Press, p. 16

146

58  Hiltner, S. (1966) "Toward a Theology of Conversion in the Light of Psychology," Pastoral Psychology 17, pp. 35-42, quoted in Conn, W. E. (1998) Ibid., p. 126

59  Sanford, J. A. (1977) Ibid., p. 20

60  Ibid.

61  Conn, W. E. (1998) Ibid., p. 128

62  From the Bereavement Services Seminar papers on November 16, 2006, organized by the Office of Bereavement Ministry, Brooklyn Catholic Diocese, New York, United States of America.

63  Bradshaw, J. (1996) Ibid., p. 4

64  Bradshaw, J. (1996) Ibid., p. 247

65  Ibid.

66  Hebrew 5:1 (RSV, Catholic Edition)

67  Bradshaw, J. (1996) Ibid., p. 257

68  Satir, V. (1988) The New People Making, Mountain View, California: Science and Behavior Books, Inc. p. 18

69  Matthew 20: 25-28; Mark 10: 42-45 (RSV, Catholic Edition)

70  John 13: 3-10 (RSV, Catholic Edition)

71  Philippians 2: 3-18 (RSV, Catholic Edition)

72  John 6: 15 (RSV, Catholic Edition)

73  Walters, C. J. (1983) To Serve As Jesus Served: A Guide to Servanthood, South Bend, Indiana: GreenLawn Press, p. 5; Matthew 20:28; John 10: 1-18.

74  Tillich, P. (1957) Dynamics of Faith, New York: Harper and Row, p. 1ff. quoted in Hill, Brennan et al (1997) Faith, Religion & Theology: A Contemporary Introduction, Revised and Expanded, Mystic, Connecticut: Twenty-Third Publications, p. 36

75  Henriot, P.J., DeBerri, E.P., & Schultheis, M.J. (1999) Catholic Social Teaching: Our Best Kept Secret, Century Edition, MaryKnoll, New York: Orbis Books, p. 3

76  Henriot, P. J. et al. (1999) Ibid., p. 7

77  Henriot, P. J. et al. (1999) Ibid., p. 8

78  Ibid.

79  Henriot, P. J. et al. (1999) Ibid., pp. 9-10

80  Henriot, P. J. et al. (1999) Ibid., p. 9

81  Henriot, P. J. et al. (1999) Ibid., p. 11

82  Henriot, P. J. et al. (1999) Ibid., p. 12

83  Henriot, P. J. et al. (1999) Ibid., p. 11

84  Henriot, P. J. et al. (1999) Ibid., p. 12

85  Ibid.

86  Ibid.

87  Ibid.

88 Henriot, P. J. et al. (1999) Ibid., p. 13
89 Henriot, P. J. et al. (1999) Ibid., p. 14
90 Webster's Universal College Dictionary, New York: Gramercy Books, 1997, p. 666
91 Tillich, P. (1963) Christianity and the Encounter of World Religions, New York: Columbia University Press, p. 4 quoted in Hill, B. R. et al. (1997) Faith, Religion & theology: A Contemporary Introduction, Revised and Expanded, Mystic, Connecticut: Twenty-Third Publications, pp. 162-3
92 Hill, Brennan R. et al. (1997) Faith, Religion & Theology: A Contemporary Introduction, Revised & Expanded, Mystic, Connecticut: Twenty-Third Publications, p. 163
93 Random House Webster's College Dictionary, New York: Random House, 1999, p.1262
94 Ibid.
95 John H. Mostyn, Workshop: Certificate in the Art of Spiritual Direction, Supervision Training, Program in Christian Spirituality, San Francisco Theological Seminary, San Anselmo, California., March 15-16, 1996, quoted in Lebacqz K. and Driskill J. D. (2000) Ethics and Spiritual Care: A Guide for Pastors, Chaplains, and Spiritual Directors, Nashville, Tennessee: Abingdon Press, p. 33
96 Lebacqz K. and Driskill, J. D. (2000) Ethics and Spiritual Care: A Guide for Pastors, Chaplains, and Spiritual Directors, Nashville, Tennessee: Abingdon Press, p. 33
97 Hill, Brennan R. et al. (1997) Ibid., p. 183
98 Ibid.
99 Hill, Brennan R. et al. (1997) Ibid., p. 182
100 Hill, Brennan R. et al. (1997) Ibid., p. 183
101 Hill, Brennan R. et al. (1997) Ibid., p. 185
102 Hill, Brennan R. et al. (1997) Ibid., pp. 186-7
103 Hill, Brennan R.et al. (1997) Ibid., pp. 187-8
104 Ogu, Heart, C. (2005) Oh! Weep Not My Country, Zaria, Nigeria: Dolphin Press, p. 44
105 Ibid.
106 Hill, Brennan R. et al. (1997) Ibid., p. 188
107 Ibid.

# CHAPTER FIVE: THE DIMENSIONS OF PRIESTLY IDENTITY

## Understanding the Priestly Identity

Priesthood is a vocation and a way of life. In the words of Fulton Sheen, an outstanding twentieth century theologian and eloquent preacher, "The priest is not his own." [1] For Fulton Sheen then, a priest is of Christ. He lives and works in Christ and for Christ. The priestly identity is a Christly identity. In the Sacred Scriptures we read: "For every high priest chosen from among (people) is appointed to act on behalf of (the people) in relation to God, to offer gifts and sacrifices for sins."[2] This is not to say that priesthood is simply an "instrument" of services (a dispatching machine for sacraments) without a personality and spirituality. A priest is more than what he does or preaches. There is need for a calculated caution in reading such categorical statements on the priesthood like these:

> The ministerial priesthood is a service to the people of God. Priests, entrusted with a divine ministry by their bishops, are ordained to fulfill the work of Christ on behalf of his members. This consists in preaching the Gospel (LG #28 and PO #4), shepherding the faithful, and celebrating divine worship. Acting on behalf of Christ, priests proclaim his mystery, unite the prayers and sacrifices of the faithful to Christ, their head, and in the Mass renew the unique sacrifice of the New Testament, making it present to the Church gathered.[3]

The above extract contains a profound teaching of the Catholic Church on the priesthood. Yet it has to be read and understood in a particular context it implied. It is true that "the ministerial priesthood is a service to the people of God" as stated above. But the ministerial priesthood is more than "a service." The priesthood is even more than the four parts of the priesthood of Christ we discussed in chapter One of this project: the priesthood as a vocation, as a sacrament, as an institution, and as a ministry. The ministerial priesthood is essentially a life of Christ, the presence of Christ, which includes all these four aspects and more.

The priestly ordination then, is a fundamental new beginning for the ordained in the life Christ. It is a new way of life which the ordained has never known before but needs now to be received and accepted wholeheartedly, lived and witnessed in life and ministry. It is a forming and transforming a priestly identity in the person of the priest. This formation process is more than a classroom education. It takes both structured and unstructured education processes: teaching, training and learning interventions at all depths and degrees of life and ministry in Jesus Christ and among the people of God.

The three processes of formation we highlighted above: the educational/academic formation, the human formation and the spiritual formation, are to be brought to a functional unity in the reflected life experiences, relationships and ministry in the person of a priest in Jesus Christ. It is more than once-in-a-while seminars or conferences or further studies. The formation needed now involves all these and more in their proper intervals and sequence. The "more" is on the critical issue of integration and a well-structured supervision in all the way round process. The kind of a priestly identity formation being proposed here is not something completely new to the Catholic priesthood. The priestly identity formation has been happening but may be, not in a structured, supervised process being proposed here.

### *The Principles of Priestly Identity*

Priestly formation is a process. Priestly formation is a process of forming a priestly identity. A priestly identity is a basic lifestyle of a priestly life and ministry. A priestly identity is an immediate goal of a formation process. The final goal of a formation process is wholeness and holiness of life. Formation is more than being knowledgeable. To "form" is not simply to "know." To form is more than to know. One may know everything about priesthood (if that is possible) and still have some serious issues with his priestly identity formation. Knowledge is a part of a priestly identity but it is not simply knowledge. Discipline is a part of a priestly identity but it is not simply a discipline. For a purpose of an illustration, let's look at the work of a potter who molds a portion of clay into a pot. The clay must be mellowed down into an indefinite form and then to be molded into a definite form, in this case, a pot. Priestly identity formation is like a work of a potter. What may be needed to mellow down "a portion of clay" (in this case, a seminarian) to an indefinite form may include education, Knowledge, instruction, discipline, etc. Yet, these items in themselves do not constitute the whole priestly formation. As I stated above, priestly formation is a process. One may have all the academic degrees and certificates and still have some issues with his priestly identity formation. Priestly identity formation is a process to follow through and to grow in what David Toups described as a "priestly character." The priestly ordination definitely is the essence and foundation of a priestly identity, yet it does not guarantee a priestly identity formation or an exercise of a priestly identity in his daily life and ministry. To follow through and grow in the priestly identity formation process, one must follow through and grow in its principles. What are the principles of a priestly identity?

The principles of a priestly identity are the make-ups of a priestly personality. David L. Toups in his book: *Reclaiming Our Priestly Character* (2008) claims that there are at least six key principles of a priestly identity which are evident in the teachings of the Catholic Church. He names them as: 1) Permanence of the priesthood; 2) In persona Christi (in the person of Christ); 3) In persona Ecclesiae (in the person of the Church); 4) Priestly presence; 5) Avoidance of functionalism (I prefer to call it: the ministerial Identity); and 6) Ongoing Formation.[4] We are now to look into each of these six principles of a priestly identity and the roots of these principles in the priestly formation process. The principles of the priestly identity must be founded and solidly *grounded* in the priestly formation process and in the sacramental ordination.

## *The First Principle: Permanence of the Priesthood*

In the Words of the Sacred Scripture, a Catholic priest is a priest forever: "You are a priest forever."[5] This statement of transubstantiation is proclaimed and sealed at the ordination of every priest in the power and Spirit of Jesus Christ, the Eternal High Priest. Richard P. McBrien in his book: *Catholicism* (1994) describes the sacraments of Matrimony and Holy Orders as "the sacraments of vocation and commitment to (permanent) life of mutual love and service."[6] The sacrament of Holy Orders or ordination confers on every priest a permanent sacramental character of priesthood.

It is an indelible mark in the soul which sets each priest out for Christ and for His Church. The permanence principle of the priesthood is not just an indelible mark, it is also a "vocation (call) and commitment to a life of mutual love and service." [7] The challenge of an ongoing formation is more on the part of a vocation and commitment to life of mutual love and service. God's call to his priests does not stop at ordination. God calls all times. Priestly ordination, in fact, broadens and deepens God's call.

Priestly ordination establishes a priest in a permanent spousal relationship with Christ and the Church. The spousal relationship of a priest with Christ and the Church is not biological but spiritual; spousal in a sense of total self-donating relationship. Hence, a priest is addressed as a "Reverend Father," a spiritual father. The name, "Reverend Father" or "Father" is not a social title a priest receives at ordination. It is a spiritual embodiment (if you like, a spiritual marriage) that signifies a self-giving relationship and responsibility with Christ and the Church that must be formed in a priest in an ongoing process. The self-giving relationship of a priest in the Church is not just something to know about or to be studied in a classroom. It is a relational commitment and identity to be formed and nurtured over time in the formation process.

At ordination, a priest is spiritually embodied with God in a special way and with every member of the Church as a father and a brother. This spiritual embodiment of every priest is both natural and supernatural. It is both a gift and a grace, to be lived, shared and witnessed at all levels of life and ministry of a priest. Understood in this sense, marriage of priests or a married priest is a contradiction of his spiritual embodiment with God and with all the people of God. It is like a father marrying his daughter or a brother marrying his sister. On theological ground therefore, a married priest is a contradiction in principle based on an authentic understanding of the sacrament of ordination as a spiritual embodiment with God and with the people of God.

A priest is a spiritual father, not a bachelor. Stressing on the challenge of forming in priests a pastoral life in tune with the priestly celibacy, Pope John Paul II writes in *Pastores Dabo Vobis, No. 22:*

> The Church as the Spouse of Jesus Christ, wishes to be loved by the priest in the total and exclusive manner in which Jesus Christ her Head and Spouse loved her. Priestly celibacy, then, is the gift of self *in* and *with* Christ *to* his Church and expresses the priest's service to the Church and the world.

The priestly ordination establishes in each priest a permanent spousal relationship in and with Christ and the Church which must be responsibly and respectfully nurtured and strengthened in life and ministry throughout a lifespan. David Toups, the author of the book: *Reclaiming Our Priestly Character,* teaches that "the priest who has the mindset that he is in a permanent relationship with Christ and His Church will not live as a bachelor or absentee-father; rather he will commit himself wholeheartedly to his family of faith."[8] To compromise in any form or shape a total self-commitment to a wholehearted permanent relationship with Christ and His Church spells doom to the priest himself and to the whole Church. It is a danger George A. Aschenbrener describes as a "bachelor syndrome." He explains:

> First, a "bachelor" syndrome has its ways of violating celibacy. Bachelors, feeling that the challenge and the vigor of life have passed them by, usually become uninvolved spectators. In self-protection, they often radiate a superior, critical attitude and condescendingly carp at people who are seriously involved with the challenges of life. Undue concern with their own security and hypochondriacal fear for their own health are often symptoms of this bachelor syndrome. [9]

The constant awareness and commitment to the demands of a spiritual father and a spiritual brother, not as a bachelor is a necessary condition for spiritual maturity. It makes a daily demand in the life and ministry of every priest in personal availability, compassion and care, listening and selflessly loving God and His people. Stressing on the implications of a daily commitment to a life of celibacy, Pope Benedict XVI proclaims in his meeting with the clergy of the diocese of Bolzano-Bressanone in August, 2008:

> [The priest must] make [himself] available to the Lord in the fullness of [his] being and consequently [find himself] totally available to men and women. I think celibacy is a fundamental expression of this totality and already, for this reason, an important reference in this world because it only has meaning if we truly believe in eternal life and if we believe that God involves us and that we can be for him. [10]

According to Pope Benedict XVI, a daily commitment to a life of celibacy is more than a belief in eternal life, it is a living, active belief that "that God involves us and that we can be for Him" in all aspects of our life and ministries. It is the heart of our spirituality. The depth of this spirituality is more than self-control and prayers. It embraces everything and builds on all we are and in all we do or say in life and ministry. Bishop Kenneth E. Untener, describes this form of spirituality this way:

> Spirituality is more than prayer. Spirituality is a vision of reality, a world-view, a way of looking at things. It includes my way of viewing God, but also the world, others and myself. It includes my beliefs and my ideas, but also my behavior, not only toward God but the world, others and myself. Spirituality is never simply in the head. It is also my behavior. Finally, it includes my openness to transcendence, a willingness to let people, the world, God, transform me.[11]

The permanence of priesthood is not something to use but to allow everything to transform and build us up in and through the Trinity in life and ministry. That is to say, a priest is constantly formed and transformed by whose he is and is becoming by how he lives, works, serves, witnesses, celebrates, preaches and relates in life.

## *The Second Principle: In Persona Christi*

The second aspect of a priestly character is "in persona Christi" – in the person of Christ. It means that through the power of ordination, every priest lives and acts in persona Christi – in the person of Christ. In the sacrament of ordination, a priest is configured into Christ to be one in and with Him, the head of His Body, the Church. It is both a natural and supernatural relationship in which a priest is made to belong totally to God and to serve him wholeheartedly in all the people of God.

In the Words of the Holy Scripture, "No one chooses for himself the honor of being a high priest. It is only by God's call that a man is made a high priest – just as Aaron was." [12] The power to live and act "in persona Christi" is not a merit or an achievement. It is a gracious gift of God to his priests for the good of all people. Stressing on this point, Joseph Cardinal Ratzinger, now Pope Benedict XVI writes: "The character guarantees the 'validity' of the sacrament even in the case of an unworthy minister, being at the same time a judgment on him and a stimulus to live the sacrament."[13] This statement highlights some critical issues of great importance in a life and ministry of a priest. While upholding the ground for the validity of priestly ministry (ex opere operato), Ratzinger's explanation does neither excuse indulgence in evil nor compromise the need for a responsible priestly life and moral growth.

In persona Christi means more than a validity of the sacraments a priest celebrates. In persona Christi is more than "ex opere operato." Ex opere operato literally means "from the work done." This Scholastic concept teaches that the effectiveness of the sacraments depends not on the faith of the receiver or "the worthiness of the minister but because of the power of Jesus Christ who acts within and through"[14] the person of a priest. In persona Christi is not only about the action of a priest, it is more of the person of a priest. A priest is not just a "pipe" through which the grace of the sacraments is run down to the people of God but a "person" of Christ.

In persona Christi therefore, is the foundation and definition of: a) the dignity of a priest; b) the personal, pastoral and spiritual presence of a priest; and c) the witness of a priest. Roderick Strange in his book: *The Risk of Discipleship,* teaches that Christ made His teaching on the person of Christ as a person of a priest a turning-point experience for His disciples in his teaching ministry in the district of Caesarea Philippi. Roderick Strange writes:

> At a turning-point in his ministry, when Jesus had reached the district of Caesarea Philippi, he raised a question with his disciples which has become famous. He asked them, 'Who do people say that I am?' And they gave him various answers. Then he pressed them personally, 'But who do you say I am?' (Mark 8:27-9 New Revised Standard Version; Mathew 16: 13-15; Luke9: 18-19). It is a personal question for every Christian, but it has particular significance for those of us who are ordained. Whatever the reality of our lives, however inadequate we may feel we are, however far short of our own hopes we seem to ourselves to fall, the answer we give reveals at least the kind of priest we would like to be. How do we see Jesus? Who do we say that he is?[15]

The Christ's question: 'Who do you say I am?' is not an intellectual question. It is a personal, pastoral, and spiritual question. It is a definitive, formative and transformative question. The ways in which we answer the Christ's question define, form and transform us in who we are in whatever situations or circumstances and in whatever we do or say in our lives and ministries as a priest of God and as a people of God. That is to say, whoever we may be, whatever we do or say anytime, anywhere, we are answering the Jesus' question: "who do you say I am?"

### *The Third Principle: In Persona Ecclesiae*

The third aspect of a priestly identity is "in persona ecclesiae" – in the person of the Church. No one is a priest for himself. A priest is ordained for the people – for the service of the people. The Sacred Scripture puts it this way: "Every high priest is chosen from his fellow-men (and women) and appointed to serve God on their behalf, to offer sacrifices and offering for sins."[16] Every priest lives and acts in persona Ecclesiae et in nomine Ecclesiae – in the person of the Church and in the name of the Church.

In the person of the Church, a priest is a spiritual ambassador, a spiritual leader of the Church. As a spiritual ambassador, a priest is "appointed to serve God" on behalf of all the people and "to offer sacrifices and offering for sin."[17] A priest is in the world but not of the world. He must be deeply in touch with the people he serves. He is with the people he serves in their sufferings, in their pains, in their difficulties, in their wounds, in their sins and in everything of their lives, otherwise, he will have nothing to offer to God on their behalf. Every priest must acquire and maintain a consistent growth in different competencies and skills of *being with* the people without taking over or being swallowed up, in his seminary formation and ongoing priestly formation through his life and ministry. It is a mission of discovering and fostering each other's gifts of God for the service of all. The mission of a spiritual ambassador shows itself in many ways of life and ministry of a priest: in spiritual generativity (helping people to discover [to give birth to] their own giftedness in grace and holiness); in leadership and good example in all aspects of life; and in community building, peacemaking and social justice. Speaking on some challenges a priest faces in this regard, Fulton Sheen writes:

> The priest is pledged to celibacy not because of human generation is wrong, but because it must be yield so that he can devote himself wholly to a higher form of generation: the begetting of children in Christ by bringing to Him those who never knew Him, by restoring to Him those lost in sin, and by arousing in those who already love Christ the inspiration to serve Him more fully as religious or priests. The energy that otherwise would be used for the service of the flesh is not buried in a napkin. It is transformed so that it serves chaste generation in the Spirit.[18]

The challenge of an ongoing self transformation in life and in deeds is very crucial. At the heart of this self transformative process is a living, active spirit of connectivity and relativity: The connectivity and relativity of a priest with other priests; a priest with his bishop/s; a priest with the professed or vowed men and women; a priest with the lay faithful. The connectivity and relativity between a priest and other priests or a priest and the vowed men and women is marked with a spirit of oneness in proclaiming the Gospel of Christ and extending His healing mission in mutual trust and support, dialogue, humility, simplicity, solidarity and collaboration. The connectivity and relativity between a priest and his bishop/s or bishop's conference is marked with respectful obedience, mutual trust and support, genuine collegiality, sincere collaboration and spiritual communion. The connectivity and relativity between a priest and the lay faithful is marked with mutual trust and support, collaborative spirit, loving care, compassion and spiritual communion. Stressing on some of the key characteristics of the relationship between a bishop and his priests, Pope John Paul II stated in one his addresses in 2004:

> Together with fostering mutual trust and confidence, dialogue, a spirit of unity and a common missionary spirit in his relationship with his priests, the bishop is also responsible for cultivating within the presbyterate a sense of *coresponsibility for the governance of the local Church.* [19]

The point being stressed here by the Pope is that the coresponsibility for the governance of the local Church derives its energy (spirit) and effectiveness (moral strength) from a coresponsibility in cultivating and "fostering mutual trust and confidence, dialogue, a spirit of unity and a common missionary spirit" among priests and bishops. Christopher Ruddy, in his book: *Tested in Every Way: The Catholic Priesthood in Today's Church* (2006), points out some character traits which may get on the way in cultivating and fostering this formative relationship among priests and their bishop/s as: "miter envy and miter ambition," inequality, favoritism, loneliness, isolation and vulnerability.[20] For Ruddy, vulnerability is not a part of the problem as it is a part of the solution. He understands vulnerability to mean "that willingness to subject (oneself) to criticism and even embarrassment (which) transforms one's life and ministry, bearing its ultimate fruit in a saintly response to" [21] life challenges and problems as opportunities for effective witnesses to the Gospel of Jesus Christ. Without a self-integrated sense of vulnerability, a feeling of loneliness and isolation generated from "being an outsider" (a loner) in one's diocese or among one's own people or community may become a real danger.

In the name of the Church, every priest is a voice of the people. A priest is both a prophetic voice of the people and a supplicatory voice of the people. With the prophetic voice, a priest proclaims the Good News as the liberating truth in the lives and conditions of the people of God. The prophetic voice of a priest proclaims the Gospel truth that does justice for all the people. A priest does not only proclaim the Gospel truth that does justice to all, he lives and witnesses it in his person and in his actions in life. The supplicatory voice of a priest defines his role as an advocate of the people of God - one who prays (the liturgy of the hours) and advocates for the people in their life journeys. These are not just roles or duties a priest should perform. They are indeed a life to live and witness in all aspects of his life and ministry. What a priest is and does forms and transforms him and others in the community.

## Priest and the Blessed Virgin Mary

A discussion on the priestly identity in relation to the Church of God will seem incomplete without a word or two on the Mother of the Church, the Blessed Virgin Mary. On the Cross, Jesus handed over the Blessed Virgin Mary to John the apostle, who stood as the representative of all priests in the Catholic world. Every priest, then, has two mothers: one's physical mother through physical birth and a spiritual mother, the Blessed Virgin Mary, through spiritual adoption in Jesus Christ. The fact of having a double mother –relationship is not as significant as the moral and spiritual implications of it.

In the first place, like Mary who was chosen among women (Luke 1:42), every priest is chosen from "among men and made their representative before God, to offer gifts and sacrifices for sin" (Hebrew 5:1). It is a humble choice, not a privileged or prestigious choice. This humble choice of God calls all priests to a humble life and a humble service to all. Like Mary's visitation in which Elizabeth was "filled with the Holy Spirit (Luke 1: 41), a priest's visitation is a moment of grace and healing service in the Holy Spirit. It is then, a call to a humbleness and holiness of life and services in Jesus Christ.

At the marriage at Cana in Galilee, Mary teaches all priests a virtue of a total surrendering obedience to the gracious will of God in all things in her last statement in the Sacred Scriptures: "Do whatever He tells you" (John 2: 5). At the presentation and the founding of Jesus in the temple, Mary teaches all priests the virtues of total detachment and persistent commitment in following Jesus Christ in life, relationships and leaderships at all times. In standing with Christ in His passion and suffering on the Cross, Mary teaches all priests a lifelong compassionate standing with the poor and the suffering ones in the world in solidarity with Jesus Christ, our Lord and Savior, who "did not come to be served but to serve and to give his life as a ransom for many" (Mark 10: 45). In these and many other ways, the Virgin Mary, the Mother of God, the Mother of the Church is not just a spiritual mother to all priests, the religious men and women as well as the other Christian faithful, she is also, a spiritual model and teacher on humility, total detachment, faithful commitment, selfless service and compassion to all in Jesus Christ.

### The Fourth Principle: Priestly Presence

Priestly presence can be seen, experienced and witnessed in different ways. Priestly presence may be evident in the person of a priest, in his words, his actions or behaviors, his relationships, his postures, his attitude and his dresses. Any of these factors may promote or belittle a priestly presence. Priestly presence is not one thing. It is everything about being a priest of Christ and a priest of the people of God: living as a priest, working and walking as a priest, relating as a priest, speaking as a priest, dressing as a priest, behaving as a priest, laughing and joking as a priest, eating and drinking as a priest, praying and playing as a priest, reading and writing as a priest, worshipping and adoring as a priest and so on. In an effort to provide a broad context for an understanding of a diverse meaning of a priestly presence, Roderick Strange writes in his book, *The Risk of Discipleship*:

> Those ordained to ministerial priesthood may be expected to be living signs of Christ's presence, as we have noticed, and that may seem very exalted; nevertheless, in the first place this vocation is a human calling. That point is fundamental. We have to be well-rounded human beings. It stands to reason. If we are to be signs of Christ's presence, of the Word made flesh, of the divine in the human, what is the condition of that humanity in which the divine is to make its home? If grace is to build on nature and so bear fruit, that nature needs to be in good repair.[22]

In this passage, Roderick Strange points out that a priest is expected to be not only the living signs of Christ's presence but more fundamentally living evidences of a human vocation in Christ – a "well-rounded human being", "of the Word made flesh;" "of the divine in the human." It is more than both holiness in healthiness and healthiness in holiness in all levels of priestly life and ministry.

Fulton Sheen, on his part, employs different images to illustrate some aspects of priestly presence. In his book, *The Priest is Not His Own,* Fulton Sheen claims that it is "more than a priest." In reference to incarnation, Sheen writes:

> Our Lord came to die. The rest of us come to live. But his death was not final. He never spoke of being our sin oblation without speaking of His glory. His Resurrection and Ascension and His glorification at the right hand of the Father were the fruits of His voluntary offering as a priest.[23]

For Sheen, "the consequences for all priests are tremendous, for if He (Jesus) did offer Himself for sins, then we must offer ourselves as victims. The conclusion is inescapable."[24] It follows then that a priestly presence is not just a victim's presence, it is also a redemptive presence, a resurrected presence, and a glorified presence. There is both relativity and connectivity involved in the process. A priestly presence does not only relate everyone to Christ's event (His suffering, death and resurrection) but it also connects all to Christ's glorification at the right hand of God. Fulton Sheen then speaks of a priest as a symbolic "cross suspended between earth and heaven:"

> We find a symbolic representation of the union of the Priest and Victim in the very position of the Cross, suspended between earth and heaven as if Jesus were rejected by (people) and abandoned by the Father. Yet He united God and man (people) in Himself through obedience to the Father's Will and through a love for (the people) so great that He would not abandon (them) in (their) sin. To His brethren He revealed the heart of a father; to His Father he revealed the heart of every son (and daughter). Our Lord, therefore, is always priest and victim. No priest was worthy of priesthood save Himself. Christ, moreover, was a victim not only in His Body, but in His soul, which was sad unto death. No external or internal sacrifice could be more united.[25]

Priestly presence is more than who a priest is (his person, relationships, capabilities, skills, acquaintances, education, spirituality, etc), or what a priest does (his ministries: celebration of sacraments, preaching, shepherding, teaching, healing, leadership). There is more to a priestly presence in terms of victim or sacrificial presence, redemptive presence, glorified presence, theological presence and spiritual presence. Every priest points beyond himself (his person) to Christ, the redemptive and glorified Christ. Every priest points beyond his place (or position) to Christ's kingdom, the kingdom of God where all people will be all-in-all in God.

### *The Fifth Principle: the Personal Identity*

If we go by a dictionary meaning of the word, identity as "the state or fact of remaining the same one, as under varying aspects or conditions" or as "the condition of being oneself or itself, and not another;" [26] how does the word, identity apply to a priest who is transubstantiated at ordination and who, according to Fulton Sheen, "is not his own." [27] Fulton Sheen sees no contradiction in speaking of a personal identity of a priest in this scenario. For Fulton Sheen, in terms of a personal identity, a priest is "Simon and Peter" – a person of two natures. Fulton Sheen explains:

> Like Peter, every priest has two "natures": a human nature, which makes him another man, and a priestly nature, which makes him another Christ. The Epistle to the Hebrews identifies these two aspects. The priest is different from ordinary men as the one who offers sacrifice in their name. "The purpose for which any high priest is chosen from among his fellow men, and made a representative of men in their dealings with God, is to offer gifts and sacrifices in expiation of their sins." Hebrews 5:1 Nevertheless, the priest is like every man in his weakness. "He is qualified for this by being able to feel for them when they are ignorant and make mistakes, since he, too, is all beset with humiliations, and, for that reason, must needs to present sin-offering for himself, just as he does for the people." Hebrews 5: 2-4 [28]

The two natures of a priest are not to be two masters. The seminary formation and the ongoing priestly formation are meant to form in every priest one master, the Christ, out of the two natures. Formation is not just a work of knowledge alone, knowing more (possessing more degrees or more certificates). Formation is a tripartite work: of the individual person, of the community and of the Holy Spirit – a work of renewal of the heart and mind of a priest. Knowledge is a part of the formation, not the whole of it. Fulton Sheen calls this transformative encounter a turning-point experience in a spiritual life journey of the priesthood. He writes, illustrating with Peter's life:

> The turning point in the spiritual life of a priest is not only his vocation, his calling. It is also that moment when he becomes obedience to the Spirit. This is a kind of second ordination, a

crisis that carries him from being a priest merely by office into the possession and manifestation of the Spirit of Christ. Before Peter possessed the Spirit of Christ, the tug-of-war between his earthly and his heavenly nature was revealed at Caesarea Philippi when he confessed the divine Christ but denied the suffering Christ. The Father has illumined his mind to recognize and proclaim, "Thou art the Christ, the Son of the living God" (Mt 16: 16). But when Our Lord announced that He would be crucified, Peter, drawing Him to his side, "began remonstrating with Him; Never, Lord, he said, no such thing shall befall Thee" (Mt 16: 22). ... Peter was willing to confess Christ the Priest, but not Christ the Victim. Men called to be rocks can become stones of stumbling. ... Our Lord did not take away Peter's vocation. He contented Himself with warning him that the flesh was with him and that in a moment of overconfidence he would fall. Peter is thus set forth by Our Blessed Lord as a constant reminder that it is in their strongest qualities, unless they are periodically renewed by divine grace, that men are most liable to fail. [29]

For Sheen then, without being "periodically renewed by divine grace" our strongest qualities may become our greatest weakness. There is a need for an ongoing experience of a "second ordination" in every priest by becoming moment by moment "obedience (listening) to the Spirit of Christ," otherwise one is hooked up in "the tug-of-war (crisis) between his earthly nature and his heavenly nature." Like Peter, such priests are called to abandon a lifestyle that denies a part of Christ, the Victim Christ in favor of the Priest Christ. Today, there is no Christ without the Cross. But there may be crosses without Christ. So, be careful! For Jesus Christ, the Cross is not a symbol of death and defeat. It is a symbol of life and victory. Christ's mandate is: "Whoever wants to be my disciple must renounce himself and take up his cross everyday and follow after me." [30] A life without the Cross is a life without Christ. It shows. For Fulton Sheen, a lifestyle of a Crossless-Christ priest shows in some of these ways: a) A *compromising* priest who maintains his two natures as two masters and tries to serve both of them. b) A *self-righteous* priest who neglects a need for ongoing conversion in desperation for what to get and what to gain in the outer world. c) A *fallen* priest who is on different paths of spiritual decline and decay. According to Fulton Sheen, an ongoing spiritual decay begins with: i.) *a neglect of prayer,* whereby one feels too weak or lazy to pray. ii.) *substitution of action for prayer,* in this case one feels too busy to replace prayers with actions or activities. To use the words of Pope Pius XII, such priests are guilt of a "heresy of action." iii.) *a neglect of mortification and meditation,* this is a situation whereby one is lukewarm because of lack of a fire or depth of the Holy Spirit in reflective meditation and moderation. The inevitable outcome is that "men called to be rocks are becoming stones of stumbling."[31] Without a commitment to a consistent and ongoing renewal in the Spirit of Christ, a life of compromise is inevitable. The need for an ongoing renewal in the Spirit of Christ is a challenge to every priest or bishop. No priest or bishop is too old or too young, too good or too bad for an ongoing renewal in life. Any form of neglect spells doom and disaster in all aspects of life and ministry. Fulton Sheen summarizes it this way:

> Every bad priest is close to being a good one; every good priest is in danger of being a bad one. The line between sanctity and sin is a fine one. It is easy to cross, and the one who crosses can quickly gain momentum in either direction. Saint Thomas Aquinas said that everything increases its motion as it nears its proper place or home. Saints grow rapidly in charity; wicked men/women rot quickly. We can see the truth of the point if we compare Peter and Judas. There seemed to be little difference in them for a long time, and then suddenly there was all the difference between being a saint and being a devil.[32]

You either "take up the Cross and follow Christ" or you step on the cross to cross over, "and the one who crosses can quickly gain momentum in either direction." It makes all the difference.

### *The Sixth Principle: Ongoing Formation (Priestly Formation)*

An ongoing formation is not Further Studies. An ongoing formation is not ongoing studies. Formation may imply studies but it is more than studies. To study is to acquire or apprehend knowledge with the mind. To form, on the other hand, is to mold or shape (reshape) the whole person, not just the mind. Ongoing formation, in this context, is an ongoing awareness, commitment and renewal in different aspects of the priestly identity. That is to say, it is an ongoing awareness, commitment and renewal in the permanence of the priesthood, in the person of Christ of the priesthood, in the person of the Church of the priesthood, in the priestly presence of the priesthood, in the personal identity of the priesthood and in the ongoing formation of the priesthood.

The key issue here is not just about knowledge but about ongoing awareness, commitment and renewal in one's priestly identity. Personal skills are fundamental. The danger here is a tendency to ignore or presume a growth in personal skills in our journey through life. Emphasizing on the damage of such a presumptuous way of life in today's society, Ralph S. Hambrick writes in his book: *The Management Skills Builder* (1991):

> Professional and administrative education seems to focus on content to the exclusion of some of the skills essential to effective performance in the workplace. Not all of these skills are always ignored, but many professional-training programs assume that the skills are unimportant, already mastered, or will be acquired on the job. Many professionals, consequently, limp through their careers, missing some of the abilities that make the difference between success, mediocrity, and failure. Further, even if they are adequately addressed in educational programs, they, like other skills and other areas of knowledge, require continual maintenance, development, and updating. A skill is not mastered once and maintained at a high level with no attention.[33]

The most neglected and often ignored skills in workplace, according to Ralph Hambrick, are what he called the seven "generic skills:" "*Writing* – a critical and often neglected skill; *Public Speaking* – a needlessly feared activity; *Interviewing* – a skill for all professionals; *Relating* – for performance and satisfaction; *Computing* – the contemporary multipurpose tool; *Researching* – putting modern technology to work; and *learning* – making skill development a lifelong habit."[34] It is not an issue of an unrecognized need for these basic skills, but rather the process of acquiring them is ignored or rationalized in real life situations. Ralph Hambrick expresses this scenario this way:

> The tendency to ignore these basic skills is commonplace. They may seem so fundamental that no attention is given to them or no special effort is made to improve them. Writing, after all, is something we have been taught since kindergarten. "If we don't know it now, we will never" may be the prevalent attitude. Public speaking is something, it seems, we must do every now and then, although, usually, if we play our cards right, we can get out of it. So no reason to really worry about that. Interviewing? That's just talking to people. We certainly know how to talk to people. Working with other people is just a normal part of life. We don't think there is much to learn there. May be we should learn

something about computers, but why rush? We might as well wait until they become cheaper and easier to use. Information search is something that researchers do, not us. The human mind has an extraordinary capacity to ignore what seem to be unpleasant tasks.[35]

The point to keep in mind here is that whatever is achieved humanly is achieved partially, not completely. Nothing is achieved completely under the sun. There is always a room for further improvement. Therefore, "the inability to totally master a skill area means there is continuing opportunity for growth. Without it, we would regress (into crisis). The potential for continuing growth in each skill is a reason it can maintain our interest." [36] The task of keeping this "interest" alive and active is a lifelong challenge. It is a task of developing learning as a "total life-style perspective." A "total life-style perspective" means that "rather than simply thinking of learning, including skills development, as something that occurs as part of our professional lives, think of them as part of our total life-style."[37]

The task of learning as a "total lifestyle perspective" invites us daily to move beyond a lifestyle of structured crisis on its three levels: 1) An updated seminary education process that is more than a school education, but more so a priestly formation (the educational agenda); 2) An ongoing human formation that is more than a professional training to be more of an ongoing awareness and commitment to potentials for growths in skills development, self autonomy and social justice (the human development agenda); And 3) an ongoing spiritual formation that is more than a series of spiritual exercises to an ongoing awareness, commitment and renewal in the Spirit of Christ and in the principles of priestly identity(the spiritual growth agenda).

### *Unique Challenge to Priestly Identity Formation in African Church Today*

The formation of priestly identity in African Church faces a unique challenge today due to a unique cultural upheaval of the 1960s, as different from that of the rest of the Western Catholic Church. To the Western and European Catholic world, the 1960s was a period of cultural upheaval in defining the Church's doctrines, their interpretations and applications. To the Catholic Church in Africa, it was a different kind of cultural upheaval in a struggle for survival as a people, as a Church and as nations in Africa.

The peculiar problem facing the African Church and the African priesthood today is an issue I would like to describe in the words of Lawrence Lucas as the *"Black Priest White Church" syndrome*. I call it a "Black Priest White Church" syndrome because there is a mish-mash of confusion and cultural conflicts of meaning with identity crisis and poverty playing into each other and reinforcing each other.

In the first place, there is a "White Church" syndrome in African Church due to some limited cultural awareness and poor leadership in the Church. Stressing on the paramount need for cultural awareness and leadership in the Church, Aylward Shorter writes in his book, *Celibacy and African Culture* (1998):

> In his post-synodal exhortation after the 1974 Synod of Bishops on Evangelization, Pope Paul VI called for "a full evangelization of culture," and he went on to say that this should not be done "in a purely decorative way as it were by applying a thin veneer, but in a vital way, in depth and right to the very roots."(*Evangelii Nuntiandi, no. 20)* This evangelization was not to be a merely verbal or semantic process, but one that was truly "anthropological and cultural" (*Evangelii Nuntiandi, no. 63).*
>
> Pope John Paul II went further in 1982. According to him, "A faith which does not become culture is a faith which has not been fully received, not thoroughly thought through, not fully lived out" (*L'Osservatore Romano, 28 June 1982, pp. 1-8).* Inculturation is therefore an essential aspect of evangelization. It is the process by which a faith becomes culture. It is the presentation and re-expression of the Gospel in forms and terms proper to a culture – processes which result in the reinterpretation of both, without being unfaithful to either. Inculturation is a creative development of faith, a new creation, resulting from the dynamic interaction of cultures. This interaction is a historical process, an essential aspect of mission, which – ideally – should have nothing to do with cultural domination, alienation or manipulation. The Gospel challenges cultures, but cultures relive the Gospel. [38]

Pope Paul VI in Evangelii Nuntiandi of 1974 called for "a full evangelization of cultures" which would follow a double process: the "anthropological and cultural process." For Pope Paul VI then, "a full evangelization of cultures would mean, first of all, a full evangelization of the people and secondly, a full evangelization of their cultures. For the African, in most cases, a full evangelization of the people was taken to mean an expansion of the Church – creating more parishes and building more Church houses. The evangelization of the people was simply recruiting or registering more people and building more Church houses.

On the issue of a full evangelization of the people's cultures, the African responded with an "inculturation" process, which in many ways is an intellectual or classroom project rather than a pastoral project. The inculturation is more of some intellectual debates among theologians and some liturgical translations among liturgists at certain levels in the African Christian communities. The Christian faith and the African culture are in some cases on a parallel relationship with each other. There are serious challenges on the road to an inculturated Christian faith in African society today. Part of the challenges is a need for an enabling environment for faith to become culture in Africa Church which has much to do with an open and respectful dialogue between faith and culture at all levels of the Christian life and witness in African states. A situation of the "White Church" and the "Black Priest" is not just a contradiction, it is a problem. It is a big problem for the formation of priestly identity because every priest is both a "persona Christi" – a person of Christ and a "persona ecclesiae" – a person of the Church. What affects the nature of the Church affects the nature of the priestly identity in a very profound way. It is not possible to separate the priesthood from Jesus Christ and the Church, His Body.

About two decades after Pope Paul VI's clarion call for a full evangelization of peoples and cultures, Pope John Paul II repeated the call, stressing that "a faith which does not become culture is a faith which has not been fully received, not thoroughly thought through, not fully lived out." That is to say, that inculturation is not just something to think/debate about or some liturgical translations into some local languages. Rather the African Christian faith, first of all, must be fully received in African cultures. Secondly, the faith must be thoroughly thought through in African cultures. And thirdly, the faith must be fully lived out in all African cultures. This is more than some intellectual debates and/or liturgical translations. The answer is not a Church with big numbers of people, with big number of parishes and Church houses. A Church with big numbers is good but not enough. The priests and the lay faithful of Africa are to experience inculturation as a process by which Christ's life becomes African life, the Christian "faith becomes culture," and the Gospel presented and re-interpreted "in forms and terms proper" to African culture. Without a true inculturation process whereby "the Gospel challenges cultures, and cultures relive the Gospel," evangelization may turn out to be another form of "cultural domination, alienation or manipulation" [39] - a new cultural colonization in African Church. There is another challenge here. It is the encroaching "global pseudo-culture" that is eroding the "religious and moral values" in the 21st century's African Church community. Aylward Shorter defines the challenge this way:

> Unfortunately, just as the African Church is beginning to realize the importance of dialogue with indigenous cultures, a global pseudo-culture is undermining their religious and moral values. Globalization exalts the economic factor as the only source of meaning and value. It teaches a neo-liberal doctrine of economic self-interest, in which the "free-market" is wrongly assumed to be objective and fair. Africa countries are exhorted to surrender to impersonal "market forces." Globalization is essentially secular, banishing religion from public life and ultimately from human consciousness. Religious and moral values are subordinated to consumer materialism. Through the power of mass media communications, globalization leads to the homogenizing of local ethnic cultures and to the domination of Africa by the first world.[40]

The confused inculturation process in African Church is complicated more by the undermining forces of "a global pseudo-culture" which is eroding the religious and moral values with its "consumer materialism." In October 2009, Pope Benedict XVI in the opening Mass of the Synod of Bishops for Africa at the Vatican, with the theme: "The Church in Africa at the Service of Reconciliation, Justice and Peace," alluded to this encroaching evil, stating that the "First World has exported … and continues to export its spiritual toxic waste, contaminating the people of Africa." [41] The Pope describes the encroaching evil as a double virus attack on African people and their values. The first virus, according to Pope Benedict XVI is "practical materialism combined with moral relativism." The second virus attack is a "religious fundamentalism, particularly when religion is used to promote particular political or economic interests." [42] The virus of religious fundamentalism is feeding some ethnic rivalries in African communities with a tendency towards inter-ethnic –religious wars. If it goes unchecked, the worst ethnic and religious crisis or wars will ensure in many African countries in recent times.

The African Church and her priesthood are under some murky water of confusion deriving from the viruses of "practical materialism," "moral relativism" and "religious fundamentalism." Practical materialism is a philosophy or a belief that money and what money can buy are ends in themselves. It is a kind of "religion" that believes that the things we earn and own are gods to be worshipped and adored by all. Sometimes, some economic systems like banking are used to promote some religious interests or beliefs that are inimical to peace and justice to all. Whichever way practical materialism is allowed to thrive, it hurts the common good, peace, justice and the values of life in general.

Moral relativism, on the other hand is a belief that nothing has value in life or has value in itself. Everything is valueless including spiritual, religious and moral values. Every value is relative to the user. The value of everything is in its usefulness to the individual. The individuals become the measure of the values in life, not God. It is a loss of meaning in everything. On the other hand, we have the religious fundamentalism or religious fanaticism, which is simply a blatant abuse of religion as a way to manipulate corruption and violent attacks on innocent people.

The point to note here is that the African people are negating what they need for what they do not need. Highlighting this point, Kenneth Kaunda, the former president of Zambia writes:

> To a certain extent, we in Africa have always had a gift for enjoying Man for himself. It is at the heart of our traditional culture, but now we see the possibility of extending the scale of our discovery by example to the whole world. Let the West have its Technology and Asia its Mysticism! Africa's gift to world culture must be in the realm of human relationships. The Colonialists may talk condescendingly about the things they have taught us, yet I honestly believe that we have been all the time much nearer to the heart of things that really matter than our Western teachers. After all, don't the scientists tell us that Africa was the cradle of Man? The way things are going, Africa may be the last place where Man can still be man. ... I believe that the Universe is basically good and that throughout its great forces are at work striving to bring about a greater unity of all living things. It is through cooperation with these forces that Man will achieve all of which he is capable. [43]

The African gift to world culture is the "communal humanism" - the Communion of all people as different from the Western Capitalism and the Eastern Communism. Pope Pius XI in 1931 in his encyclical teaching, *Quadragesimo Anno (The Reconstruction of the Social Order)* warned us of the danger of a world built principally on the principles of Capitalism with its "unregulated competition" and of a world built essentially on the principles of Communism with its "promotion of class struggle" and its limited leadership of a few people. [44] Pope Benedict XVI in his opening Mass of the Synod of Bishops for Africa in October 4, 2009 describes the African communal humanism – the Communion of all people as "the world's spiritual lung," pointing out that it will "inspire renewed solidarity with our African brothers and sisters" and with the whole world. [45]

An openly honest and respectful dialogue will lead the way in this new way of being a "communion of all people" in today's world of extreme individualism, materialism and terrorism. The African people must lead in this process of heart-to-heart dialogue between cultures and among the peoples. Aylward Shorter cautions that the much needed dialogue is not yet a reality in many African communities:

> In practice, however, no explicit dialogue between faith and indigenous culture had taken place before the mid-1970s. Euro-American culture was entrenched in the language and forms of universal communion, leading to a feeling of alienation among many Catholics. Africans worshipped with a liturgy that was not theirs. They were ruled by an alien Canon Law, and they reflected on their faith, using theological systems that have been developed elsewhere. We now realize more and more clearly that the Church must be a communion of cultures. [46]

The Africans may not lead until they themselves become a communion of cultures that is at the same time a communion of all peoples. It is a commitment to a better formation or a greater frustration. There are at least two mapped out approaches: the practical approach and the process approach, which will launch us onto the path of a better formation, a better formative community in the Catholic Church.

The process approach, as discussed earlier in this work, is for the Catholic Church and its leaders to structure a total-lifestyle-perspective of learning process on the three levels of priests/peoples' lives and leaderships: 1) An Educational process that is more than a school education with emphasis on priestly identity formation (see chapters two and five). 2)

An ongoing human formation that is more than a professional training with emphasis on human identity formation (see chapter three). And 3) an ongoing spiritual formation that is more than spiritual exercises with emphasis on a continuous conversion and renewal in the paschal mystery of the Trinitarian God, as well as in establishing God's kingdom of love, peace and justice. (see chapters 4 and 6). What is the most emphasized issue is critical, because, what is emphasized gets most of the attention and defines the vision and focus. It is very important to be clear on what is the most emphasized issue and why?

On a practical approach to the issue of the structures of crisis in the Church and priesthood today, I base my response on the November 2000 brilliant, pastoral paper, "Facing the Crisis in the Priesthood" by a great modern theologian and scholar, Donald Cozzens. To put the whole situation of crisis in the Church in context for us, Cozzens writes:

> The ambivalence of the last decades of the 20th century and the first unsteady days of our new era have created their own crisis in the Church, destabilizing the equilibrium of large numbers of priests and bishops. Priests in particular have wrestled with their new and emerging identities as servant-leaders, with the suspicion that their very integrity was at stake and with the dawning awareness that their celibate lifestyle were fraught with dangers they dare not admit, let alone confront. While the crisis is multifaceted, it is undeniably a crisis of nerve. It comes down to this: Do our bishops and priests, our laity and religious leaders, have the will and courage to address this crisis candidly and confidently – inspired, not by the fear and suspicion that characterized the greater part of Pius IX's papacy, but by the openness and trust that marked the papacy of John XXIII? The answer to the question will define the issues and shape the structures of the Church in the 21st century. [47]

Donald Cozzens in a way is saying that "the ambivalence of the last decades of the 20th century" has left us with a destabilizing crisis that calls for a personal response from priests and the lay faithful of the Church of the 21st century. This crisis, we must note, is "multifaceted." The crisis in the Catholic priesthood of today is not simply a problem of few priests in the Catholic Church. It is indeed the crisis of the entire Catholic Church, the priests, the bishops, the professed or vowed men and women, and the lay faithful. Everyone has a part to play in fixing the problem of crisis in the Catholic Church of the 21st century. As wisely suggested by Donald Cozzens, it must begin with asking ourselves serious questions by speaking out with courage, listening attentively with the heart, and courageously affirming what we hear by living it out selflessly in love, peace and justice. It is simply a three-step approach, namely: "Courage to speak;" "Courage to listen;" and "Courage to affirm."[48]

## Courage to Speak

First of all, every member of the Church, the priests and the lay faithful alike must face the truth of our communal life and speak that truth with courage. Without speaking the truth with courage, we are all in bondage because "only truth will set us free," the Sacred Scripture tells us. Donald Cozzens believes that we will never begin to address and contain the present crisis in the Church if priests and the lay faithful alike lack the inner freedom, conviction and courage to speak "about their experiences and insights." This means that "they are consistently, (relentlessly ready) to speak honestly about their lives and their concerns relating to pastoral issues and to the Church itself in any but the most protected situations."[49] That is, we must have the voice to speak out about our feelings, experiences and insights. We must also courageously and honestly be the voice of the voiceless at all time and in all places. It is a constant and continuous invitation to speak the truth in love, in justice and peace to all and with all.

## Courage to Listen

Our courage to listen is primary and fundamental to our courage to speak. Without listening, we will either speak out of content or out of context or even both. In these cases, our speech may lack truth, meaning and/or purpose. Listening is more than paying attention. Listening is an art of giving attention that acknowledges and honors one's presence in acknowledging and honoring Other's presence.

Listening is an art of being a presence in Other's presence. Some forms of listening are: 1) *Personal listening*, which may focus mainly but not separately on personal issues and experiences with a personal attitude about them. Personal listening is fundamental to an art of respectful listening. If one cannot respectfully listen to oneself, it may be difficult, if not impossible to listen to others. 2) *Pastoral listening*, which may focus mainly but not exclusively on pastoral issues and experiences with a pastoral attitude about them. 3) *Communal listening*, which may focus mainly but not exclusively on communal issues and experiences with a communal attitude about them. These three forms of listening: personal, pastoral and communal listening, I would like to describe as the more positive ways of listening. In a real life situation, these forms of listening interplay into each other in a respectful conversation or dialogue. The other two less positive forms of listening are: a) *Professional listening,* is a way of listening with a superior knowledge to offer solutions to problems and answers to questions. Here, the sense of presence may be lost to the power of professionalism. b) The other form of less positive listening is *hierarchical listening.* In hierarchical listening, one listens with an authority of one's office to give an advice or correction. The truth is that everything goes wrong when we fail to listen as to learn and to live wholeheartedly with an attitude of love, truth, honesty, humility, patience, genuineness, simplicity, faithfulness, forgiveness and openness to new visions in life and in relationships.

### *Courage to Affirm*

To affirm is "to assert positively; to maintain as true." [50] The courage to affirm the truth of everything and everyone's dignity, respect, rights and responsibilities is a living truth that will set us free. It is the courage not only to know the truth but also to live and witness the kind of truth that sets all free.[51] These three practical stepping-stones to a better formative community, namely: Courage to speak the truth of our communal life, courage to listen wholeheartedly to one another, and courage to affirm the dignity, respect and rights of all, if they are lived and witnessed in all honesty, patience, humility and faithfulness will launch us onto a path of better and better formative community in the Church, otherwise, we fall back to a path of greater frustrations or more crisis.

1  Sheen, Fulton J. (1963) The Priest is not His Own, New York: McGraw Hill Book Company.

2  Hebrew 5:1 (Revised Standard Version (RSV), Catholic Edition)

3  Philibert, Paul J. (2004) Stewards of God's Mysteries: Priestly Spirituality in a Changing World, Collegeville, Minnesota: Liturgical Press, p. 25

4  Toups, David L. (2008) Reclaiming Our Priestly Character, Nebraska: Institute of Priestly Formation, pp. 133-195

5  Hebrew 5:6 (RSV, Catholic Edition)

6  McBrien, Richard P. (1994) Catholicism, Revised Edition, New York: HarperSanFrancisco, pp. 851-2

7  Ibid.

8  Toups, David L. (2008) Ibid., p.144

9  Aschenbrener, (2002) Quickening the Fire in Our Midst: The Challenge of Diocesan Priestly Spirituality, Chicago: Loyola Press, p. 124

10  Pope Benedict XVI (2009) The Priesthood: Spiritual Thoughts Series, Vaticana: Libreria Editrice, p. 12

11  Untrener, K. E. "Using the Wrong Measure" in The Spirituality of the Diocesan Priest, (1997, Minnesota: The Liturgical Press, edited by Donald B. Cozzens, p. 26

12  Hebrew 5:4  (Good News Bible)

13  Ratzinger, J. "Life and Ministry of Priests," in Priesthood: A Greater Love, 122 quoted in Reclaiming Our Priestly Character by David L. Toups (Nebraska: IPF Publications, 2008) p. 150

14  McBrien, R. P. (1994) Catholicism, Completely Revised and Updated, New York: HarperSanFrancisco, p. 1239

15  Strange, R. (2004) The Risk of Discipleship: The Catholic Priest Today, London: Darton, Longman and Todd Ltd, p.9

16  Hebrew 5:1 (Good News Bible)

17  Ibid.

18  Sheen, F. (1963) The Priest is not His Own, San Francisco: Ignatius Press, p. 60

19  Pope John Paul II's Ad Limina Address in his visit to the Bishops of Region IX in November 2004 quoted in "The Priest's Relationship to the Bishop" by John Strynkowski in Priests for the 21st Century, (New York: The Crossroad Publishing Company, 2006) edited by Donald Dietrich, p. 100

20  Ruddy, C. (2006) Tested in Every Way: The Catholic Priesthood in Today's Church, New York: The Crossroad Publishing Company, p. 79

21  Ruddy, C. (2006) Ibid., p. 83

22  Strange, R. (2004) Ibid., pp. 56-7

23  Sheen, F. (1963)Ibid., p. 15

24  Sheen, F. (1963) Ibid., p. 14

25  Sheen, F. (1963) Ibid., pp. 16-17

26  Random House Webster's College Dictionary (1999) New York: Random House Inc., p. 653

27  This is the title of Fulton Sheen 1963 book.

28  Sheen, F. (1963) Ibid., pp. 162-3

29  Sheen, F. (1963) Ibid., pp. 165-6

30  Luke 9:23 (RSV, Catholic Edition)

31  Sheen, F. (1963) Ibid., p. 166

32  Sheen, F. (1963) Ibid., p. 170

33  Hambrick, Ralph S. (1991) The Management Skills Builder: Self-Directed Learning Strategies for Career Development, New York: Praeger Publishers, p. 2

34  Hambrick, Ralph S. (1991) Ibid., p. v

35  Hambrick, Ralph S. (1991)Ibid., pp. 2-3

36  Hambrick, Ralph S. (1991) Ibid., p. 191

37  Ibid.

38  Shorter, A. (1998) Celibacy and African Culture, Nairobi (Kenya): Paulines Publications Africa, pp. 9-10

39  Shorter, A. (1998) Ibid., p. 10

40  Shorter, A. (1998) Ibid., pp. 11-12

41  The Long Island Catholic, Newspaper for the Diocese of Rockville Center, New York, October 7, 2009,  pp. 1,6.

42  Ibid.

43  Booth, N. S. "An Approach to African Religion" in African Religions: A Symposium, 1977, edited by Newell S. Booth, New York: Nok Publishers, Ltd. P. 7

44  Henriot, P. J., DeBerri, E. P. & Schultheis, M. J. (1999) Catholic Social Teaching: Our Best Kept Secret, Century Edition, New York: Orbis Books, p. 8

45  Published in Long Island Catholic, the Newspaper for the Diocese of Rockville Center, October 7, 2009,  New York: p. 6

46  Shorter, A. (1998) Ibid., p. 11

47  Cozzens, D. "Facing the Crisis in the Priesthood," November 4, 2000 in http://www.americamagazine.org/content/article.cfm?article_id=2296 December 8, 2009, p. 1

48  Cozzens. D. "Facing the Crisis in the Priesthood," Ibid., pp. 1-4

49  Cozzens, D. "Facing the Crisis in the Priesthood," Ibid, pp. 1-2

50  Webster's Universal College Dictionary (1997) New York: Random House Inc., p. 14

51  In John's Gospel, Jesus declared: "If you obey my teaching, you are really my disciples; you will know the truth, and the truth will set you free." John 8:32 (RSV, Catholic Edition)

# Chapter Six: The Structuring of a Formative Community in the Catholic Church Today

The Catholic Church is at the verge of repeating history or reshaping history of the 16th century Church in the 21st century. It is a challenge of rooting a path to new "reformation" or a path to greater "frustration," based on the response to the crisis in priesthood today. The crisis in the Church and priesthood of the 16th century called for a reformation. Martin Luther with his 517 theses he placed at "the door of the Wittenberg Cathedral in 1517," opted to champion the course of reformation in the Church. However, the Reformation process shifted from "a pastoral program to renew the local Church" to be "a religious protest against the localization of God's activity in the human and the created." [1]

The Catholic Counter-Reformation, on the other hand, as streamlined in the Council of Trent, took a defensive approach to channel all efforts in "safeguarding priestly power by emphasizing even further the indelible character which was received at ordination" and "the essential difference between the clergy and the laity."[2] It was simply a legalistic teaching on the "cultic power" of the ordained and this power "resided in the individual rather than the Church."[3] The felt-need and the opportunity to build a formative community in the 16th century Church was a loss opportunity. Another opportune moment for building up a formative community has shown itself again in this

---

[1]   Bernier, P. (1992) *Ministry in the Church: A Historical and Pastoral Approach,* Connecticut: Twenty-Third Publications, p. 151

[2]   Strange, R. (2004) *The Risk of Discipleship: The Catholic Priest Today,* London, Darton: Longman, & Todd Ltd, p.42

[3]   Ibid.

21$^{st}$ century Catholic Church with the ongoing crisis in the priesthood. Two roads are opened to the Church today: a developmental road to a "new reformation" or a destructive road to a "greater frustration" in the Church. It is a call to "reshape history" or to "repeat history." There are three operative themes here: "formation", "crisis" and "priesthood". This study makes a case that poor formation is the principal factor to the crisis in Catholic priesthood today. The chief operative principle here is "crisis." The principal root factor is "formation." And the "victim" in the whole process is the "priesthood."(The victim in this context may mean, in one way, the "victimizer" and in other way, the "victimized." The umbrella term, priesthood, implies the priesthood of Jesus Christ, the author and the foundation of priesthood, the ministerial priesthood, and the universal priesthood of the people of God. In this study, it is the ministerial priesthood that is the principal focus of interest.

## Crisis, the Operative Principle

"Crisis" is like some "smoke" that calls attention to a "burning-fire" inside the Church. In this study, we defined "crisis" as a turning-point event or experience in life. Anything can create a "turning-point event or experience in life. Crisis may appear in different forms. Whether we understand "crisis" in the words of A. W. Richard Sipe (1995) as a "sexual crisis," or in Donald B. Cozzens (2000) as a "crisis of soul," or in Alan Abernethy (2002) as a crisis of "fulfillment and frustration," or in Michael S. Rose (2002) as a crisis of liberalism or in Andrew M. Greeley (2004) as a "calling in crisis," or in Roderick Strange (2004) as "the risk of discipleship," or in the Catholic Bishops Conference of Nigeria (CBCN)(2004) as a "crisis of identity." In all, it is still some "smoke" which points beyond itself to an "inward-burning fire," that is, a poor formation process which is undermining the transformative qualities and practices of many communities in our Church and the world.

As rightly pointed out by a Sociologist, Richard Sennett in speaking of Eriksonian perspective, he said: "The essence of human (and spiritual) development is that growth occurs when old routines break down, when old parts are no longer enough for the needs of the new organism" (1970, p. 98). Crisis, then, is a substratum for great possibilities, especially for human and spiritual growth and formation. It depends on the response to the crisis. The response is a community task, not just a personal one. It is the community response that inaugurates and authenticates the personal response into a growth process. There are at least four ways a community may approach a crisis moment of its members: " to *ignore*, to *distract*, to *blame*, and to be *involved*. "[4]

## *To Ignore*

The community may choose to ignore the person in crisis, pretending that by so doing, the crisis will go away. The crisis may not go away, it rather grows worse. For instance, we have the sexual abuse crisis in the Catholic Church today because the early signs of the abuse in the 60s, 70s, 80s and 90s were ignored by some leaders in the Church community. What happened? The crisis became compounded and complicated in many ways. Today, the crisis has eaten deep into the Catholic Church worldwide. The crisis has cost the Catholic Church so much resources and personnel: About 26 bishops have resigned worldwide in connection with sexual abuse crisis, not to talk of hundreds of priests who also resigned and about two billion dollars have been spent in settling lawsuits. It follows then that when the community response to crisis is lacking in any form, the individual response is weak and feckless. To *ignore* is a poor and weak strategy in handling a crisis.

## *To Distract*

The community may decide to distract a person in crisis by sending him/her away on a study abroad or on a vacation, or just transfer the person to another area of work. Evelyn and James Whiteheads (1979) point out that this is not an act of "kindness but an act of banishment" [5] which removes the person in crisis from the much needed enabling environment for dealing effectively with the crisis. What happens is that the person in crisis loses "the network of friends" with the challenges, support and encouragement that they may provide. The person in crisis is then in a worse state than ever before. To *distract* also is a weak and ineffective strategy in dealing with crisis.

---

[4]  Whitehead, Evelyn E., and Whitehead, James D., (1979) *Christian Life Patterns: The Psychological Challenges and Religious Invitations of Adult Life,* New York: The Crossroad Publishing Company, pp. 56-58.

[5]  Whitehead, Evelyn E., and Whitehead, James D., (1979) Ibid., p.57

## *To Blame*

To blame is the third strategy a community may adopt in response to a person in crisis. In this way, the person in crisis is reproached or reprimanded for being in crisis. This is a way of finding faults with, instead of finding help for the person in crisis. It breaks down the morale and strength of both parties in the long run. To blame as a strategy for dealing with crisis serves no one any good. Blaming destroys people and blurs the road to growth and formation.

## *To Work Through With and To Be Involved*

In actual fact, the three strategies discussed above, that is, "to ignore," "to distract," and "to blame," are simply a **reaction**, not a **response** to a person in crisis. "To work through with and to be involved" is an appropriate and authentic response to a person in crisis, an important strategy that is recommended by this study. There are three steps to follow in this strategy, namely: a) Identification and recognition; b) Confrontation and challenge; and c) Support and encouragement.

In the first step, the identification and recognition, the community reaches out to identify with and to recognize the "person" and the "evil" of the individual in crisis "within the supportive bounds of the community."[6] In this way, the person in crisis does not feel isolated or banished from the network of friends that will assist him/her in dealing with the "evil" of the crisis at this critical moment. The welcoming attitude of the community to the "person" of the individual in crisis is to foster the awareness that the "person" of the individual *has* crisis, not that the individual person *is* crisis itself. This important distinction between "someone who has crisis" and "someone who is crisis" is critical to begin a necessary journey of recovery and growth process. Crisis often points back to a misstep or a neglected growth process that needs to be reclaimed. The first step of identification and recognition, in a way, re-orientates the person in crisis in a proper setting for a re-working of a neglected growth process in life.

The second step in the fourth strategy of an appropriate response to a person in crisis is to *confront and challenge*. In the first step, the community reclaims the "person" of the individual in crisis as a valued

---

6    Whitehead, Evelyn E. and Whitehead, James D., (1979) Ibid., p. 57

member of the community who has crisis. To acknowledge the "person" of the individual in crisis, is not to deny the crisis in his/her life. While the community has a duty to recognize the person of the individual in crisis, it has even greater responsibility to confront some actions of the person that are harmful to the good of the community and to challenge his/her habits/character that are inimical to the growth process in life. To confront and to challenge is not to condemn and to criticize. "To confront" is to point out some needs to be addressed in one's life, while "to condemn" is an attack on the person or the good of the person. The spirit of confrontation would then imply a deep sense of humility that everyone could be a victim of crisis any time, and a heartfelt compassion that everyone needs help in one way or another.

The third and final step in the fourth strategy of an appropriate response to a person in crisis is *to assist, support and to encourage.* It is not enough to confront a person in crisis as to point out some neglected needs for growth, it is equally important to *assist* the person in crisis to define the needs, to *support* the person to design appropriate ways and means to meet these needs, and to *encourage* him/her to follow through faithfully in genuine processes of accomplishing the targeted goals of life. It is critical to bear in mind that "to assist" is not "to take over" or "to replace" the person in crisis. Both the community and the professionals must bear this in mind, not to pretend to replace the person in crisis. Every attempt "to replace" instead of "to help" will spell doom to both parties and may block the "road" to growth and further formation.

### Formation, the Task In Crisis

There is a "ground plan" for our life (to use Erikson's term). This "ground plan" follows a formation process or a growth process which is spread out all through our lifespan, in stages. At each stage, there are two forces at work that define our personality at that particular stage in our ground plan: a) A maturity step to be taken; and b) A society-structured challenge to be accomplished. There is then, an inner pressure for maturity and a society-structured challenge for adaptability and commitment to the desired community life and responsibility. This two-way process of growth and formation is described as a moment of crisis, the fruit of which is formation or missed formation (a frustration) in a life process. Therefore, no one grows or is formed alone. We grow and are formed in a community. When there is a missed formation or a frustration, because nature abhors vacuum, nature has a way of calling us back to accomplish the unaccomplished life task at one's second stage in a life process.

The formative community may take any form: 1)the familial ones like the family, kindred; 2) the social/political ones like the society, groups, associations, organizations, political parties, government offices /agencies etc; 3) the Ecclesial ones like the Church, Parish, seminary, convent, religious institutions, formation houses; 4) the Educational ones like schools, colleges, universities and so on . A formative community is not just a group of people or a gathered people with some specializations. A formative community has both some *qualities of life* and some *practices of life* connected to it, which make all the difference.

In her book, *The Church As Learning Community*, (2002), Norma Cook Everist, points out what she considers as the three qualities of life of a formative community: a) "Gathered to learn;" b) "Challenged to grow;" and c) "Sent to serve" (P.7). First of all, a formative community must "gather to learn" about themselves, about others, about God, about the demands of mutual selfless love, truth, justice and peace to all. The community must form itself into a nurturing "community of teachers and learners," a creative "learning environment" for every member of the group to make a difference individually and collectively. Individual gifts and talents must be recognized, honored, and celebrated for the enrichment of both the individuals and the community. The spirit of mutuality, collaboration and cooperation must be cultivated, not cutthroat competition and control. Everyone in the community must be encouraged to learn to live/lead collaboratively, to live in love faithfully, and to love to learn in all honesty and humility throughout one's lifespan.

Secondly, a formative community must "challenge the members to grow" in all aspects of their life together, namely: the intellectual formation, the human or identity formation, the spiritual formation as well as the priestly/personal identity formation. All these dimensions of formation have been dealt with in some details in this study. The reader may do well to go back and read them up again for a good understanding and application in a community life.

Thirdly, a formative community must send the members to serve as Jesus served, for Jesus said: "The Son of Man did not come to be served but to serve and to give his life as a ransom for many" (Mark 10:

45). How did Jesus serve? Jesus served in humility as a servant, not as a taskmaster. He served others in needs, healing the sick, welcoming strangers, feeding the hungry and the homeless. Jesus served in self-sacrifice, he died and resurrected that we may have life, life in abundance (John 10:10). Jesus served in total obedience to the will of his Father. Jesus never served for money, for popularity, for power or position. A formative community serves in the spirit of, and in obedience to Jesus Christ and God and the people.

In his book, *Five practices of Fruitful Congregations,* (2007) Robert Schnase identifies some five practical ways a formative community may witness a transformative, mission-oriented community. He listed them as follows: 1) "Radical hospitality;" 2) "Passionate worship;" 3) "Intentional faith development;" 4) "Risk-taking mission and service;" and 5) "Extravagant generosity" (pp. 8-9). In other words, Robert Schnase is of the view that a fruitful congregation or what I described here as a formative community must practice, live and witness individually and collectively a profound spirit of *"radical hospitality"* such that there is "the active desire to invite, welcome, receive, and care for those who are strangers so that they find a spiritual home and discover for themselves the unending richness of the life of Christ" (p. 11). In such a community, no one feels as a stranger, abandoned or isolated even in great difficulties and problems of life. There is a robust spirit of care and compassion shared and lived by all.

There also a *"passionate worship,"* in their celebrations such that their "worship bends hearts toward God as it stretches hands outward toward others" (p.35) in support and help to all. Evident in the community is what Schnase called "intentional faith development," which is a faith-filled life that seeks opportunities for growth in God and things of God. Equally in such a community, there is "risk-taking mission and service as well as "extravagant generosity." It means that the community is not only deeply mission-oriented in different ways, it also serves all with extravagant generosity.

The inescapable point to be drawn from the above is that formation is not simply a matter of instruction and knowledge. It is more of how formative is the community where the individual lives and interact. A formative community then is on how genuinely nurturing it is to its members and a witness of it to others, outside the community. When a community fails to form, the individual lives in crisis and the task of a reformation is called to question.

## A CONCLUDING SUMMARY

We live in a different world today, a world of problems and difficulties, but also of possibilities and opportunities. In the midst of problems and difficulties of this world, we also discover some possibilities and opportunities for a change. Based on this fact, this project makes a case on the current crisis in the Catholic priesthood on two grounds: 1) the need to foster a comprehensive understanding of the priestly life, identity and ministry in priesthood and how to witness the priestly life and identity honestly and responsibly in the Church and in the world. This number one grounding-issue in the Catholic priesthood today is rooted on the second grounding-issue. 2) The need to foster a functioning formative community in the seminary schools and an on-going formation in priestly life and ministry in the parish and diocesan communities. That is to say that a functioning formative community in the seminary schools must find a living extension in all levels of life in the Church, especially the family, the school, the parish and diocesan communities.

There is a big challenge among the Catholic priests today that is yet to be addressed in a proper and consistent manner. It is this, that some priests are ordained with a poor understanding of the enormity of the challenges and the uniqueness of the demands of the priestly life, the priestly identity and the priestly ministry in the Church and in the world of today. It is a less challenge to work through the secured environment of the seminary formation processes to the altar of ordination. Then, you are "let loose" in the "nakedness" and "wickedness" of the world to fend for yourself, to be on your own to "swim well" or "to drown." I call it the challenge of "being grounded" in the Catholic priesthood before and after ordination and down the road of the priestly life and ministry. It should never be taken for granted without some dangerous risks of crisis and abuses among the priests themselves and in the whole Church and the world at large. The challenge of "being grounded" in the Catholic priesthood has four phases, namely the priestly life, the priestly identity, the priestly ministry and a formative community.

## 1. The Priestly Life

It is true that "a priest is not his own," Bishop Fulton Sheen would insist, yet every priest has a life to live, to grow, to mature and become an adult person with all that it means and implies in the Church, in the society and in the world. Being a priest does not excuse or exempt anyone from this life-ordained process and responsibility. No one may pretend to deny or presume this natural process of growth and maturity without a big price to pay in one's life and in the community with other people.

The personal life of a priest includes: the cognitive life, the affective life, the moral life, the religious life and the spiritual life. Every priest is to know intentionally and to have a good grasp of what each of these aspects of his personal life means for him and for others in his relationships and leadership, as well as the challenges that flow from them. It is not enough to know these challenges intentionally, one must live them out honestly and responsibly in all levels of life and ministry otherwise, crisis ensues and abuses set in for everyone in the community.

## 2. The Priestly Identity

The priestly identity, though spoken of in singular, is not one but many. It is a multi-faceted priestly identity. Every priest has a personal duty to oneself and to others in his relationships and leadership to identify and name the different faces of his identity and the different challenges they make on him and on the demands of his leadership. I tried to name and discuss the six basic priestly identities in the Catholic Church (see chapter five).

In relationships and leadership opportunities of priests and others where identities are not properly identified and named, the risk of blurring the boundaries is inevitable. Once the boundaries are blurred, the danger of "pushing" and "pulling" off balance is real and abuses are enthroned into the whole community. It is not enough to identify and name identities in relationships and leadership, it is even more critical to honor and respect the demands of the identities and all that they entail, otherwise, the problem of "blurred boundaries" and "off balancing" is still real and active.

## 3. The Priestly Ministry

The priestly ministry carries with its very nature a priestly presence that is uniquely Christlike, Christ-centered and Kingdom oriented. There may be no separation or distortion without some dangerous misrepresentations and misinformation in the process. In everything a priest does or says, appropriate attention and commitment must be paid to a priestly presence that is uniquely Christlike, Christ-centered and Kingdom oriented, otherwise, the door is opened for crisis and a possibility of abuses.

The priestly ministry is not just sacramental, like celebrating the Holy Mass, the sacrament of reconciliation or confession, and the anointing of the sick or the dying. Priests have ministries outside the altar and outside the Church. Priests have ministries in social life in the local communities, in the political life of the political parties and the governments, and in the world life of the poor, the neglected, the abandoned and the most vulnerable ones like children and women. This is not to say that a priest is just a social worker or a politician. It rather means that a priest shares in the mission of caring of the social worker and in the peaceful political organization of politics and the politicians with a witness of Christ's Gospel of truth, justice and peace for all peoples and cultures.

## 4. A Formative Community

The priestly life, the priestly identity and the priestly ministry are like the branches of a tree. The root of the tree that will foster the growth and fruition on the tree's branches is a formative community in the seminary schools and its continuity in the family, school, parish and diocesan communities in the life and ministry of priests. A formative community is not a community without problems and difficulties, crisis and abuses. There is nothing like a perfect community under the sun. God did not create a perfect community on earth but a good one. The Book of Genesis states that "God looked at everything He had made, and He found it very good" (1:31). God, in His divine wisdom and plan, created a good world that could be made better, leading to the best. We are not yet there in the best world. The world as we know it is still in the process of being perfected, not yet fully perfect. The challenge is not on how to fashion a community without problems or crises or abuses. It is on how to work from "crisis" to "creation." It is on how to transform what is "bad" to "better," and from what is better to something much better and better and better.

A formative community does not fall down from heaven. Every member of the community especially priests, teachers and parents, has an important part to play to make it happen. It means that everyone must take the formation agenda seriously and be honestly and faithfully committed to live and promote its principles in all levels of life, relationships and leadership in the family, the Church and the society. As we discussed earlier, the three principal parts of the formation agenda are as follows: The first is "gathered to learn." That is to say that everything in life invites us to learn something different or new about the demands of respectful, selfless love, of working in truth and honesty for justice and peace with, and to all. The second is "challenged to grow." This means that everything in life challenges us to grow in all aspects of life, intellectually, morally, affectively, religiously and spiritually. And the third is "sent to serve." This also implies that everything in life invites us to serve God and other people redemptively as Jesus served in humility, in generosity, in care and compassion without prejudice, favoritism, exploitation and oppression.

An active formative community then, has all it takes to form and transform its members. In a formative community, the people are open to see the needs of others and they go out of their way to help in a spirit of honesty, peace, respect, and responsibility to all without prejudice or discrimination. In this way, it is a functional formative community that makes all the difference on how a community may grow from a crisis community to recreate itself into a nurturing, vibrant community.

# THE BIBLIOGRAPHY

Abernethy, A. (2002*)* *Ministry in Today's Church: Fulfillment and Frustration*, Dublin: The Columba Press.

Arinze, F. A. (1970) *Sacrifice in Ibo Religion,* Ibadan-Nigeria: Ibadan university Press.

Aschenbrenner, G. A. (2002) *The Challenge of Diocesan Priestly Spirituality: Quickening the Fire in Our Midst*, Chicago: Loyola Press.

Aumann, J. (1985) *Christian Spirituality in the Catholic tradition*, San Francisco: Ignatius Press.

Badru, P. (1998) *Imperialism and Ethnic Politics in Nigeria*, New Jersey: African World Press Inc.

Baur, J. (1994) *2000 Years of Christianity in Africa: An African Church History*, 2nd edition, Kenya: Paulines Publications Africa.

Bernanos, G. (1965) *The Diary of a Country Priest*, New York: Carroll and Graf Publishers.

Bernier, P. (1992) *Ministry in the Church: A Historical and Pastoral Approach*, Connecticut: Twenty-Third Publications.

Bleichner, H. P. (2004) *View from the Altar: Reflections on the Rapidly Changing Catholic Priesthood,* New York: The Crossroad Publishing Company.

Boran, G. (1999) *The Pastoral Challenges of A New Age*, Dublin: Veritas Publications.

Booth, N. S. ed. (1977) *African Religions: A Symposium*, New York: Nok Publishers Ltd

Bradshaw, J. (1996) *The Family: A New way of Creating Solid Self-Esteem,* Revised Edition, Deerfield Beach, Florida: Health Communications, Inc.

Bradshaw, J. (1988) *Healing the Shame that Binds You,* Florida: Health Communications, Inc.

Catholic Bishops' Conference of Nigeria, (2004) *I Chose You: The Nigerian Priest in the Third Millennium*, Nigeria: Madol Press Ltd.

------ (2004) *The Church in Nigeria: Family of God on Mission*, Enugu-Nigeria: CIDJAP Printing Press.

Cencini, A. (1994) *Vocation* Animation*: A Sign of Renewal*, Bombay: Paulines publications.

Chrittister, J. D. (2003) *Twelve Steps to Inner Freedom: Humility Revisited,* Pennsilvania: Benetvision.

Clowes, B. (1997) *Call to Action Or Call to Apostasy: How Dissenters Plan to Remake the Catholic Church in their Own Image,* Virginia: Human Life International.

Collins, P. (1997) *Papal Power: A Proposal for Change in Catholicism's Third Millennium,* Australia: HarperCollinsPublishers.

Congregation for the Clergy (1994) *Directory for the Life and Ministry of Priests,* Vatican: Libreria Editrice Vaticana.

Conn, W. E. (1998) *The Desiring Self: Rooting Pastoral Counseling and Spiritual Direction in Self-Transcendence,* New York: Paulist Press.

Cooke, B. (1976) *Ministry to Word and Sacrament*, Philadelphia: Fortress Press.

Cozzens, D. B. ed. (1997) *The Spirituality of the Diocesan Priest,* Minnesota: The Liturgy Press.

Cozzens, D. B. (2000) *The Changing Face of the Priesthood: A Reflection on the Priest's Crisis of Soul,* Minnesota: The Liturgical Press.

Crampon, E. P. T. (1975) *Christianity in Northern Nigeria,* London: Geoffrey Chapman.

De Caussade, Jean-Pierre (1975) *Abandonment to Divine Providence,* New York: Image Books.

Dietrich, D. ed. (2006*) Priests for the 21ˢᵗ Century,* New York: The Crossroad Publishing Company.

Donovan, D. (1992) *What are They Saying about the Ministerial Priesthood?* New York: Paulist Press.

Edwards, T. H. (1980) *Spiritual Friend: Reclaiming the Gift of Spiritual Direction,* New York: Paulist Press.

Ezeh, M. N. (?) *Nigeria: Cogs in National development,* Owerri-Nigeria, Ihem Davis Press Ltd.

Ehusani, G. (2002) *Witness and Role of Priests and Religious in Nigeria,* Ibadan-Nigeria: Daily Graphics Nigeria Ltd.

Ferder, F. & Heagle, J. (1992) *Your Sexual Self: Pathway to Authentic Intimacy,* Indiana: Ave Maria Press.

Gramick, J. and Furrey, P. eds. (1988) *The Vatican and Homosexuality: Reactions to the "Letter to the Bishops of the Catholic Church on the Pastoral Care of Homosexual Persons,"* New York: The Crossroad Publishing Company.

Grannis, C. J., Laffins, A. J. & Schade, E. (1981) *The Risk of the Cross: Christian Discipleship in the Nuclear* Age, New York: The Seabury Press.

Greeley, A. M. (2004) *Priests: A Calling in Crisis,* Chicago: Chicago Press.

Groeschel, B. J. (1995) *Spiritual Passages: The Psychology of Spiritual Development,* New York: Crossroad Press.

Hambrick, R. S. (1991) The Management Skills Builder: Self-Directed Learning Strategies for Career *Development,* New York: Praeger Publishers.

Henriot, P. J., DeBerri, E. P. & Schultheis, M. J. (1999) *Catholic Social Teaching: Our Best Kept Secret*, New York: Orbis Books.

Hill, B. R., Knitter, P. & Madges, W. (1997) *Faith, Religion & Theology: A Contemporary Introduction*, Connecticut: Twenty-Third Publications.

Hoge, D. R. & Wenger, J. E. (2003) *Evolving Visions of the Priesthood: Changes from Vatican II to the Turn of the New Century*, Minnesota: Liturgical Press.

Holland, J. & Henriot, P. (1998) *Social Analysis: Linking Faith and Justice*, Revised and Enlarged Edition, Washington DC: Dove Communications and Orbis Books.

Iperu Formation Community (1992) *A Handbook on Formation*, Ibadan-Nigeria: Ambassador Publications. Gift and Mystery: On the fiftieth

John Paul II (1996) *On The Fiftieth Anniversary of My Priestly Ordination*, New York: Doubleday.

Keating, T. (1986) *Open Mind, Open Heart: The Contemplative Dimension of the Gospel*, Massachusetts: Element.

Kelsey, M. (1998) *Spiritual Living in a Material World: A Practical Guide*, New York: New City Press.

Kelsey, M. (1996) *Companions on the Inner Way: The Art of Spiritual Guidance*, New York: The Crossroad Publishing Company.

Kelsey, M. (1981) *Reaching for the Real: Reflections on Becoming Real Human Beings*, New Mexico, Dove Publications.

Maciel, M. (1998) *Integral Formation of Catholic Priests*, Philadelphia: The Legion of Christ, Inc.

McBrien, R. P. (1994) *Catholicism*, Completely Revised and Updated, New York: HarperSanFrancisco.

McGinnis, K. and McGinnis, J. (1990) *Parenting for Peace and Justice: Ten Years Later*, New York: Orbis Books.

McInerny, R. M. (1998) *What Went Wrong with Vatican II: The Catholic Crisis Explained*, New Hampshire: Sophia Institute Press.

Murphy, C. M. (2006) *Models of Priestly Formation: Past, Present, and Future*, New York: The Crossroad company.

Nichols, T. L. (1997) *That All May Be One: Hierarchy and Participation in the Church*, Minnesota: The Liturgical Press.

Nouwen, H. J. M. (1992) *Life of the Beloved: Spiritual Living in a Secular World*, New York: Crossroad.

Nouwen, H. J. M. (1972) *The Wounded Healer: Ministry in Contemporary Society*, New York: Image Books, Doubleday .

Obiefuna, A.(1985) *Idolatry in a Century-Old Church*, Enugu-Nigeria: Cecta Nigeria Ltd.

Okehie-Offoha, M. U. & Sadiku, M. N. O. eds. (1988) *Ethnic and Cultural Diversity in Nigeria*, New Jersey: African World Press, Inc.

Ojemen, C. A. ((2003) *Parish Life and Ministry*, Benin-Nigeria: Pastoral Initiative Commission.

Ojo, G. A. (2004) *Catholic Laity in Nigeria: Yesterday, Today, Tomorrow*, Ibadan-Nigeria: Daily Graphics Nigeria Ltd.

O'Keefe, M. (1995*) Becoming Good, Becoming Holy: On the Relationship of Christian Ethics and Spirituality*, New York: Paulist Press.

Okeke, C. U. (2003*) Expectations of Life as a Priest: A Comparative Study of Igbo Catholic Diocesan and Religious Seminarians*, Rome.

Okonkwo, A. (1999) *The Priests of God: Yesterday, Today & Tomorrow*, Rome.

O'Meara, T. F. (1999) *Theology of Ministry*, Completely Revised Edition, New York: Paulist Press.

O'Murchu, D. (1999) *Poverty, Celibacy and Obedience: A Radical Option for Life*, New York: The Crossroad Publishing Company.

Onyeneke, A. O. (1987*) The Dead Among the Living: Masquerades in Igbo Society*, Enugu-Nigeria: Chuka Printing Co, Ltd.

Osudibia, K. C. (1995) *Nigeria: The Case of Fragmentation*, Umuahia-Nigeria: Guinea-Chim Industries, Ltd.

Rahner, K. (1983) *The Practice of Faith: A Handbook of Contemporary Spirituality*, New York: The Crossroad Publishing Company.

Ratzinger, J. (2007*) Jesus of Nazareth: From the Baptism in the Jordan to the Transfiguration*, New York: Doubleday.

Rohr, R. (1991) *Simplicity: The Art of Living*, New York: The Crossroad Publishing Company.

Rose, M. S. (2002) *Goodbye Good Men: How Liberals Brought Corruption into the Catholic Church*, New York: The Crossroad Publishing Company.

Ruddy, C. (2006) *Tested in Every Way: The Catholic Priesthood in Today's Church*, New York: The Crossroad Publishing Company.

Satir, V. (1988) *The New PeopleMaking*, California: Science and Behavior Books, Inc.

Schaef, A. W. (1987) *When Society Becomes an Addict*, San Francisco: Harper & Row Publishers.

Sipe, A. W. R. (1982) *Sex, Priests and Power: Anatomy of a Crisis*, New York: Brunner Routledge.

Sheen, F. (1963, 2005) *The Priest is not His Own*, New York: McGraw-Hill Book Company.

Schillebeeckx, E. (1985*) The Church with a Human Face: A New and Expanded Theology of Ministry*, New York: The Crossroad Publishing Company.

Shorter, A. (2000) *Religious Obedience in Africa*, Nairobi-Kenya: Paulines Publications Africa.

Shorter, A. (1999) *Religious Poverty in Africa*, Nairobi-Kenya: Paulines Publications, Africa.

Shorter, A. (1998) *Celibacy and African Culture*, Nairobi-Kenya: Paulines Publications Africa.

Sofield, L. & Juliano, C. (2000) *Collaboration: Uniting Our Gifts in Ministry*, Indiana: Ave Maria Press.

Sofield, L. & Kuhn, D. H. (1995) *The Collaborative Leader: Listening to the Wisdom of God's People*, Indiana: Ave Maria Press.

Tavard, G. H. (1983) *A Theology for Ministry*, Delaware: Michael Glazier, Inc.

Taylor, C. W. (1991) *The Skilled Pastor: Counseling as the Practice of Theology*, Minneapolis: Fortress Press.

Toups, D. L. (2008) *Reclaiming Our Priestly Character,* Nebraska: The Institute for Priestly Formation Inc.

Veling, T. A. (1995*) Living in the Margins: Intentional Communities and the Art of Interpretation*, New York: The Crossroad Publishing Company.

Walsh, J. et al. (1995) *Grace under Pressure: What Gives Life to American Priests*, Washington DC: National catholic Educational Association.

Wilkinson, B. (1998, 2003) *Set Apart: Discovering Personal Victory through Holiness*, Oregon: Multnomah Publishers, Inc.

Whitehead, E. E. & Whitehead, J. D. (1979) *Christian Life Patterns: The Psychological Challenges and Religious Invitations of Adult Life*, New York: The Crossroad Publishing Company.

Zeller, H. V. (1992) *And So to God*, Massachusetts: St. Bede's Publications.

CPSIA information can be obtained at www.ICGtesting.com
Printed in the USA
BVOW010739011212

306859BV00010B/7/P

9 781468 553161